Ayn Rand at the Movies

Ayn Rand at the Movies

By Denise Noe

BearManor Media
2023

Ayn Rand at the Movies

This book is an independent work of research and commentary and is not sponsored, authorized or endorsed by, or otherwise affiliated with, any motion picture studio or production company affiliated with the films discussed herein. All uses of the name, image, and likeness of any individuals, and all copyrights and trademarks referenced in this book, are for editorial purposes and are pursuant of the Fair Use Doctrine.

The views and opinions of individuals quoted in this book do not necessarily reflect those of the author.

The promotional photographs and publicity materials reproduced herein are in the author's private collection (unless noted otherwise). These images date from the original release of the films and were released to media outlets for publicity purposes.

Published in the USA by
BearManor Media
1317 Edgewater Dr. #110
Orlando, FL 32804
www.BearManorMedia.com

Softcover Edition
ISBN: 979-8-88771-266-6

Printed in the United States of America

Dedicated to a more nuanced understanding of Ayn Rand

Also by Denise Noe

Hard copy books

The Complete Married... with Children Book: TV's Dysfunctional Family Phenomenon (2017)

Teletubbies On the Screen and Behind the Scenes (2020)

Christmas Gifts from the Chanukah Crowd: The Extraordinary Contributions of Americans Jews to Christmas (2020)

Maury: The Story of an American Pop Culture Institution (2021)

Wishbone Behind the Scenes (2022)

The Bloodied and the Broken (2021)

Justice Gone Haywire (2021)

I Spy, You Spy, They Spy (2022)

A Sheep In Wolf's Clothing: The Life of Marie Windsor (2023)

Ebook-Only Books by Denise Noe

Suffer Little Children (Unsure)

Obsessions & Exorcisms in the Work of Joyce Carol Oates (2018)

Voices from the Inside: Letters from Famous Prisoners (2022)

Hard Copy Books by Rachel Heath (a Denise Noe pen name)

The Man Who Was Put On Earth To Serve Women (2015)

Ten Stinging Stories (2016)

Rachel Heath's Lesbian Erotica (2017)

Ebooks by Rachel Heath

Will and Trish: A Domestic Discipline Romance

Grant and Deirdre: A Domestic Discipline Romance

Vince and Sheila: A Domestic Discipline Romance

Ferd Learns: Fidelity and sobriety — or else!

Lady Cherokee

Contents

Introduction

Ayn Rand is one of the most polarizing figures in modern America. Famous for regarding selfishness as good, even authoring a book entitled *The Virtue of Selfishness*, Ayn Rand is idolized and despised, loved and hated, revered as a prophet of capitalism and reviled as a quintessentially "mean girl."

Oddly, even the pronunciation of her first name causes disagreements! Is it "Ann" or "Ian"? It is usually said to rhyme with "pine" or "mine" and is "I-an." However, many people understandably have difficulty with the name.

Rarely is Ayn Rand regarded as this author views her: an individual richly talented and deeply wounded, outstanding in her accomplishments but limited in much of her outlook, extraordinary in some insights but afflicted by large blind spots. I have never followed her philosophy of Objectivism but I believe she has written some vibrantly interesting stories and made some brilliantly on target (Objective?) observations. In this author's opinion, Ayn Rand is fascinating even for her foibles.

This book is not a biography of Ayn Rand. Neither is this book an examination of the philosophy of Objectivism that she founded. Nor is it a work of literary criticism of her writings.

Ayn Rand at the Movies is about Rand's relationship with the motion picture industry, both during her lifetime and after it. The book discusses her love for cinema and the work she did in it. The book examines films on which she worked in one capacity or another, films inspired by her work, and films about her. It is the author's hope that readers of this book will understand that the relationship between Ayn Rand and the motion picture industry was rich, multi-layered, and deeply meaningful.

Alisa Rosenbaum and Communist Oppression

Although this book is not a biography of Ayn Rand, a modest overview of her life, and her works, is necessary to understand the relationship of Rand with motion pictures that is this book's subject.

The writer and philosopher destined to become famous as Ayn Rand was born Alisa Rosenbaum on February 2, 1905, in St. Petersburg, Russia. She was the first of three children, all daughters, born to pharmacist Zinovy Rosenbaum and housewife Anna Rosenbaum. Throughout history families have rejoiced unreservedly at the births of sons; they have experienced joy mixed with disappointment at the births of daughters. That the Rosenbaums had three female babies in a row, and never a male baby, had to have been a source of anguish for a couple in the early 20th century. (Even in our era, with so much open to women, many couples would suffer severe disappointment under such circumstances.)

Little Alisa did well in school academically but, like many precocious children, was less successful at making friends and was something of a loner. Unlike many who do well in verbal subjects but poorly in math and sciences, Alisa excelled in both. Early in childhood, Alisa set a firm career goal — a goal from which she would never waver. "I decided to be a writer at the age of nine, and everything I have done was integrated to that purpose," the adult Ayn Rand recalled.

It was also at the age of nine that Alisa would drastically change her belief system. She was already in a minority because she was Jewish in a nation in which the overwhelming majority of people were Russian Orthodox Christians. Nine-year-old Alisa decided she did not believe God existed. Just as she never wavered in her career goal of being a writer, neither did she waver in her steadfast atheism.

Probably hoping to stimulate the imaginations of her three daughters, and perhaps not wanting those imaginations stifled by the gender limitations of the period, Anna Rosenbaum purchased a subscription to a French magazine aimed at pre-adolescent boys for her girls. The magazine ran a serial entitled "The Mysterious Valley." In this story, a group of English officers found themselves attacked by trained tigers. Alisa found the story most intriguing. She would later describe herself as "mesmerized" by a drawing of the story's hero, a character named "Cyrus." In adulthood, she would name a fictional heroine "Kira," the Russian female form of "Cyrus."

A vociferous reader, little Alisa was entranced by the works of Victor Hugo. She relished reading his dramatic stories with their larger-than-life characters and colorful plots. Alisa promised herself that she would someday write in a Romantic manner as did Hugo.

When Alisa was twelve years old, her country suffered that historical convulsion known as the Bolshevik Revolution, violently changing from a monarchy to a communist government. Czar Nicholas II and his wife Czarina Alexandria, along with their five children, were brutally "executed" by the fanatical communist revolutionaries. Some individuals close to the royal family were murdered alongside them. Contrary to legend, the royal daughter named Anastasia was killed with the rest of the family.

Even as a pre-teenaged child, Rand saw through the false promises of communism. She later asserted, "When, at the age of twelve, at the time of the Russian revolution, I first heard the Communist principle that Man must exist for the sake of the State, I perceived that this was the essential issue, that this principle was evil, and that it could lead to nothing but evil."

Although the Rosenbaums had not been wealthy under the rule of the czars, they had been comfortably upper-middle-class. The Bolsheviks slapped "Red seal" on the door of Zinovy Rosenbaum's pharmacy and confiscated it, plunging the family into sudden and extreme poverty.

Fleeing the harshness of city life in revolutionary Russia, the family traveled to the Crimea — where they sometimes went hungry. It is understandable that such a sharp fall in fortunes psychologically scarred Alisa.

After a period, the Rosenbaums returned to the city from which they had fled. That city was no longer St. Petersburg but Petrograd.

A teenaged Alisa Rosenbaum enrolled at the University of Petrograd where she concentrated on learning history but also studied philosophy and literature, three subjects that were excellent preparations for a writing career. Experience had led Alisa to despise communism; the knowledge she acquired through her studies deepened that feeling and she grew into a fiercely anti-communist adult. The *Internet Encyclopedia of Philosophy* reports, "As a youth, she had been repelled by the communists' political program, and now as an adult, she was more fully aware of the destructive effects that the revolution had had on Russian society more broadly."

In 1924, Alisa graduated from the University of Petrograd. She enrolled in the State Institute for Cinema Arts to study screenwriting. This was an appropriate move since Alisa adored the then-new art form of motion pictures. Starting in her late teens, Alisa had visited cinemas on a regular basis where she relished watching silent movies. In her diary, she recorded information about the films she saw, often "grading" them. She also "graded" performers through an underlining system by which she underlined a name once if she especially liked an actor or actress, twice if she really liked that performer, and three times if she really super-liked that performer. Directors Fritz Lang and Cecil B. Demille were among her favorite filmmakers. She would later call Lang's *Siegfried* a "source of inspiration." A friend of Rand's, Mary Ann Sure, told an interviewer that *Siegfried* was Rand's "top favorite" and that Rand "remarked on how beautifully each scene was composed. She said that each frame looked like a painting." What was this silent flick that so impressed Rand? It impressed many people and is considered by film experts to be an artistic and technical triumph. The film is based on a Nordic legend and tells the story of Siegfried traveling to King Gunther's castle, slaying both a dragon and an evil dwarf on the way to that destination.

In 1925, Rand published a biographical article on her favorite actress, an article entitled by the name of its talented and acclaimed subject: "Pola Negri." The performer Rand admired had been born in 1897 in Poland. She lived in poverty in her early years. She loved dancing and was so talented that, as a teenager, she was accepted into the Imperial Ballet. Then she came down with an illness that ruled out a dancing career. She changed course and was accepted into the Warsaw Imperial Academy of Dramatic Acting. Her talent was so great that she was considered a stage star at the tender age of seventeen. Then she turned to the emerging medium of the motion picture. She traveled to Germany where she was cast in the films of renowned director Ernst Lubitsch. In 1922, both Negri and Lubitsch got contracts to work in Hollywood. Along with professional success, Pola Negri enjoyed an active personal life with her name being romantically linked to Charlie Chaplin and Rudolph Valentino. It was during this time period, when Pola Negri was both an admired actress and the subject of titillating gossip, that Rand 's "Pola Negri" was published. It was a monograph that was part of a series about motion picture performers. It was published under the name "A. Rosenbaum." This author believes it possible "Alisa" was not used for fear that readers would be less apt to take the writing seriously if they knew the writer was female. Rand noted Negri's "mysterious contemptuous smile" and applauded the actress for projecting an image of a "strong, powerful woman" who is "powerful even in her suffering." This actress, Rand suggested, "portrays the woman victorious" and possessed "the eternal, unconquerable power of a woman."

Young Alisa adored serious philosophical and political discussions. Sadly, her intellectual bent turned some people off as there was still a deeply entrenched sexist prejudice against female intellectuals. This might have led Alisa, who had never been good at making friends, to feel especially isolated.

Even as Alisa explored serious matters, she possessed a frivolous side that she would never lose. She was a big fan of the light-hearted music that was popular in the early 20th century and that she called "tiddlywink music."

Having studied the history and culture of the United States, and believing America's system of republic government and capitalist economy vastly superior to the communism she loathed, Alisa resolved that she would someday live in the United States. In 1925, Alisa received permission from the Soviet government to visit relatives residing in Chicago, Illinois. The implicit understanding, of course, was that she would return home to the Soviet Union. However, she privately planned to stay in the United States indefinitely if at all possible.

The aspiring writer turned twenty-one on a boat sailing to America. In Chicago she moved in with relatives and started learning English. (She would become thoroughly conversant in English but retain a heavy Russian accent throughout her life.) She also spent much time working with concepts for stories and movie scripts. Alisa applied for an extension of her visa and the Soviets granted it.

Alisa started writing in the language of her adopted country. In 1926, she published a booklet entitled "Hollywood: American City of Movies." She tried her hand at short stories written in her second language. Two short stories that she penned in 1926 are featured in the *The Early Ayn Rand*, a book that includes short stories, unpublished excerpts from her novels, a screenplay, a script for a play, and observations about Rand from authors Richard E. Ralston and Leonard Peikoff, both of whom have written extensively about her. Never published during her lifetime, the short stories she wrote in 1926 were "The Husband I Bought" and "The Night King." Peikoff calls these stories "a beginner's exercises written as literary practice, and never meant for any audience."

Peikoff reports that she signed "The Husband I Bought" with "a pseudonym invented for this one case and never used again: Allen Raynor." It might be significant that she used a male pen name; it is obvious that she clung to her real initials. Peikoff believes the story exemplifies a tendency in Rand's early fiction in which "female protagonists predominate." Since Rand had not yet crystallized her philosophy when she crafted the tale, it is not shocking that some of the attitudes expressed in this story could be viewed as opposing her later systematized philosophical beliefs. However, Peikoff believes there is no contradiction between the values in the tale and Objectivist precepts — although he acknowledges that some readers might see a contradiction. Peikoff writes, "On the surface, this story might appear to be quite conventional. I can imagine someone reading it as the tragic story of an unloved wife 'selflessly' removing herself from her husband's path." Since "selfless" was a strongly negative quality according to the Objectivist ethos Rand eventually developed, Peikoff argues that the story's "actual meaning is the opposite" and is about "a passionate valuer" and the triumph of those values. The author of this book believes that Peikoff may be straining for consistency and that we should not expect a short story written as an experiment in Rand's youth to be consistent with her mature philosophy. Then again, I must also allow that Peikoff may have the correct assessment.

"The Husband I Bought" begins: "I should not have written this story. If I did it all — I did it only by keeping silent. I went through tortures, such as no other woman on earth, perhaps just to keep silent. And now — I speak."

The narrator/protagonist then goes on to tell the story of how she was strongly attracted to a man who was "tall and slim, and beautiful, too beautiful." Henry Stafford is the fellow's name. In the fictional small town in which our characters reside, Henry Stafford is the "aim and target of all the girls and 'homemade' vamps." The man is considered a true marital "catch" since he was not only handsome but had inherited a big business from his father. She continues: "I tell the whole truth here, so I must tell that I was beautiful. And I was clever. I knew it; you always know it when you are." She tells us that she loved Henry Stafford and he loved her. They are starting a romance when disaster strikes the object of her affections. His inherited business fails. He is not at fault but the victim of "circumstance."

Some people in the small town sympathize with the rich man brought down; others, especially those who envied him, happily gloat at the comedown.

It is here that we learn our narrator/protagonist is Irene Wilmer who, although attractive and intelligent, is not as gorgeous as the "town's prize vamp" Patsy Tillins. There was resentment among some people that he had gone for second best in Irene rather than the supposed best of Patsy so those people feel a smug satisfaction that Irene has had to witness Henry's fall.

When Irene tries to comfort Henry, he tells her to leave him and never speak to him again. She does not belong with a failure and he will not tie her to a penniless man.

She is still wealthy. He has nothing. But she still wants him — she always wanted him for himself and not his money — so she finally convinces him that it is no sacrifice on her part to unite them. To the shock of their neighbors, they marry.

As newlyweds, they are happy. Irene pays off her husband's debts and they put that behind them. Rand writes, "We could live just for one another, with nothing to disturb us, in the maddest, the wildest of happiness two human beings had ever experienced." Eventually he gets a job in engineering.

They enjoyed four years of "perfect, delicious happiness." Then? Claire Van Dahlen, a divorcée from New York with "the body of an antique statuette" and "slow, soft, fluent movements" and "arms that undulated like velvet ribbons" attracts Henry.

Henry refuses to have anything to do with her or attend any event at which she might be present. Our alert and sensitive Irene knows that he is in love with Claire but that his gratitude to Irene prevents him from acting on that love. He is the husband she "bought" and his debt to her, combined with his sense of honor, means he cannot leave Irene for Claire.

Irene deeply loves Henry but, knowing he will never again be truly happy with her, cannot hold onto him. She realizes that if she just tells him she no longer loves him, he is sure to discern the lie. So she decides on a ruse that might actually fool him. She leads him to believe she has fallen in love with another man, a handsome man-about-town named Gerald Gray.

It works. Henry Stafford is able to divorce his "unfaithful" wife without sacrificing his moral code. He finds renewed happiness with Claire.

Gray has fallen in love with Irene but she has no genuine interest in him. She disappears from the town, leaving behind the man she "bought" and then deliberately discarded for the sake of his own happiness. She also leaves behind Gerald Gray, the man she courted but never really wanted.

Taking up residence in another town, she gets a job in a department store. She works long hours and eschews a social life of any kind. Her life contracts to working, eating, and sleeping, a routine free of passion. However, she is satisfied she did the right thing for her ex-husband, having "bought his happiness" and "paid with everything I had."

During the period in which Rand was still learning English and experimenting with writing, she moved to Hollywood, California where she would soon have real life experiences that sound tailor made for movie scripts.

Richard E. Ralston comments that the early short story "The Night King" was probably written while the budding writer "was living at the Hollywood Studio Club." She "was still learning English" and in "The Night King" is particularly tentative in her "use of American slang and how to re-create the same on the printed page."

"The Night King" resembles a story she would pen a few years later entitled "Escort" in reflecting Rand's admiration for another author, O. Henry. Peikoff states that these stories, with their twist endings, are "her own private salute to O. Henry."

Written in the first person, "The Night King" tells the story of career criminal Steve Hawkins who plans well in advance a big-time caper: "I sacrificed two years of my valuable life to that one job." He worked as a valet in order to get the information necessary to steal an extraordinarily valuable black diamond called "The Night King." It is unnecessary for this author to give the game away but Rand does indeed pull off a powerful twist with "The Night King" — a twist worthy of O. Henry.

1927: Finding Her King on *The King of Kings*

Alisa Rosenbaum had only been in Hollywood two days when she spotted famous director Cecil B. DeMille in his car. The starstruck young woman could not help staring. DeMille stopped the car and asked why she was staring. Alisa let him know that she recognized him as the renowned film director. She also told DeMille that she had recently come to America from the Soviet Union, that she loved movies, and yearned to someday work as a professional screenwriter. DeMille must have been impressed by the honesty and sincerity of the young foreigner since he gave her a ride to the set on which his latest project, *The King of Kings*, was being filmed. He soon signed her on as an extra. Thus, Alisa Rosenbaum got to be a face in a crowd scene in a silent movie.

One of the most whimsically humanizing anecdotes of Ayn Rand's life concerns how she first became acquainted with the man who would become the central figure in her life, the man she would put above all others, the extraordinary man who would in a very real sense make her career possible — the man who would be her king.

While working as an extra on the 1927 film *The King of Kings*, a handsome actor caught her eye. That actor's name was Frank O'Connor and he had previously had an uncredited bit part as a party guest in the 1921 D. W. Griffith movie *Orphans of the Storm*. O'Connor was walking by when Ayn mischievously put her leg out so he would stumble over it. The little kerfuffle led Ayn and Frank O'Connor to strike up a conversation. After their work on the film ended, they briefly lost contact with each other. Ayn feared she might not see him again but had a strong feeling that she would find him — and she did. They happened to be in the same library and caught sight of one another. She was 22, Frank was 29 when they started seeing each other regularly. Ayn Rand's visa was about to expire and she dreaded returning to a country she considered a vast prison. Although her desire to remain in America was a spur to their nuptials, there is no question that they were very much in love at the time of their 1929 marriage and would remain so until "death did them part."

Perhaps it is beautifully appropriate that Rand met the man who would become her personal king on the set of a film entitled *The King of Kings*.

Since she was an extra and O'Connor had a very small bit part, neither of them has their name in the credits of the motion picture. But they could take pride in playing even tiny roles in a very special film. *The King of Kings* was the middle of a Biblical trilogy DeMille created, being preceded by *The Ten Commandments* (1923) and followed by *The Sign of the Cross* (1932).

The King of Kings starred H. B. Warner as Jesus Christ, Dorothy Cumming as the Virgin Mary, Jacqueline Logan as Mary Magdalene, and Joseph Schildkraut as Judas Iscariot. It is filmed in black and white save for the opening scene and the resurrection scene. DeMille set those two scenes off from the rest of the movie by filming them in glorious Technicolor. DeMille showed his way with imagery by having Mary Magdalene, depicted as hard-partying and affluent, riding on a chariot drawn by zebras! The director sought to arouse a special sense of reverence by having the audience first see Jesus through the eyes of a small sick child Jesus healed and who sees Jesus with a halo around him.

Performers are, well, performers so there is no necessary link between the roles an actor plays and the type of person he or she is in real life. However, DeMille realized that audiences all-too-often confuse actors with their parts and sought to ensure such confusion would not negatively impact ticket sales. Thus, DeMille insisted H. B. Warner and Dorothy Cumming sign contracts barring them from appearing in movies that might be seen as offensive to religious people for a period of five years after *The King of Kings*. Their contracts also stated that they could not be seen engaging in activities like nightclubbing or card playing that are regarded as at least morally problematic, if not downright sinful, by a fairly large number of Christians.

Perhaps there is a sliver of irony in the fact that Rand, who prided herself on her reason-based thinking and ironclad atheism, worked on a movie glorifying Christianity. However, the irony is quite mild as writers and performers often work on projects crafted from a belief system they do not happen to share. I wrote a book entitled *Christmas Gifts from the Chanukah Crowd: The Extraordinary Contributions of American Jews to Christmas* that pointed out that much of popular Christmas celebration, especially in the United States, originated with Jewish people. I am not Jewish. Just as Jewish songwriters frequently write Christmas songs, and non-Jews occasionally try their hand at Chanukah tunes, hard-core skeptics often write religious, fantasy, and horror fiction.

Interestingly, Ayn Rand was not the only *King of Kings* extra who would someday achieve fame. Oddly, that other extra achieved that fame using the same surname. Sally Rand was destined to become famous for her daring 1933 World's Fair "Fan Dance." Since "Rand" was not a birth name in either instance, it should come as no surprise that the two women named Rand were not related.

In 1927, the same year Alisa met her future husband while working as an extra on *The King of Kings*, she penned a short story entitled "Good Copy." Leonard Peikoff believes that this short story "reminds us" of Rand's "view that suffering is an exception, not the rule of life." Peikoff elaborates that the Ayn Rand rule was that life — usually — should not be "pain or heroic endurance, but gaiety and light-hearted joy in living."

According to Peikoff, many years after it was written, "Good Copy" was read out loud in a course on fiction-writing that Ayn Rand gave to a group of young admirers. She told the assembled students that this was a story written by a writer who was just starting out and asked if the students thought the writer of "Good Copy" had a future as a writer. Some of the young acolytes realized that Rand was the author; others did not. When the latter found out, they were astonished that Rand would write something so "unserious." Peikoff summarizes their criticism: "It doesn't deal with high issues like [Rand's] novels; it has no profound passions, no immortal struggles, no philosophic meaning."

What is "Good Copy" about? Newspaper reporter Laury McGee is desperate for a sensational story to cover. Frustrated by the lack of attention-grabbing events, "His steps rang like gunshots in the sweet peace of the summer afternoon."

Chewed out by his boss at the newspaper for not reporting anything of interest, Laury comes up with an odd solution. He will not just report news but make it. Then he makes news through kidnapping! His victim is young heiress Juliana Xenia "Jinx" Winford, called the "dime-a-hair girl" because people believe the fortune she will inherit amounts to a dime for each hair on her head.

The story is written as a broad cartoon-like comedy. Rand is deliberately and flamboyantly unrealistic, especially in her depiction of Jinx. The rich young woman is not the least bit frightened at being kidnapped. Instead, she kind of "takes over" the house of her kidnapper, redecorating it and even pointing out to Laury that she could have easily phoned the cops for help but did not. He rips the phone out before asking her why she did not use it and she replies that she was too busy with her self-assigned housekeeping chores. She also insists that he revise his ransom note to ask more from her father because she finds it offensive to suggest her freedom can be purchased cheaply.

Another way Rand underlines the comic unreality of the story's world is through her cheekily alliterative titles: Laury works for a newspaper called Dawn in the town of Dicksville and the alter ego he adopts as kidnapper is Damned Dan!

In the cartoon world of "Good Copy," the kidnapping revives and revitalizes Laury's flagging journalistic career. However, he suffers a quasi-punishment through the awful shame he feels when he must shop for Jinx in the lingerie section of a nearby department store.

Rand works in several twists, all of them only credible in the cartoon-land in which she has situated "Good Copy," and all of them crafted to make the short story a fun and breezy read. One "serious" aspect of "Good Copy" is that it implicitly criticizes certain aspects of the media as would some of her later work.

The Great Man Behind the Great Woman

"Behind every great man is a great woman" is a proverb that some people might dislike repeating in our "post-feminist" era. However, there is powerful truth in it: our great men were often helped along by the women in their lives whether mothers, wives, sisters, daughters and, yes, even girlfriends, mistresses, and courtesans.

At least in some cases, a great woman is backed up by a great man. One example is that of the famous poet Edna St. Vincent Millay. Her husband, Eugene Jan Boissevain, was a successful business executive in the coffee business. He to a large extent dedicated his life to hers, taking over domestic duties like cooking and cleaning to give his wife more time to write. He had no trouble justifying it since, as he once observed, "Anyone can buy and sell coffee. Not anyone can write great poetry." That may have been a bit self-deprecating as it takes a special individual to be good in business. However, it may also reflect his recognition of the truth that the level of "specialness" was greater in a fine poet. Their marriage was one in which each partner was free to pursue other romantic/sexual liaisons but always kept their basic commitment to each other as of most importance.

Frank O'Connor was, in a major way, the great man behind the great woman. Ayn Rand dedicated both *The Fountainhead* and *Atlas Shrugged* "To Frank O'Connor." That a young Ayn Rand would find herself powerfully attracted to him is understandable as he was indisputably handsome. There obviously is more than a physical attraction in a good marriage, especially one that lasts for life as did the marriage of Ayn Rand and Frank O'Connor. When discussing the dedications to her husband, Rand explained, "I knew what values of character I wanted to find in a man. I met such a man — and we have been married for twenty-eight years. His name is Frank O'Connor."

There is no question that Frank O'Connor contributed mightily to his wife's writing. "Every hero was modeled after him," she readily acknowledged. "I sometimes took an entire monologue from him and slipped it into my books." An example of words originally uttered by Frank O'Connor that were transferred to his wife's fiction is one of the most memorable exchanges in both the novel and the film versions of *The Fountainhead* occurs when hero Howard Roark is challenged by villain Ellsworth Toohey: "Why don't you tell me what you think of me?"

"But I don't think of you," is Roark's unforgettably withering retort. Frank O'Connor once told someone exactly that and Rand was impressed by her husband's dry wit and ability to make a striking point in few words. Frank O'Connor also suggested the title for her largest and most influential novel. She worked on it as *The Strike*. Frank suggested the more witty title *Atlas Shrugged* — so *Atlas Shrugged* it became. This author believes that the vibrancy of Frank O'Connor's suggested title contributed mightily to the book's success, underlining his importance as the great man behind the great woman.

Some might argue that Rand's doctrine that selfishness is a virtue is belied by her devotion to her husband. She asserted there was no contradiction because "romantic love is a selfish emotion." She described romantic love as the "choice of a person as a great value." She once said she would step in front of a loaded gun if it were aimed at her husband. That would not be altruism, she elaborated, because he was a value she did not want to live without.

Ayn Rand published short stories, articles, novels, essays, and collections of essays. She authored books that have never gone out of print. She wrote movie scripts. She founded a school of philosophy that garnered a major following and continues to attract new followers many years after her death. What did she regard as her proudest achievement? "Marrying Frank O'Connor," she replied. Some would reflexively characterize this as an "anti-feminist" statement that places women in an inferior position. This writer does not think it should be so regarded. After all, it is quite possible that a man could consider marrying his wife as his proudest achievement. I suspect that, had Frank O'Connor been asked the same question about what his proudest achievement was, he might well have answered, "Marrying Ayn Rand."

A Fledgling Writer Takes A New Name

Early in her career, Alisa Rosenbaum adopted Ayn Rand as her pen name. A story has circulated that while residing with relatives in Chicago in 1926, she took the name "Rand" from the Remington Rand typewriter. This cannot be true since the Remington and Rand companies did not merge until 1927 with the word "Rand" not appearing on their typewriters until the early 1930s. In 1936, she explained her choice of pen surname by saying, "Rand is an abbreviation of my Russian surname." Her initials remained A. R. and she later wittily stated, "Two kinds of people keep their initials when they change their names — criminals and writers."

After her extra work on *The King of Kings* was completed, DeMille kept her on for a period as a script reader. She took a succession of odd jobs. During this period, she and her husband financially struggled and sometimes had very little to eat.

Hired as a filing clerk in the RKO Wardrobe Department, she disliked the job but did her best and was suitably rewarded by a raise after working at it for six months and a promotion to department head within the year. Her adoring husband presented her with a radio along with a desk and typewriter to continue to hone her writing skills.

And hone them she did with a couple of short stories believed to have been written in 1929: "Escort" and "Her Second Career." Much briefer than "The Night King," "Escort" also clearly shows the influence of O. Henry. It is a spry and witty tale of a man who keeps his occupation secret even from his own wife. He is not a criminal but a professional "escort" who squires women around the town. No sexual favors are included but our hero feels demeaned by the job as it is not a serious or genuinely respectable position.

"Her Second Career" is more like "Good Copy" in its elements of parody combined with cartoon-like characters and situations. At the center of the story is movie star Claire Nash whose vanity in her acting abilities is oddly offset by a prickly sensitivity to criticism. Wanting to prove her stardom not just a matter of luck, the actress decides to seek employment under a different identity. Will she shoot to stardom with "Her Second Career"? The situations that result from Claire's pride-based experiment are darkly comic.

The year 1932 would be a turning point for the author. It was the year she sold a film synopsis and screenplay, *Red Pawn*, to Universal Studios. It was also the year in which saw the producing of her first stage play, *Night of January 16th*.

The apparent suicide of Swedish entrepreneur Ivar Kreuger inspired Rand to write *Night of January 16th*. Kreuger (1880-1932) had built a vast financial empire. He was nicknamed the "Match King," because manufacturing matches was his major business. He also owned a gold mine, banks, businesses that created pulp, and real estate. After the end of World War I, Kreuger started many highly speculative transactions. People began to suspect some of the holdings he claimed to possess did not actually exist and that he was persuading people to invest in phantom holdings. In 1932, he was found dead in a hotel room of a single gunshot wound. His death was ruled a suicide but his family and others speculated he might have been murdered. The *Encyclopedia Britannica* states that after his death it was discovered "that the assets and profits that were recorded for the business were largely fictitious." What's more, "The concern disintegrated and many of its component companies went bankrupt."

Rand revealed about *Night of January 16th*, "The springboard for the story was the collapse of Ivar Kreuger — or, more precisely, the public reaction to that collapse." She continued, "His death was followed by the crash of the vast financial empire he had created, and by the revelation that that empire was a gigantic fraud. He had been a mysterious figure, a 'lone wolf,' celebrated as a man of genius, of unswerving determination and spectacular audacity. His fall was like an explosion that threw up a storm of dust and muck." Rand believed there was a negative side to the publicity surrounding his demise. She speculated that his ambition led to "hordes of envious mediocrities rejoicing at his downfall." She pointedly asserted that the legendary Icarus would have garnered gloating obituaries had there been a world press in existence when he flew too close to the sun.

Rand viewed the fallen entrepreneur sympathetically as someone "of unusual ability" who made a fortune through "legitimate means" but then ventured into "mixed-economy politics" and was "destroyed." She concluded, "Seeking a world monopoly for his match industry, he began to give large loans to various European countries — loans which were not repaid, which he could not collect and which led him to a fantastic juggling of his assets and bookkeeping in order to conceal his losses. In the final analysis, it was not Kreuger who profiteered on this ruin of the investors he had swindled; the profiteers were sundry European governments." She wryly noted that governments are not said to "swindle" but engage in "deficit financing" when pursuing policies similar to those that brought Kreuger down.

Rand wrote that she was not interested in the political ramifications of the Kreuger story "but the nature of those public denunciations" that she took as denunciations of "greatness." She hoped in her play to "dramatize the sense of life that was vaguely symbolized by Ivar Kreuger, and set it against the sense of life blatantly revealed by his attackers."

The character modeled after Ivar Kreuger in Rand's play is entrepreneur Bjorn Faulkner — who has died before the story opens. He never appears in the play either in flashback or as an apparition. The play takes place entirely in a courtroom and is the trial of secretary-mistress Karen Andre who is on trial for murdering him. The "sides" in the play pit entrepreneur Bjorn Faulkner and his secretary-mistress Karen Andre against Bjorn Faulkner's wife and her father John Graham Whitfield.

The prosecution alleges that she pushed him from the roof of his New York penthouse and sent him hurtling to his death. Among those testifying on the witness stand are Faulkner's betrayed wife, his father-in-law, and gangster Lawrence "Guts" Regan.

In describing the events that unfold in *Night of January 16th*, Rand asserted, "The factual evidence for and against the accused is (approximately) balanced. The issue rests on the credibility of the witnesses. The jury has to choose which side to believe, and this depends on every juror's own sense of life."

Here we come to a facet that makes Rand's play excitingly special. A trial takes place in this play but there is no jury made up of performers. Instead, the play calls for a jury to be impaneled in every showing of the play — a jury made up of audience members! Those twelve audience members decide whether or not Karen Andre is guilty of the murder of Bjorn Faulkner. The play has two different endings with each acted out according to the decision of that showing's jury.

In an introduction to the play, Rand asserted that she believed *Night of January 16th* should not be classified as "Romantic Realism" (a genre of literature in which she often wrote) but as "Romantic Symbolism." She elaborated that it "is not a philosophical, but a sense-of-life play," an "untranslated abstraction" and "its events are not to be taken literally" but are meant to "dramatize certain fundamental psychological characteristics, deliberately isolated and emphasized in order to convey a single abstraction." The playwright continued that, in "dramatizing the conflict of independence versus conformity," a criminal or any other "social outcast" can be "an eloquent symbol."

The "presentation of an ideal man" was always a goal for Rand but she did not intend Bjorn Faulkner to be viewed as an ideal man.

However, she did intend Karen Andre's view of him to represent "a woman's feeling for her ideal man."

When Rand was writing this play, her tentative title was *Penthouse Legend*. (This author is glad that *Penthouse Legend* did not remain the title because, in more modern times, it could conjure an association with the men's sex magazine *Penthouse*!) In another introduction to *Night of January 16th*, one written in 1968, Rand opined, "This [*Penthouse Legend*] is still its best title; it gives some indication of the play's nonrealistic, symbolic nature." At the insistence of producers, the title was first altered to *Woman on Trial* and then to *Night of January 16th*. Rand acceded to the wishes of producers who believed that the original title would "be a serious handicap to the play." One producer claimed people disliked the word "legend" which caused films with "legend" in the title to bomb. Rand did not insist on her original title because she regarded the issue as "unimportant." However, in the 1968 introduction, she said she regretted allowing the play's title to change "because *Night of January 16th* is an empty, meaningless title." Still, it was the "least offensive" of those titles that the producers suggested. After the play received recognition, it became pointless to alter its title so she felt pretty much stuck with it.

As Rand would throughout much of her writing career, she experienced a great deal of rejection with this play. Residing in Hollywood when she wrote the play, she sent it to an agent in New York City who submitted the play to one producer after another (mostly producers in NYC since Broadway was considered the best place for a play to be staged). It was rejected by one producer after another. A reason often given was that the audience would be turned off by what Rand regarded as "the most original feature of the play," creating a jury made of audience members and giving an ending depending on their verdict. Producers derided this feature, claiming it would "destroy the theatrical illusion."

After being repeatedly rejected, the play was accepted by two people at the same time! One was New York producer A. H. Woods and the other was British actor E. E. Clive who ran a theater company at the Hollywood playhouse. Woods demanded the right to make alterations according to his judgement. Rand could not go along with this demand so she signed a contract for production only with E. E. Clive.

The play debuted at the Hollywood Playhouse in 1934 under the title *Woman on Trial*. Barbara Bedford, a silent film star, played protagonist Karen Andre. E. E. Clive played a small role and also directed the play. Rand praised him as "a brilliant character actor" who "loved my play and seemed to understand it." However, Rand believed this production was "handicapped by lack of funds" which led to a production that was "competent, but somewhat unexciting." Despite the "handicap," *Woman on Trial* enjoyed positive reviews and, Rand stated, "a modestly successful run."

When that production finished, A. H. Woods again offered to put the play on Broadway. The contract was revamped and Rand's agent assured her that any changes would require "mutual consent" but she was skeptical about this and feared Woods had complete control. Despite misgivings, she decided to take a chance on it. Rand related that this led to "hell" as there was "a sickening struggle between Woods and me." She believed that struggle meant "the play became an incongruous mongrel slap-dashed out of contradictory elements." Woods innovations included "a gun, a heat test to determine its erased serial number, a flashy gun moll." However, Rand believes it is "to his credit as a showman" that he realized "the jury gimmick was a great idea" and it was that gimmick that led him to want to put this play on.

Rand had negative reactions to Woods's innovations but liked his most important casting decision. Rand wrote, "He gave the part of Karen Andre to a talented unknown, a young actress he had discovered — Doris Nolan." Rand found Nolan "very attractive" and applauded her "excellent performance." Rand suggested Walter Pidgeon for the part of Lawrence "Guts" Regan. Woods, after seeing Pidgeon in another play, eagerly signed him for the production *Night of January 16th* that Woods put on under that very name.

It opened on Broadway in September 1935. *Night of January 16th* received mixed reviews but was successful with the public, running for six months. On opening night, Woods arranged for the jury to be made up of celebrities. Thereafter, the jury was made up of audience members as Rand had intended. However, for the first two weeks, Woods made sure he had "stooges" backstage in case not enough audience members volunteered as jurors. Then he realized it was unnecessary as audience members enthusiastically volunteered to serve on the jury.

Rand related that an "interesting incident" was a "benefit performance for the blind." Most of the audience and all jurors were blind with Helen Keller serving as foreperson. Newscaster Graham McNamee narrated one of the proceedings for the blind audience. The jury decided that night on a guilty verdict.

During the Woods run, a stage manager informed Rand that verdicts generally ran three to two for "not guilty."

There have been other stage productions of *Night of January 16th*. And a film was made of it. That film will be discussed at length later in this book.

1933: *We the Living*, a Novel Set in the Soviet Union

In 1933, Rand finished her first novel, *We the Living*. She had worked on it for years. The story was set in Russia in the years immediately following the communist revolution. Rand said that it was not an autobiographical novel but the closest she would ever come to one. Rand stated, "The plot is invented; the background is not." Rand did not look like Kira or share her subject of study but she shared a basic outlook: "The specific events of Kira's life were not mine; her ideas, her convictions, her values were and are."

The story told starts in 1922 and ends during 1925. The heroine is Kira Argounova whose father had owned a textile factory before the communist takeover and had the business confiscated by the Bolsheviks. As the story starts, the family is returning to Petrograd after leaving it. The home they used to live in has been seized by the government and converted into a multi-family dwelling unit.

The entire situation in Petrograd is described as bleak with people barely making it as they wait in long lines for food and fuel rations. Kira manages to get government permission to work and attend an educational institution. She enrolls at a college where she studies engineering and meets Andrei Taganov, officer in the Soviet secret police and dedicated communist. Andrei is unique among Rand characters as he is the only communist character depicted as an honorable person who genuinely believes in communist doctrines.

Although Kira despises communism and Andrei embraces it, the two of them like and respect each other.

Kira meets Leo Kovalensky and this pair also become close. The initial meeting is hardly promising as Leo mistakes Kira for a street-walker! But they have a powerful sexual attraction as well as respect and affection based on their shared distaste for communism.

Our heroine faces many trials and tribulations in a society in which those of "bourgeois" background are apt to lose educational and career opportunities. Kira tries to keep her spirits alive in the face of adversity but Leo sinks into depression and physical illness as well.

Throughout the novel, Kira is torn between her feelings of affection for different men and her frustration at the way the society around her claims to champion the common people yet catapults toward tyranny. Rand describes a heroine with whom we deeply sympathize and a culture we are meant to despise. The aspiring author submitted *We the Living* to publisher after publisher after publisher. She received rejection after rejection after rejection.

In 1934, while Rand was still submitting *We the Living* to various publishers, she penned a play entitled *Ideal*. Leonard Peikoff writes, "The story was written originally as a novelette and then, probably within a year or two, was extensively revised and turned into a stage play." Peikoff elaborates that Rand's theme is again "the role of values in men's lives" but that the "treatment is not jovial" but "sober."

Ideal was inspired by an offhand remark a Rand female acquaintance made, that she worshiped a particular actress so much she would give her life to meet her. Although Rand recognized the hyperbole of the comment, she used it to create a fictional scenario in which an actress whose beauty is so great that, in Peikoff's phrasing, "she comes to represent to men the embodiment of their deepest ideals," actually comes into the lives of her worshippers. The actress in *Ideal* is Kay Gonda. Peikoff notes that she suffers acute "alienation" because she does not wish to accept anything less than that which is "ideal."

A successful author is apt to require the characteristic of persistence. The persistent Ayn Rand kept submitting the multiply rejected *We the Living* until, in 1936, three years after she began submitting it, her persistence paid off: Macmillan published it in the United States and Cassell published it in England. Rand always said that *We the Living* was not her life story but that it was the most autobiographical of her novels. The *Internet Encyclopedia of Philosophy* relates that the novel's theme was "the brutality of life under communist rule in Russia." It elaborates, "*We the Living* did not receive a positive reaction from American reviewers and intellectuals. It was published in the 1930s, a decade sometimes called the 'Red Decade,' during which American intellectuals were often pro-communist and respectful and admiring of the Soviet experiment."

Even as Ayn Rand bore down on her career, she could not help but be concerned about her family who had remained behind in the Soviet Union. She wanted to get her parents and two sisters out of Russia but could not. As Stalinist Russia became increasingly oppressive, Rand stopped writing to her family — not because she ceased to care about them but because it had become actually dangerous to even write to people in the Soviet Union.

There was one thing Rand never learned to do that is often considered routine for Americans. She never learned to drive a car. The automobile is often seen as symbolic of individual freedom so some have wondered why someone so strongly committed to individual freedom never learned this skill. In the "Trivia" section about Rand in the Internet Movie Database, it states, "Her friends and associates believed that this was on purpose, so she would always depend on her husband Frank to do the driving, leaving him in control of that part of their relationship." However, a passage from Barbara Branden's *The Passion of Ayn Rand* contradicts that assertion. That book stated, "Frank had promised to teach her to drive their new Cadillac convertible, so that she would not be dependent on him. He gave her several driving lessons, then they both gave up the attempt in mutually enraged despair." That book described Rand as finding "mechanical objects impossible to master" and being "unable to learn" to drive.

This author would like to suggest a possible reason Rand never learned to drive. Driving requires that an individual maintain a constant awareness of immediate surroundings and respond instantly to changes in those surroundings. Artists, writers, and other creative types often tend to kind of "live in our heads," being mentally preoccupied with what's going on in our imaginations rather than what is going on in the immediate environment. For this reason, we often do not make safe drivers. A gut feeling that she would not be a safe driver may have kept Rand from learning this skill. Thus, the absence of a driver's license in her life did not reflect hypocrisy but responsibility on Rand's part. (In case the reader is curious, the author of this book does not drive.)

In 1935 Rand began working on a novel she tentatively entitled *Second-Hand Lives*. The novel would be about the philosophy of individualism that she was developing. It would contrast living according to one's own vision and goals, living "first-hand," with varied ways of living "second-hand," through and for other people.

Rand decided that she would use architecture as the backdrop to her novel. It would not be about "architecture" but it would be set among architects. To understand that profession, she sometimes took jobs in architectural offices.

Even as the busy author researched architecture and worked at her new novel, she occasionally took time off from the major novel to work on briefer projects. One of those briefer projects was a novella she would entitle *Anthem*.

1937: *Anthem*: Novel of a Foul Future

Written in 1937, Rand's *Anthem* is a dystopian science fiction story in the mold of George Orwell's classic *Nineteen Eighty-Four* (1949) and Margaret Atwood's brilliant *The Handmaid's Tale* (1985). Anthem takes place in a super-collectivistic future society. The year is never specified but it is a culture in which technology has regressed to a very simple level and in which independent thinking is a crime. There are no personal possessions and even the word "I" has disappeared from the language.

Our hero is Equality 7-2521, a 21-year-old man who chafes bitterly against the rules of this society. He writes his story in a tunnel inside the earth and is guided by the light of a candle since advanced technics like the light bulb no longer exist in this world. In telling his life story, he uses words like "we" and "our" to discuss himself because this is a world that lacks even the concept of individualism. Like other children in his culture, much of his childhood was not spent with his family or blood relatives. Rather, he was in the Home of Infants when very small and transferred to the Home of Students when he was five years old, remaining there until through his fifteenth year. Equality 7-2521 learns easily and his mind is filled with questions. Taking the super-collectivistic values of his culture as good, he believes both his intelligence and his tendency to question constitute a kind of "curse."

Equality 7-2521 is interested in science so he hopes that the Council of Vocations will assign him to become a Scholar. Instead, they assign the teenager to become a Street Sweeper.

Having no choice but to follow the path selected for him by his superiors, he spends his days sweeping. Others with whom he works include Union 5-3992 and International 4-8818.

Our protagonist "knows" curiosity is opposed by the norms of his culture but cannot keep himself from exploring an underground tunnel. Why is the tunnel even in existence? He concludes it must be something left over from what are called the Unmentionable Times that preceded the current social structure. At night, he sneaks away from the community to the tunnel where he conducts experiments with trash he has stolen from the Home of the Scholars. The very journal we are reading is said to have been written on paper pilfered from the Home of the Clerks and the candles were stolen from the Home of the Street Sweepers.

Equality 7-2521 is doing his cleaning job when he happens upon a young female, Liberty 5-3000, who is working at her job in the fields. He begins obsessively thinking of Liberty 5-3000 although he knows he is not supposed to do this. When he turns 20, he will, like other males in his culture, be assigned a woman at the Time of Mating. He knows this but cannot keep himself from desiring the attractive brown-eyed blonde Liberty 5-3000. As he fantasizes about her, he stops thinking of her by her true name but, in his own mind, re-names her "The Golden One."

The two of them start talking one day and he learns that the strong attraction is mutual. He tells her he does not think of her as Liberty 5-3000 but as The Golden One. Then she reveals that she has secretly given him a nickname: "The Unconquered."

Even as the two continue their illicit flirtation, Equality 7-2521 continues his — also illicit — secret scientific experiments in the tunnel. This leads to his re-discovery of electricity! He also finds a use for electricity when he finds a glass box with wires in it and — wow! — it gives off light when he passes electricity through it.

Equality 7-2521 believes that these great discoveries will lead the World Council of Scholars to make him a Scholar. He knows he has been violating laws but believes showing them a way to make light that is superior to the candle will lead them to overlook his wrongdoing.

Before he can go before the Council, a nocturnal absence from his proper place at the Home of the Street Sweepers is noted. This leads to severe punishment including a whipping and incarceration in the Palace of Corrective Detention. Just before the World Council of Scholars is scheduled to hold a meeting, Equality 7-2521 escapes.

The hero presents his discoveries (he does not know they are re-discoveries) to the World Council of Scholars. He expects this learned group will be enthralled by what he demonstrates to them. Instead, they are upset that he performed independent experiments and order that this "wretch" be punished. They also wish to destroy the box that he can light. Equality 7-2521 grabs the box and flees the World Council of Scholars. He escapes into a place outside city limits called the Uncharted Forest.

Events that follow reunite him with the Golden One. Even more importantly, they lead him to discover the meaning and power of the word "I."

Anthem is a startlingly beautiful work of the imagination and a hymn to the beauty and power of individualism.

A publisher in England called Cassell brought out *Anthem* in 1938. Rand submitted it to Macmillan Publishers, which had previously published *We the Living*, but they rejected it. *Anthem* was not published in the United States until 1946 when a small publishing house owned by Leonard Read and William C. Mullendore, both friends with Rand, brought out a copy.

When *Anthem* was published in England in 1938, reviews were mixed. *Sunday Times* reviewer Dilys Powell praised *Anthem* for its "simplicity and sincerity." Maurice Richardson, writing for *The Observer*, believed it showcased "some extremely eloquent writing" but was ultimately "unconvincing."

In 1987, the Libertarian Futurist Society gave *Anthem* its Hall of Fame Award. In 2014, it was nominated for a Retrospective Hugo Award in the "Best Novella" category.

Ayn Rand herself called this novella a "hymn to man's ego." A radio adaptation of it aired in 1950. This author did not find more information about that adaption. *Anthem* has been made into stage productions.

1939-40: *Unconquered*, *Think Twice*, "The Simplest"

Rand wrote a stage adaption of *We the Living* that was produced in 1939 on Broadway as *The Unconquered*. It was not a success. Also in 1939, Rand penned her third, and last, stage play. That play is entitled *Think Twice* and tells the story of a murder mystery as it explores philosophical implications in its story.

In 1940, Rand wrote a short story entitled "The Simplest Thing in the World." The protagonist is writer Henry Dorn. The entire story is largely the thoughts of a frustrated writer trying to come up with a commercially viable project. It opens: "Henry Dorn sat at his desk and looked at a sheet of blank paper. Through a feeling of numb panic, he said to himself: this is going to be the easiest thing you've ever done." All he needs to do is "relax" and write a simple, even "stupid," story that the public will like. He chides himself for thinking he "can't be stupid."

Then we are told he is "tired" although he has not gotten up from his desk, nor has he even written a single word on the page. Perhaps only a writer writing about a writer would understand and write how just thinking about a writing project can be wearying.

Henry Dorn turns to examine his published book that is entitled *Triumph*. He tells himself it "was not a good book." Then he thinks: "All right, it was a good book. It's a great book." He believes it would be easier on him emotionally if he could believe the book he authored was really bad. If he believed that, he would believe it deserved the negative reviews it received. And then he thinks that it was not the negative reviews that bothered him as much as the good reviews — because those who liked it did not interpret it the same way Dorn did. He is mentally harassed by a compliment from reviewer Fleurette Lumm "who said it was the best book she'd ever read — because it had such a touching love story." Why in the world would that bother author Dorn? "He had not even known that there was a love story in his book." What's more, the things he most liked in his own book were things Lumm had not even mentioned in her positive review.

Dorn reminds himself that he has not even started typing a new story! He turns and looks into his bedroom to see "Kitty" — presumably his wife — "at a table, playing solitaire." As Dorn gazes at her playing solitaire, the doorbell rings. He could answer it but Kitty brushes past him to answer it. A salesperson is at the door and Kitty says they do not need what is offered.

Dorn tells himself to think of reviewer Fleurette Lumm, imagine what would appeal to her, then write it. He recalls people advising him to stop being "intellectual all the time" and give the public what it wants. He tells himself to stop being "complicated" and opt for the "simple" in his writing. Is he so "conceited" that he cannot write a simple story? He must avoid the "profound" and "important" and not be a "world-saver" or "Joan d' Arc." He ruminates obsessively on his mission of writing this simple story. Dorn considers a story inspired by Mr. Crawford, a lawyer "who's glad when a client of his loses a suit" despite the fact "he loses money" and "it hurts his reputation."

Soon Dorn imagines a tale about "a middle-aged millionaire who tries to seduce a poor young working girl." The man is created in Dorn's mind as "ruthless" and possessing "millions" yet "miserable." The girl? She will be met "in the five-and-ten" but Dorn decides to not bother with that character. Instead, his middle-aged protagonist will meet a youth who is nice and likable but without ambition. He starts developing that story but does not get far with it.

Dorn imagines a young woman living in a storeroom over a loft. On a summer's day, she relaxes on the roof when "a window in the next building cracks open" and a man jumps out of that window to land on the roof with her. There is more rumination about the female character and her circumstances. Perhaps he will have the man who lands on the roof have just committed a shooting. Or perhaps . . . He gropes for a larger meaning. He tells himself to stop seeing larger meanings and just write a story.

"You're not settling world problems," he remonstrates with himself. "You're writing a commercial story." He could write a murder mystery and/or detective story. More fantasizing follows and Dorn resolves that he will create a character who is a professional blackmailer and, about to be exposed for his blackmailing, the blackmailer murders. That would be "as low a motive as you could imagine." Then Dorn wonders if he could soften the motive by having the blackmail victims be so evil that they deserve their fates. Perhaps he could create "a crusading blackmailer." He meditates more and realizes that his mind goes blank — as blank as the paper on which he has written nothing.

This short story ends on a note that is not tragic, not comic, not dramatic, but tellingly prosaic: "Then he pushed the sheet of blank paper aside and reached for the *Times*' 'Help Wanted' ads."

"The Simplest Thing in the World" is obviously autobiographical in its obsessive concern with the special problems of being a writer. It is a short story that perfectly captures the frustrations of writer's block, the yearning for inspiration that feels so close yet so terribly out of reach. The back and forth of Henry Dorn's internal dialogue is completely credible as the thoughts of a writer trying to write a story. The conflict a writer feels between wanting to create something artistically satisfying and needing to write something that will sell is made palpably believable. Rand brings to life the often gapingly large distance that can exist between how an author interprets his or her work and how a critic may view it. The story's ending will hit home with any writer as it so concisely describes the conflict between the creative urge and the practical need to just earn a living. In the opinion of the writer of this book, "The Simplest Thing in the World" is a perfectly penned wail to the woes we writers must suffer.

Written in 1940, it was not published until 1967 when it appeared in the November issue of a magazine Rand put out, *The Objectivist.*

While Rand worked "regular" jobs in various architectural offices to research a major novel, while she adapted *We the Living* into a play and wrote a fresh play, and while she penned a strikingly brilliant novella and a short story, a motion picture was made of *Night of January 16th.*

1941: A Film Called *The Night of January 16th*

In 1934, Metro-Goldwyn-Mayer optioned the right to turn *Night of January 16th* into a motion picture. MGM also hired Rand to work on the screenplay. However, the studio apparently lacked enthusiasm for the project as the option lapsed without a movie getting made. Rights to the play were resold to RKO Pictures in January 1939. RKO planned to star either Claudette Colbert or Lucille Ball in the film. Paramount Pictures bought the rights to the play in July 1939.

Paramount Pictures brought in other writers to craft a screenplay so Rand played no part in scripting the movie. While the film was being made, its working titles were *Private Secretary* and/or *Secrets of a Secretary.* A 1931 motion picture that has no relationship to this movie had already been made with the latter title. Paramount wanted Don Ameche to play the major male part but he did not accept the role because he believed he was not right for the part. Paramount filed a lawsuit against Don Ameche demanding $170,000 for his refusal but dropped the suit when Ameche agreed to act in *Kiss the Boys Goodbye* (1941).

Ray Milland and Paulette Goddard were cast in the film and Warner Bros. loaned William Clemons to Paramount to direct it. Three writers worked on the screenplay: Delmer Daves, Eve Greene, and Robert Pirosh. Milland and Goddard did not work on it.

As previously noted, changes must always be made when a story goes from one medium to another. Changes from the play entitled *Night of January 16th* to the movie that, whatever its working title, would be released as *The Night of January 16th* in 1941, were major.

The hero of the story is a character named Steve Van Ruyle who did not exist in Rand's play. He is played by Robert Preston, a handsome actor experienced on both stage and screen. In 1957, he was cast as Professor Harold Hill in a Broadway production of *The Music Man*. He won a Tony for his stage portrayal of that character and reprised the role in the 1962 film *The Music Man*. In movies generally, he often played the leading character's pal. Commenting on his career, Preston said, "I'd get the best role in every B picture and the second best in the A pictures."

Secretary-turned-murder suspect Karen Andre has been rechristened Kit Lane and is played by Ellen Drew, a dark-haired actress with fresh-faced girl-next-door good looks. Drew's "discovery" as an actress took place in an archetypically accidental fashion. She was working in a Hollywood ice cream parlor when actor William Demarest, who would eventually become known to America for playing Uncle Charley on *My Three Sons*, noticed her and told her he would try to get her into movies. He was instrumental in getting her signed with Paramount Studios when she was 21. Prior to playing in *The Night of January 16th*, she acted in several movies including the 1938 Bing Crosby musical *Sing, You Sinners*.

The character of Bjorn Faulkner exists in the film with the name Rand bestowed upon him. The actor who plays him, Nils Asther, was born in Denmark and raised in Sweden. After attending the Royal Dramatic Theater School in Sweden, he returned to his native Denmark to act in the theater. Then it was back to Sweden for movie roles. He worked in Germany before journeying to Hollywood where he co-starred with such female greats as Pola Negri (the actress so admired by Ayn Rand), Greta Garbo, and Joan Crawford. He left Hollywood for Britain in 1934 and returned to Hollywood in 1938.

The play has Faulkner dead before the proceedings begin. In the movie, he is very much alive when the story begins. The story in the motion picture is far from confined to a courtroom. Indeed, relatively little time spent in a courtroom in this movie. Early in the story, we see a meeting take place of a company's board of directors. Wearing his sailor's uniform, Steve stands out like a sore thumb among men in standard business suits. Why is he there? Much to

Steve's surprise, an uncle to whom he was not close left him a seat among the directors together with a hefty inheritance.

Financial shenanigans come to light when the board finds $20 million dollars missing from the company's funds. The understandably perplexed board of directors demands Faulkner explain this. Faulkner tells them he cannot explain it right then but promises to do so soon.

After that board meeting, in the night, Faulkner meets with a shadowy character named Anton Haraba. We see the two men fiercely struggling, both figures darkened so we cannot make them out to identify either one.

It appears from what we see that Haraba tosses Faulkner from the balcony to his death. Only minutes later, Kit Lane arrives for a visit. Bad timing makes her a murder suspect.

Wanting his missing $3 million, sailor-turned-board-member Steve Van Ruyle then turns amateur detective as he tries to put the pieces together. A variety of twists and turns occur as Van Ruyle and Lane join forces to ferret out what really happened to Faulkner. This leads to adventures both comic and dramatic. Characters have been created for the film primarily to lighten the mood and produce chuckles. For example, veteran supporting actor Cecil Kellaway plays Oscar, a lovable drunk still mourning because his wife deserted him. Cliff Nazaro plays a gas station attendant with a comical obsession with good manners that leads to his not selling as much gas as he could because, "I make my point." Perhaps the most interesting bit player in the film is four-footed. The small dog named Spooky in the film is played by a cocker spaniel/poodle/terrier mix whose official name is given as Daisy by the Internet Movie Database because she played Daisy in the *Blondie* film series but whose "real name" is given as Spooks — a variation on the name of her character in *The Night of January 16th*.

Worth mentioning is a little globe that was not in the play but is in the movie and features strongly in the unraveling of the story's basic mystery. That little globe is held up by a figure of the mythological Atlas. Of course, this is only a coincidence as the filmmakers could not possibly know that the writer whose play inspired their motion picture would someday write a novel entitled *Atlas Shrugged*.

New York Times reviewer A. W. praised the movie as "an engrossing mystery melodrama" and continued, "The picture, although making no pretense to cinema grandeur, is a compact and adult thriller of better than average quality." That reviewer found the performances of Preston, Drew, and Asther "neatly and often humorously turned." A. W. concluded, "Put this entertainment down as a minor but gratifying offering."

A critic for the *Motion Picture Herald* called it "a murder-mystery the unity and impact of which place it near the all-time top of its class." The review continued that the makers of the movie "have concocted a story certain to please all lovers of this type of drama" because "from its arresting beginning to its climax, the story runs along smoothly" and elaborated that its "parts fit as neatly as a jigsaw puzzle." The review stated that the "cast is uniformly excellent," asserting, "Nils Asther makes a most attractive villain-tycoon" and praising Preston for "a neat performance." The critic applauded the film's "excellent comedy sequences" and stated "sets throughout the picture are lavish, elaborate, and ahead of their time in decor."

More recent reviews of what is now an oldie have tended to concur in its value as an enjoyable minor movie. Writing for a website called Mystery File, David Vineyard called it "a fairly decent mystery to wrap a bright comedy mystery around." He believed the screenwriting trio of Daves, Green, and Pirosh turned in a "good fast-paced script," that Clemens delivered "capable direction" and that Preston and Drew were "attractive leads." Vinyard concluded it was a "bright little B film." On the Classic Movie Review website, Derek Winnert found Drew and Preston "an attractive star couple" but faulted the film as "dully acted" and "insufficiently reworked for the cinema." He continued that Clemens's direction was "uninspired" and concluded the film just "isn't much of a story."

The writer of this book believes *The Night of January 16th* is a fast-paced and feisty film that holds interest until its genuinely surprising end. Perhaps the most significant strength of a mystery is to keep things mysterious until the revelation and this film succeeds in doing that.

One person who disliked *The Night of January 16th* was Ayn Rand. She wrote, "There is nothing of mine in that movie, except the names of some of the characters and the title (which was not mine)." She dismissed the movie as "cheap, trashy vulgarity."

The year after one of her plays hit the big screen, a version of Rand's first novel *We the Living*, appeared in movie theaters. However, those movie theaters were in neither Rand's native land of the Soviet Union nor in her adopted country of the United States. They were in Italy.

1942: *We the Living* Made in Fascist Italy

World War II was being fought when an Italian film company, Scalera Films, produced a motion picture based on Rand's *We the Living*. Part of the reason Scalera Films wished to film the work is that the novel sold very well in Italy. Producer Duncan Scott stated, "I believe the idea to film the book originated with Scalera's daughter." Massimo Ferrara, who had been general manager for Scalera Studios, recalled, "She read the book and enjoyed it. I read the book and liked it."

Since Italy and the United States were on opposite sides of the conflict, there was no way for Scalera to secure Rand's permission to use her story for this film so the company created it without Rand's consent or even knowledge. What's more, the company never gave her any compensation for the use of her novel.

In order to make this film — or any film — a motion picture company in Fascist Italy required the approval of Fascist authorities. Because Benito Mussolini's son, Vittorio Mussolini, advocated filming *We the Living*, Scalera secured that approval. Since Italy was at war with the Soviet Union and *We the Living* was an indictment of communism and a grim portrait of how people suffered in communist Russia, we can surmise that Fascists believed the movie might rally Italians to fight ever harder against the Red enemy.

Goffredo Allessandrini, who was at the height of his career as a filmmaker, directed *We the Living*. Some of his best work was filmed when Italy was Fascist: he won the Mussolini Cup for Best Italian Film in 1938 for one of his films and won it again in 1939 for another.

Two Italian novelists co-wrote a screenplay based on *We the Living*. They made significant changes from Rand's novel, one of the most striking being that Kira became a ballet dancer instead of an engineering student. It is possible that, in the 1940s, they believed an audience would be more apt to want to see a heroine in a traditionally "feminine" occupation. It is also possible that this occupation would give the filmmakers greater opportunity to display the heroine's legs!

However, Allessandrini disliked their script. The upshot was that the movie was made without a complete script in a kind of "on the fly" manner with a part of a script often written a day before the camera filmed it or scenes were filmed as directly taken from the novel. Kira is an engineering student as she was in Rand's novel. The odd manner of filming resulted in a movie that was in fact more faithful to its source material than is usually the case since both dialogue and action were often lifted directly from the novel. On the negative side, it also resulted in a movie that was extremely long. After the film was completed, it was decided that this super-long motion picture would be released as two separate films, one entitled *Noi Vivi* (*We the Living*) and another entitled *Addido Kira* (*Farewell Kira*).

Three of Italy's most popular performers were cast in the main roles of Kira, Andrei, and Leo. Dark-haired beauty Alida Valli played Kira, Fosco Giachetti played Andrei, and Rossano Brazzi played Leo. Massimo Ferrara recalled, "Alida Valli was a good friend of mine. Brazzi was quite popular. Giachetti was a major star, a virile leading man."

It was very difficult to secure location permits due to the wartime conditions so all scenes in the film, including those taking place in a snowy Russian winter, were filmed on a soundstage. While this worked against authenticity, one thing that worked for it was that many extras were in fact Russians who had fled Russia due to their opposition to Bolshevism. Those who crafted banners and posters were also Russian expatriates which again worked to promote a sense of authenticity. Duncan Scott noted that there are advantages to shooting outdoor scenes inside since "you can control lighting."

Fascist officials monitored the film throughout and came to the editing room.

There is an irony about one of the film's Italian extras. Raf Vallone was little known at the time this movie was made but would achieve renown in Italy as a leading man during the 1950s and '60s. He was also a dedicated communist even though he participated in the making of this profoundly anti-communist motion picture. Before World War II, Vallone had been culture editor for *L'Unitá*, the official newspaper of Italy's Communist Party. Even as a he worked as an extra on this film, he was a secret agent for an anti-Fascist and Communist-associated group called the "Brigade Garibaldi."

When the two motion pictures hit the theaters, they were an instant hit. People in war-torn Fascist Italy identified strongly with the deprivations and constrictions that harmed the people of Bolshevik Russia. The films became so well-known to Italians of the time period that some started using ironic slang based on the movies like calling themselves "Noi Morti" ("We the Dead) and saying "Addio, Lira" (Goodbye to the Italian currency called "lira"). Duncan Scott commented, "The films became a kind of *Gone With The Wind* for Italy. People named their kids Kira and Andrei." Part of the reason for the popularity, Scott asserted, "The public could relate to things like the shortages depicted."

Producer Massimo Ferrara-Santamaria attempted to sell *Noi Vivi* in Nazi Germany where, of course, any film had to be approved by authorities before it appeared in theaters. Thus, it was shown to Reich Minister of Propaganda Joseph Goebbels in a private screening in Berlin. Goebbels watched this cinematic attack on Nazi Germany's enemy but was not persuaded that it belonged in the theaters of his own nation. The official reason given for banning the movie was that it was "too mild" in its depiction of Russian Communism. The more likely reason is that Goebbels realized that the citizens of the Reich would realize it was an attack on *all* tyrannies.

As Mussolini's cronies also realized not too long after Italians crowded into theaters to see the films. Although Fascist officials originally approved the making of the movies that blasted their Soviet enemy, when the common people of Italy viewed the movies, they recognized the similarities between Fascism and Communism. As Leonard Peikoff observes, "People grasped AR's broader theme and embraced the two movies, in part as a way of protesting their oppression under Mussolini."

The Fascist government figured out that the public saw the aforementioned parallels so, five months after the government approved release of the films, the government banned them.

It was not until the end of World War II that Ayn Rand found out that her novel had been, in a sense, hijacked by filmmakers in Italy. However, when she saw the movies, she liked them overall — but was offended by a few pro-Fascist additions the filmmakers had inserted into them. It seems likely those insertions were a kind of sop to the Fascist government in the hope that a few positive nods to Fascism would prevent Fascists from seeing, as they eventually did see, that these movies opposed totalitarianism regardless of how it is branded.

Since the war was over and relations were restored between Italy and the United States, her permission was needed for a re-release of the movies. She refused to grant those literary rights and the films were not seen anywhere. In the early 1950s, the company that had made the movies, Scalera Films, folded. The films based on Rand's *We the Living* essentially disappeared from public consciousness with few people even knowing where copies of them were kept. "Filmmakers hid the negatives of the original films in the basement of somebody's home," Scott stated.

In the 1960s, two of Rand's attorneys, husband-wife team Erika Holzer and Henry Mark Holzer, traveled to Italy to look for copies of the movies. In 1968, the couple found a business that possessed dozens of copies of the film. They brought some copies back to the United States.

In America, Rand, assisted by Duncan Scott, worked on crafting a re-edited version. "She was unhappy that she'd never seen a dime from the originals," Scott remembered. "She got money from the condensed version we created but it was not a grand sum. It was more the principle of the thing that mattered to her."

According to Scott, "Rand thought Fosco older than she envisioned Andrei as being but she believed his older age worked well. Everyone was blown away by Alida Valli's performance." One thing was necessary and that was to edit out all scenes that seemed to support Fascism, as this form of "collectivism" was as anathema to Rand as communism.

They combined the films into a single three-hour long motion picture with English subtitles called *We the Living*. It was re-released as such in 1986, four years after Rand's death.

The premiere of the revised *We the Living* took place in Colorado in 1986 at the Telluride Film Festival. Then it was released in theaters throughout the United and Canada as well as in other countries. Duncan Scott Productions sells a two-disc DVD of *We the Living*.

Reviews of *We the Living* have tended toward the positive. *Washington Post* critic Hal Hinson called it "a mixture of robust naturalism and operatic romance." He said it projects "a sort of Hollywood-style neorealism." Hinson elaborated that the "characters make speeches and posture outrageously — they make spectacles of their passion." Hinson noted that the absence of work on location is obvious when "a layer of gummy artificial snow" is seen on the boots of Kira and Leo. Hinson asserts, "In her love scenes, Alida Valli is like an Italian Debra Winger; there's heat in her soulfulness" and that Brazzi as Leo "is her passionate equal." Even though Hinson finds flaws in the film, he concludes it is "pure delight."

Reviewer Derek Winnert stated that Valli, Giachetti, and Brazzi all "give outstanding performances." Winnert continued that it is "an indictment of any kind of dictatorship," a "good and important film," and "a stunning social document."

Ayn Rand liked the revised and pared-down movie version of her debut novel. A film restoration co-producer, Henry Mark Holzer, said, "She said from the beginning it was a pretty good film." Film restoration co-producer Erika Holzer asserted, "Rand found it quite exciting."

The author of this book wants to say she was strongly impressed by Alida Valli's fiery performance as Kira. Alida Valli appears to speaks from her heart, and from that of her creator, when she predicts a "glorious funeral march" will follow when "Bolshevism is disinfected from history." There is an appropriate joy when she says, "Do they really wear black underwear abroad? How silly. And how lovely." When challenged that engineering is not a "profession for a woman," the stoutly individualistic Kira is true to herself when she refuses to allow stereotypes to dictate her goals. She seems a precursor to Howard Roark when she happily asserts, "I want to build skyscrapers of glass and steel. And a huge bridge, made of aluminum. White, shining — the most beautiful in the world." In this writer's estimation, the filmed version *We the Living* gave the world a true and vibrant Ayn Rand heroine.

1943: *The Fountainhead*: Novel of Moral Idealism

The novel Rand began in 1935 would be published in 1943. Her tentative title for the novel was *Second-Hand Lives*. It would not be published not under the title *Second-Hand Lives* but under the far more inspiring title *The Fountainhead*. This change was significant because it altered the focus from the people who lived "second-hand" lives to the individualism and creativity that Rand viewed as the "fountainhead" of progress.

Before the novel actually saw print, history repeated itself as twelve publishers rejected *The Fountainhead*. The persistent Ayn Rand kept going with it. Editor Archibald Ogden of Bobbs-Merrill told his superiors, "If *The Fountainhead* isn't the book for you, then I'm not the editor for you." Bobbs-Merrill accepted the novel. Published in 1943, *The Fountainhead* was an immediate best-seller!

The Fountainhead in 1943 put Ayn Rand on the map as a writer and a public person. Set in the early 1920s through early 1930s, its protagonist, Howard Roark, was created by Rand to epitomize a "moral ideal." The story begins in 1922 with twenty-two-year-old Howard expelled from the Stanton Institute of Technology where he was studying architecture.

From childhood, Howard wanted to become an architect. Rand describes her hero as viewing the world through an architectural prism: "He looked at the granite. To be cut, he thought, and made into walls. He looked at a tree. To be split and made into rafters. He looked at a streak of rust on the stone and thought of iron ore under the ground. To be melted and to emerge as girders against the sky. These rocks, he thought, are here for me: waiting for the drill, the dynamite and my voice, waiting to be split, ripped, pounded, reborn; waiting for the shape my hands will give them."

When the story starts, young Howard Roark has just been expelled from architectural school. The youth has not been expelled for lack of talent or industriousness but because he refuses to learn traditional architectural styles. He believes strongly in modern architecture and will not emulate the architectural styles of ancient Greece or medieval Europe or colonial America or any other past era. When assigned to design something in a period mode, Howard turned in a drawing that is obviously modernistic. The academics who run the institution regard modernism as a passing fad — one that has already passed.

Before going further with *The Fountainhead* plot, it is necessary to comment on the literary school to which Rand subscribed. She wrote in "romantic realism." Thus, some of the history in *The Fountainhead* was deliberately distorted to make a larger point. Some critics have pointed out that, at the time the novel is set, modern architecture was becoming quite popular. Contrary to what is depicted in the novel, the architectural establishment of the 1920s-1930s did not persecute modernistic architects. Rather, modern architects like Le Corbusier and Frank Lloyd Wright did much of their work during that era and were successful right from the start of their careers.

However, to give us a sense of the individual-against-the-collective, Rand depicts a staid, moribund architectural community committed to past styles with no room for modernists. Howard states his architectural principles: "What can be done with one substance must never be done with another. No two materials are alike. No two sites on earth are alike. No two buildings have the same purpose. The purpose, the site, the material determine the shape. Nothing can be reasonable or beautiful unless it's made by one central idea, and the idea sets every detail." He elaborates, "A man doesn't borrow pieces of his body. A building doesn't borrow hunks of its soul."

At the same time that Howard, completely committed to his own brand of modern architecture, is expelled, his friend Peter Keating is graduating with honors. Peter often had difficulty with problems concerning the engineering side of design. He had sometimes gone to Howard with those difficulties and Howard was happy to point out solutions. Ironically, in view of his graduating with honors, Peter does not really like architecture. He yearns to become an artist and specifically a painter but, Rand writes, "It was his mother who had chosen a better field in which to exercise his talent for drawing." Mom believed it was a more practical aspiration, one that would lead to an affluent and socially respectable lifestyle. Still, Peter ruminates: "He was ready to do great things, magnificent things, things unsurpassed in . . . in . . . oh, hell . . . in architecture." He soon finds a job with the distinguished architecture firm headed by Guy Francon. It is called Francon & Heyer but partner Lucius N. Heyer is relatively inactive as he is aging and in ill health.

Howard seeks work with Henry Cameron, a proponent of modern architecture who was popular decades previously but now gets few commissions. He is best known for the modernistic Dana Building, a structure created with such originality that a passerby "would come upon it unexpectedly in the moonlight and stop and wonder from what dream that vision had come." It was also appreciated by its tenants who "said that they would not exchange it for any structure on earth; they appreciated the light, the air, the beautiful logic of the plan in their halls and offices." With few clients, Cameron has deteriorated and taken to drinking. When Howard asks for a job, he displays the drawings that got him expelled. Cameron tells the newcomer he has much to learn before hiring him.

While Cameron's office gets a few commissions here and there, Francon & Heyer does brisk business giving the public what it wants, grafting facades of the past onto buildings of the present. One of the book's most pivotal characters is introduced when Francon displays a positive review of the Francon-designed Melton Building. The reviewer is Ellsworth Toohey. "It stands in white serenity as an eloquent witness to the triumph of Classical purity and common sense. The discipline of an immortal tradition has served here as a cohesive factor in evolving a structure whose beauty can reach, simply and lucidly, the heart of every man in the street. There is no freak exhibitionism here, no perverted striving for novelty, no orgy of unbridled egotism." The flattered Francon points out that Toohey has "a tongue like an icepick, when he feels like using it" so it is especially welcome when he praises.

Peter works at Francon & Heyer, making good money and favorably impressing his colleagues. Thoughts of an affluent young man are apt to turn to marriage and Peter finds a woman whom he considers a good match. At first he finds young Catherine Halsey "homely and dull" but as he gets to know her, he finds himself enchanted by her humility, kindness, and honesty. When she phones him "the sound of her clear voice was like a hand pressed soothingly against his hot forehead." Then he is startled to learn she is the niece of none other than Ellsworth Toohey, who is, among many other things, a respected architecture reviewer.

After a year at the firm, Peter gains "the whispered title of crown prince without portfolio." He still has trouble with design issues so he takes work to Howard and requests assistance. Rand writes, "Keating stood watching the pencil in Roark's hand. He saw his imposing entrance foyer disappearing, his twisted corridors, his lightless corners; he saw an immense living room growing in the space he had thought too limited; a wall of giant windows facing the garden, a spacious kitchen." Howard says he simply cannot help with the facade but advises, "If you must have it Classic, have it good Classic at least" and suggests Peter drop decorations that are "too much."

It is through Peter's employment at Francon & Heyer that the reader learns that Guy Francon's daughter is Dominique Francon who works for a newspaper called *The Banner* that was created by rags-to-riches "success story" Gail Wynand. The publisher rose from the poverty of "Hell's Kitchen" to wealth through the creation of a newspaper that combines scandal-mongering and sensationalism with clichés and platitudes. This winning formula makes Gail feel powerful, as if he in a sense controls the public through *The Banner*. Like Peter Keating, Gail Wynand is a second-hander, devoting himself to his supposed power over his readers.

Howard is startled to see a copy of *The Banner* in Cameron's office. Cameron believes the newspaper has a "sense of symbolism" about all things mediocre. Rand writes, "The front page carried the picture of an unwed mother with thick glistening lips, who had shot her lover . . . a crusade against utility companies; a daily horoscope; extracts from church sermons, recipes for young brides, pictures of girls with beautiful legs . . . a poem proclaiming that to wash dishes was nobler than to write a symphony; an article proving that a woman who had borne a child was automatically a saint." However, Cameron purchased this popular newspaper largely to sneer at it which is, of course, Howard's reaction to it as well.

Rand once described Dominique as "myself in a bad mood." Dominique is deeply pessimistic about the world, believing that beauty and greatness have no place in the same world in which *The Banner* flourishes. Despising *The Banner*, she works for it, writing a column entitled "Our House" that deals with architecture and interior decorating. Her in-house rival is the aforementioned Ellsworth Toohey whose column deals with architecture but also with varied other matters including politics, social trends, art, and entertainment events.

Rand bestowed upon Dominique a name suitable for a romance novel heroine — which to some extent the character is as there are elements of that genre in this novel. There is also a suggestion in her name of "dominant," which is alternately appropriate or ironic depending on where you are in the novel. Dominique is an adult who often has a teenaged *Rebel Without A Cause* air about her. For example, she writes sarcastically of a house she knows was designed by her father's company (specifically by Peter Keating), pointing out "dead ducks and rabbits hanging on the wall panels" that are "bad plaster imitations" and that anyone in the house will "look at dimpled soles [of cupids] every time you glance out to see whether it's raining." Peter overhears her outraged Dad take her to task for the review and is struck by the way she laughs at the remonstrance, at once "so gay and so cold." Dominique is so perverse that she sometimes deliberately praises houses and other buildings that she knows are decorated or built in an atrocious style. She explained this once by saying something was "so awful that to pan it would have been an anticlimax" so she found it more "amusing to praise it to the sky." She writes her column to "have something to do" that is "more disgsting" and, therefore, "more amusing" than many other possible activities. |

At least during much of the novel, Dominique is cynical and bitter. She has no special ambition. But she is not lazy. As part of an investigation for *The Banner*, this child of privilege spends a couple of weeks living in a slum tenement. Rand writes, "She wore frayed skirts and blouses. The abnormal fragility of her normal appearance made her look exhausted with privation in these surroundings; the neighbors felt certain that she had T.B." Yet we are told she moved as she had in high-class drawing rooms, "with the same cold poise and confidence." Additionally, "She scrubbed the floor of her room, she peeled potatoes, she bathed in a tin pan of cold water. She had never done these things before; she did them expertly." She possessed "a capacity for action" and "was indifferent to the slums as she had been indifferent to the drawing rooms."

Rand describes Ellsworth Toohey as a very different character. *Sermons in Stone* is a successful book Toohey authored to acquaint the general public with the history of architecture. In that book, Toohey stated that he wished "to bring architecture where it belongs — to the people." More philosophically: "He said that architecture was truly the greatest of the arts, because it was anonymous, as all greatness." The discerning reader should sense something amiss when reading that Toohey "listed no architect by name in the text of his book" and "names appeared only in footnotes." Several footnotes mentioned Guy Francon "who has a tendency to the over ornate, but must be commended for his loyalty to the strict tradition of Classicism." In a single note Toohey mentioned Henry Cameron, "Prominent once as one of the fathers of the so-called modern school of architecture and relegated since to a well-deserved oblivion." Riding the success of the book, he signs on to write a column called "One Small Voice" in *The Banner.* Rand writes, "It had started as a department of art criticism, but grown into an informal tribune" from which Toohey "pronounced verdicts on art, literature, New York restaurants, international cases and sociology — mainly sociology."

We soon learn that the elderly, ailing, and alcoholic Cameron eventually retires and closes his office, leaving Howard jobless.

While Peter finds himself increasingly drawn to Catherine Halsey, his mother, without mentioning Catherine by name, warns him against her by relating "every newspaper account of a celebrity divorcing his plebeian wife who could not live up to his eminent position."

When Peter learns that Howard is unemployed, Peter asks Guy Francon to hire the old college pal as a draftsman. Howard goes to work for Francon & Heyer. But Howard insists on conditions: "I'm not going to do any designing . . . No Louis XV skyscrapers. Just keep me off esthetics . . . Put me in the engineering department."

Howard does not last long at Francon & Heyer. Oddly enough, the beginning of the end started when Guy Francon offered him a special opportunity. Francon explains that a client who is a bit "odd" has given the company an $8 million dollar office building commission. The client wants something that looks like the Dana Building that Cameron designed. The client rejected sketches made by three other employees so Francon offers Howard a chance to try. However, Francon attaches a condition, saying it can't be as "crude" as the Dana Building but, to keep up the reputation of Francon & Heyer, must have Greek ornaments.

Howard wants the opportunity but asks that there be no conditions. "Mr. Francon, let me design it the way the Dana Building was designed," Howard requests. He continues, "Just let me do it my way and show it to him. Only show it to him. He's already turned down three sketches, what if he turns down a fourth? But if he doesn't . . ." He begs for the chance to just show the client a building without Classic ornamentation. Francon says he can only have the chance if he follows the "instructions as to the Classic treatment of the facade" and Howard answers, "I can't do it."

Believing Howard "impertinent," Francon fires the draftsman.

Our hero finds work with the architectural firm of John Erik Snyte who employs designers of "various types," choosing from among their designs and then adding "improvements" from the others. The designers nickname each other according to their specialties. There is a "Classic," a "Gothic," a "Renaissance," and a "Miscellaneous." Howard becomes "Modernistic."

Snyte assembles the five and announces they are all to try to create a house for Austin Heller, a hard-to-please client who has already rejected the offerings of three architectural firms. Snyte adds that Heller is sure there is a "building he could love" but no one has yet come close. Later Snyte and the formidable five visit the site Heller chose. It is a "lonely, rocky stretch of shore" with a "cliff rising in broken ledges from the ground to end in a straight, brutal, naked drop over the sea, a vertical shaft of rock forming a cross with the long, pale horizontal of the sea."

After examining what his underlings have sketched, Snyte edits them into a version he will show Heller. Rand writes, "It was Roark's house, but its walls were now of red brick, its windows were cut to conventional size and equipped with green shutters, two of its projecting wings were omitted, the great cantilevered terrace over the sea was replaced by a little wrought-iron balcony, and the house was provided with an entrance of Ionic columns supporting a broken pediment, and with a little spire supporting a weathervane."

It is presented to Heller who says it is "the nearest anyone's ever come to it" but that he does not like it. He continues that it is "so near" but "not right." Trying to pull his thoughts together, Heller rambles about the need for "some unity," for "some central idea" and the need for it "to live." Searching for a word, he realizes he needs to see a design that is "integrated."

That is Howard's cue: "He seized the sketch, his hand flashed forward and a pencil ripped across the drawing, slashing raw black lines over the untouchable water-color. The lines blasted off the Ionic columns, the pediment, the entrance, the spire, the blinds, the bricks; they flung up two wings of stone, they rent the windows wide; they splintered the balcony and hurled a terrace over the sea." Snyte reached to stop Howard "but Heller seized his wrist and stopped him" so the upstart's "hand went on razing walls, splitting, rebuilding in furious strokes." Howard stopped and "the house — as he had designed it — stood completed in an ordered pattern of black streaks."

An infuriated Synte shouted, "You're fired!" A very pleased Heller added, "We're both fired." He invited Howard to meet privately with him.

Realizing his mistake, Snyte hurried to tell Heller he can have what Howard sketched "if that's what you want."

Heller is uninterested. He and Howard exit. The two make a contract and Howard designs the house for Heller.

Flush with victory, Howard opens his own office. Of course, the first project is the construction of the Heller house. Heller himself is unsure of what it is he liked about Howard's plan so Howard tells him, "A house can have integrity, just like a person and just as seldom."

By November 1926, the Heller house is finished. It is ignored by the *Architectural Tribune* and all the real-estate sections of New

York newspapers. It is ignored by the Architects' Guild of America. It is unmentioned by Ellsworth Toohey in "One Small Voice."

In private conversations, architects grumbled about it as a "blot on the Profession." Snyte himself comments that clients avoid architectural firms because "they see a house like that and they think all architects are crazy." One architect calls the house "funny" and quips "it looks like a cross between a filling station and a comic-strip idea of a rocket ship to the moon." Guy Francon believes Heller will come to regret commissioning the house, saying, "Those modernistic stunts never last more than a season. The owner will get good and sick of it and he'll come running home to a good old early Colonial."

Howard's construction of a decidedly modernistic house leads to a kind of negative fame for the building that some wags nickname "The Booby Hatch."

As Howard tries his wings in his own office, Peter continues regularly getting high-paying clients and making friends at Francon & Heyer. He also becomes well-acquainted with beautiful and aristocratic Dominique Francon. Peter knows that an alliance with Dominique would help his career. Her father, Guy Francon, is sure she has done nothing "dishonorable" but is dismayed that she is twenty-four and still a virgin. With her looks and social opportunities, it seems abnormal that she is single. He tells Peter, "I wish to God she'd get married." Peter naturally takes that as a green light to court the boss's daughter.

Peter finds himself in a jarring situation when a clearly distressed Catherine comes unexpectedly knocking at his door. Mrs. Keating is there and Catherine says to Peter, "I want to be married now, tomorrow, as soon as possible." She needs to marry because of a sense she is "in mortal danger, that something was closing in on me." The triggering was her Uncle Ellsworth Toohey who was in the next room surrounded by piles of papers. She says, "I couldn't see Uncle in the living room, but I saw his shadow on the wall, a huge shadow, all hunched, and it didn't move, only it was so huge!" Continuing, "It wouldn't move, that shadow, but I thought all that paper was moving, I thought it was rising very slowly off the floor, and it was going to come to my throat and I was going to drown. That's when I screamed. And, Peter, he didn't hear. He didn't hear it! Because the shadow didn't move." Then she wrapped coat and hat and raced out of the house. Uncle naturally asked where she was going but she could neither look back nor answer. She remembered, "I was afraid of him. Afraid of Uncle Ellsworth who's never said a harsh word to me in his life!"

Does Peter marry Catherine? Mrs. Keating says of Catherine, "I like her very much. . . . She's a respectable girl and I'd say she'd make a good wife for anybody. For any nice, plodding, respectable boy." However, she adds that if he wants to get to the top of the architectural profession, he should try to wed a woman who can help with that — like Miss Dominique Francon. Mrs. Keating adds that an "elegant society" type would probably edge "dowdy, uneducated" Mrs. Keating straight out of the house. The reason to aim for Dominique is that she can help him in his profession. He does not really even like Dominique. But to make it to the top . . .

Peter loves Catherine. He wants her. But he does not marry her.

A commission that is apt to help Peter's career comes his way when he is assigned to design the Cosmo-Slotnik building. However, he finds there are structural difficulties he is unable to adequately address. He goes to Howard and asks for guidance. Howard puts down a basic plan and leaves the facade — which must be Classical — to Peter. After the building goes up, Peter's prestige rises with it. He has a certain trepidation that word might get out that he did not design it himself. He goes to Howard, who is struggling financially, and writes out a check. He presents it to Howard as a payment for his help but both are aware it is really a bribe for Howard not to reveal his part in designing it. Howard takes that check and writes it back to Peter. Handing the check back, Howard makes it clear that he does not want Peter to reveal his part in the creation of the Cosmo-Slotnik building. Peter is miffed at the way his "generosity" is rejected.

One day Howard is at the Heller house when an admirer of it asks if Howard is willing to design a gas station. He is. Howard creates: "Two small structures of glass and concrete forming a semicircle among the trees: the cylinder of the office and the long, low oval of the diner, with the gasoline pumps as the colonnade of a forecourt between them. It was a study in circles; there were no angles and no straight lines; it looked like shapes caught in a flow, held still at the moment of being poured, at the precise moment when they formed a harmony that seemed too perfect to be intentional. It looked like a cluster of bubbles hanging low over the ground, not quite touching it, to be swept aside in an instant on a wind of speed; it looked gay, with the hard, bracing gait of efficiency, like a powerful airplane engine."

Howard is given a seemingly golden opportunity by a man named Nathaniel Janss of the Janss-Stuart Real Estate Company. Janss likes the idea of the sort of building Howard designs but the board of directors has the final say. They reject his design.

Department store owner John Fargo asks Howard for a building design. Then Howard gets a commission for a country house from Whitford Sanborn who had once owned an office building designed by Henry Cameron. Sanborn gets in squabbles with his wife who wants a more traditional abode. The house is finished but Mrs. Sanborn refuses to live in it. Their son insists on living in it. Of an age to live alone, he moves into it. The incident is mentioned in an AGA bulletin in which it is said to have been "erected at a cost of well over $100,000" but "found by the family to be uninhabitable." The item concludes, "It stands now, abandoned, as an eloquent witness to professional incompetence."

The Manhattan Bank Company offers Howard a chance to design a new building for them. After his design is examined, he receives a welcome phone call asking him to come to the office. He is told, "The commission's yours."

Howard is delighted. The board chairman tells Howard there had been squabbling over his selection as "some of our members just couldn't swallow your radical innovations." There is more talk but Howard is lost in "thinking of the first bite of machine into earth that begins an excavation."

Our hero's ears perk up when he hears that the contract will be signed "on one minor condition." What could that be? "Only a slight alteration in the façade," is the answer. He is shown a sketch illustrating that change: "It was his building, but it had a simplified Doric portico in front, a cornice on top, and his ornament was replaced by a stylized Greek ornament."

Howard cannot accept such alterations: "He explained why an honest building, like an honest man, had to be of one piece and one faith; what constituted the life source, the idea in any existing thing or creature, and why — if one smallest part committed treason to that idea — the thing or creature was dead; and why the good, the high and the noble on earth was only that which kept its integrity."

The board is adamant that they must have something classic on the façade. Howard is adamant that under no circumstances will he compromise on the appearance of a building he designs.

The chairman is flabbergasted. "We want your building. You need the commission. Do you have to be quite so fanatical and selfless about it?"

"What did you call me?" Roark asked incredulously.

"Fanatical and selfless."

"That was the most selfish thing you've ever seen a man do," he explains.

This scene should be an eye-opener to those who see Ayn Rand as just an advocate of simple greed, a prophet of profit. Her belief was that true "selfishness" is not greed or social climbing or hedonism but being true to one's self and one's values. Thus, her "moral ideal" turns down a commission that could have catapulted him to wealth and fame rather than compromise his artistic vision.

Indeed, after this pivotal scene, the out-of-work architect has little choice but to shut down his office. Then he accepts work as a day laborer in a quarry. Along with high school drop-outs and paroled convicts, he labors in the scorching sun.

The quarry in which Howard sweats for his bread is owned by Guy Francon. It is while doing this manual labor that Howard meets Dominique Francon who is spending the summer "in the great Colonial mansion of her father's estate."

She visits the quarry. She and Howard begin an odd flirtation that culminates in an encounter that will be dealt with in more detail in another section of this book.

A letter is sent to Howard by the wealthy Roger Enright who wants Howard's services as an architect. Enright has been favorably impressed by buildings Howard designed.

Rand returns to other characters. Peter Keating learns that Ellsworth Toohey has discussed Keating in a "One Small Voice" column. In the column, Toohey praises Keating. Rather, he praises a building Keating designed with the secret assistance of Howard Roark. "There is no personality stamped upon that building — and in this, my friends, lies the greatness of the personality. It is the greatness of a selfless young spirit that assimilates all things and returns them to the world in which they came, enriched by the gentle brilliance of its own talent. Thus, a single man comes to represent, not a lone freak, but the multitude of all men together." Toohey continues, "This column wishes to thank Peter Keating for affording us the rare — oh, so rare! — opportunity to prove our delights in our true mission, which is to discover young talent — when it is there to be discovered."

After the erection of the Enright House, others come to Howard who appreciate his distinctive modernistic architecture. Even as his fortunes appear to rise, he faces bad press. Even as she is secretly enjoying sex with Howard, Dominique Francon enters into a pact with Ellsworth Toohey to destroy Howard's career. Their weapons are alternately to write spiteful things about his work or ignore it. As Howard gets more commissions, Dominique begins to have second thoughts, believing that perhaps greatness does have a chance. However flawed the world is, it is not so flawed that true achievements cannot be recognized and appropriately rewarded. One day she suggests, "He's beating you, Ellsworth. Ellsworth, what if we were wrong about the world, you and I?"

That leads Ellsworth to hit upon a truly devious plan to gut Howard's career. The tool is the super-wealthy Hopton Stoddard. The rich fellow wishes to build a temple that will not be a temple for any particular denomination but a "non-sectarian monument to religion, a cathedral of faith." Who would be the best architect for this project? Toohey enthusiastically recommends Howard Roark as "the best there is."

Stoddard calls in Howard to ask him to design and oversee the creation of what Stoddard calls the Temple of the Human Spirit.

Howard says, "I don't believe in God." Stoddard retorts that the architect is a religious man "in your own way" and Howard agrees with that assessment. He also agrees to build the Stoddard Temple of the Human Spirit. Stoddard gives Howard complete leave to construct what he wants — as Stoddard will be out of the country during the construction.

Of course, Howard throws himself into the project. The structure is a "small building of gray limestone. Its lines were horizontal, not the lines reaching to heaven, but the lines of the earth. It seems to spread over the ground like arms outstretched at shoulder-height, palms down, in great, silent acceptance. It did not cling to the soil and it did not crouch under the sky. It seemed to lift the earth, and its few vertical shafts pulled the sky down." Rand elaborates, "It was a joyous place, with the joy of exaltation that must be quiet. It was a place where one would come to feel sinless and strong, to find the peace of spirit never granted save by one's own glory. There was no ornamentation inside, except the graded projections of the walls, and the vast windows. The place was not sealed under vaults, but thrown open to the earth around it, to the trees, the river, the sun — and to the skyline of the city in the distance, the skyscrapers, the shapes of man's achievement on earth. At the end of the room, facing the entrance, with the city as background, stood the figure of a naked human body." The body was modeled after Dominique Francon.

After the construction of the Stoddard Temple of the Human Spirit, Stoddard returned from his trip to look at it. He also met with Toohey. Then Stoddard issued a statement saying there would be no opening. He gave no explanation.

Toohey devoted a column to the structure. He began with a poem: "The time has come, the walrus said/To talk of many things/ Of ships — and shoes — and Howard Roark/And cabbages — and kings/And why the sea is boiling hot/And whether Roark has wings." In discussing Howard, Toohey wrote of how "a fly acquires delusions of grandeur." Toohey continued that Howard had been "commissioned to erect a great monument" and that what he "delivered constitutes the equivalent of spiritual embezzlement." Instead of a "non-sectarian cathedral symbolizing the spirit of human faith," Howard designed something which "might be a warehouse — though it does not seem practical" or "might be a brothel" but is "certainly not a temple." He continued, "It seems as if a deliberate malice had reversed in this building every conception proper to a religious structure. Instead of being austerely enclosed, this alleged temple is wide open, like a western saloon. Instead of a mood of deferential sorrow, befitting a place where one contemplates eternity and realizes the insignificance of man, this building has a quality of loose, orgiastic elation. Instead of the soaring lines reaching for heaven, demanded by the very nature of a temple, as a symbol of man's quest for something higher than his little ego, this building is flauntingly horizontal, its belly in the mud, thus declaring its allegiance to the carnal, glorifying the gross pleasures of the flesh above those of the spirit. The statue of a nude female in a place where men come to be uplifted speaks for itself and requires no further comment." Finally, the column turned back to the architect and suggested it was "an obituary for Howard Roark's career."

Stoddard could not understand why Toohey had suggested Howard Roark for the job. The reader knows that it was precisely because a building designed by Howard would be unconventional — and that Toohey could use it to try to bury Howard's career. To Stoddard, Toohey says he made a mistake in his expectations. Then he suggests Stoddard file a lawsuit which he does.

The matter sets off a "clamor of indignation against Howard Roark" as he is denounced by ministers in sermons and journalists in newspapers. Also, "The A.G.A. issued a dignified statement denouncing the Stoddard Temple as a spiritual and artistic fraud."

In the civil suit, Howard acts as his own attorney. Rand writes, "The case of Hopton Stoddard versus Howard Roark opened in February of 1931."

The first witness for the plaintiff was Ellsworth Toohey. He testified that a temple should arouse "a sense of awe and a sense of man's humility." He called the Stoddard Temple "a brazen denial of our entire past."

Howard asked no questions. He would ask no questions of any of the plaintiff's witnesses.

Peter Keating noted that Howard had once worked for Francon & Heyer but was fired for "incompetence." He continued that Howard "didn't care what the clients thought or wished, what anyone in the world thought or wished." Zeroing in the architectural deficiencies of the Stoddard Temple, he said it had "an improperly articulated plan, which leads to spatial confusion. There is no balance of masses. It lacks a sense of symmetry. Its proportions are inept."

Other witnesses for the plaintiff were called and derided Howard's building plans.

The biggest stir in the courtroom occurred when Dominique Francon was called to testify for Hopton Stoddard. She called the Stoddard Temple "a threat to all of us." Ears pricked up when she explained the reasons for that threat: "Howard Roark built a temple to the human spirit. He saw man as strong, proud, clean, wise and fearless. He saw man as a heroic being. And he built a temple to that. A temple is a place where man is to experience exaltation. He thought that exaltation comes from the consciousness of being guiltless, of seeing the truth and achieving it, of living up to one's highest possibility, of knowing no shame and having no cause for shame, of being able to stand naked in full sunlight. He thought that exaltation means joy and that joy is man's birthright. He thought that a place built as a setting for man is a sacred place." Later in her testimony, she declared, "I condemn Howard Roark. A building, they say, must be part of its site. In what kind of world did Roark build his temple?" She rhetorically asked, "When you see a man casting pearls without getting even a pork chop in return — it is not against the swine that you feel indignation. It is against the man who valued his pearls so little that he was willing to fling them into the muck and to let them become the occasion for a whole concert of grunting, transcribed by the court stenographer." There is naturally confusion as she appears to praise Roark so Stoddard's attorney inquires, "Miss Francon, for whom are you testifying? For Mr. Roark or Mr. Stoddard?" She answers, "For Mr. Stoddard, of course, I am stating the reasons why Mr. Stoddard should win his case." At the judge's prodding, Dominique proceeds, stating, "Let us destroy, but don't let us pretend that we are committing an act of virtue. Let us say that we are moles and we object to mountain peaks. Or, perhaps, that we are lemmings, the animal who cannot help swimming out to self-destruction."

After the plaintiff's lawyer rests, the judge invites Howard to put on his case. He goes up to the bench and takes out ten photographs of the Stoddard Temple which he places on the judge's desk. Then he says, "The defense rests."

Howard lost the case, was ordered to pay expenses for the building's alterations, and did not appeal that decision.

Dominique wanted to re-print her testimony in her column but could not because Gail Wynand fired her rather than allow that to happen. Shortly after this, Dominique and Peter Keating marry. Dominique is punishing herself for failing to effectively stick up for Howard Roark and the Stoddard Temple; Peter is so eager to please his boss that he is willing to marry a woman for whom the union is a form of self-punishment. Their wedding night was truly unique, even in the annals of fiction. Dominique tells Peter she must leave, their marriage will really start the next day. Then she spends that night with Howard Roark! Adultery on the wedding night!

After the Stoddard Temple debacle, Howard gets only a few commissions for such things as "remodeling rooming houses." One evening he happens to run into Ellsworth Toohey. The latter deliberately provokes Howard, suggesting, "Why don't you tell me what you think of me? In any words you wish. No one will hear us."

"But I don't think of you," Howard replies.

The story returns to Peter Keating and the new Mrs. Keating. Dominique does all her marital "duties," doing housework and socializing by her husband's side. She also does her sexual duties — which are indeed duties. She never refuses him. She never enjoys it. Sex is neither painful nor pleasurable. Peter Keating is all-too-aware that there is no passion on her part.

Marital duties take an odd turn when Keating seeks a commission with publisher Gail Wynand — and Dominique, with her husband's knowledge and support, agrees to sex with Wynand in order to secure that commission.

The commission is secured but Wynand ratchets up the price: instead of the one-night stand Dominique expected, he demands marriage. Dominique divorces Peter and marries the publisher. Gail loves Dominique who cares no more for him than she did for Peter. It is Dominique's second passionless marriage. Despite her "rigid indifference," the brief discussion of this union gives Rand a chance to expound on her beliefs about the sexes: "man was the life force and woman could respond to nothing else."

Gail Wynand decides he wants a house built for himself and Dominique. Whom does he hire? None other than Howard Roark. He does not remember the Stoddard Temple scandal and how negative things were published in *The Banner* about that building. He has no idea of the romantic feelings between Dominique and Howard.

Howard agrees to design the house. He also becomes close friends with Gail. Dominique, Gail, and Howard are often together — but *not* doing threesomes! At one point, Wynand is reminded of the Stoddard Temple catastrophe. He decides to test Howard. Wynand says he wants Howard to be the architect of all Wynand structures and that Howard will "build Colonial houses, Rococo hotels, and semi-Grecian office buildings." Howard plays along and makes a sketch of a building in an old-fashioned style. Wynand realizes he does not want that from Howard and laughs at the idea. There is no point in tempting Howard to violate his principles.

The story returns to Peter, now the head of a firm called Keating & Dumont. By this time, Heyer is dead, Francon retired, and Peter is partnered with architect Neil Dumont. Peter's business begins dissipating as fewer people come to him with commissions. Even as he frets about his lack of architectural business, he privately tries to return to his real love: painting.

There might be a way Peter Keating can get back to the top of the architectural game. There is a government housing project called Cortlandt Homes: "It was planned as a gigantic experiment in low-rent housing." Neil Dumont tells Peter that they can revive a flagging reputation if they get that commission.

Peter knows Ellsworth Toohey has influence and asks the well-known columnist and architectural expert for help. Toohey emphasizes the difficulty of the project: "It must be the most brilliant, the most efficient exhibit of planning ingenuity and structural economy ever achieved anywhere." Toohey promises to let Peter try. He gives him the information on what is wanted so Peter can work out "a preliminary scheme." Toohey adds, "If you come anywhere near it, I'll submit it to the right people and I'll push it for all I'm worth."

Toohey turns over a briefcase with all the specifications as to what is needed to build Cortlandt Homes. Peter sits up all night gazing at "the charts and figures spread before him." He realizes the project is beyond his capabilities. Peter goes to Howard, asking him to do the project and let Peter present the design as his own. After explaining the situation, he leaves the material with Howard who promises to look it over and decide what to do about it. The pair meet again the next day.

Howard says he might take on the project if he is well-rewarded. Peter promises to give him all the fees and even double the amount. Howard scoffs at such a temptation.

Then Peter points out that Howard would save Peter from ruin.

Howard is unmoved.

Peter points out that it is a "humanitarian undertaking" and asks Howard to "think of the poor people who live in slums."

But Howard is not an altruist. He will not work on it to help Peter or to aid the impoverished.

Finally Peter says, "You will love designing it."

"Yes, Peter. Now you're speaking my language."

Howard has little interest in money or fame and none in charity or altruism. He loves "the doing" of his work. He will take on the design and allow Peter to keep the fees as well as present it as his own. He has only one condition: "It will be built exactly as I design." There must be no changes of any kind.

The agreement is made. Howard even draws up a contract about it. He readily admits it is not legally enforceable and adds that when the building has been built, he will send his copy of the "contract" to Peter who can then destroy it if he wishes.

Before leaving, Peter wants to show Howard something he has not shown anyone else. He takes out six of his paintings.

Howard looks over them. Rand writes: "He took a longer time than he needed. When he could trust himself to lift his eyes, he shook his head in silent answer to the word Keating had not pronounced.

"It's too late, Peter," he said gently.

Rand tells us much of her basic beliefs with this scene: "When Keating had gone, Roark leaned against the door, closing his eyes. He was sick with pity . . . this was pity — this complete awareness of a man without worth or hope, this sense of finality, of the not to be redeemed. There was shame in this feeling — his own shame that he should have to pronounce such judgment upon a man, that he should know an emotion which contained no shred of respect. This is pity, he thought, and then he lifted his head in wonder. He thought that there must be something terribly wrong with a world in which this monstrous feeling is called a virtue."

When Peter presents the drawings of Cortlandt Homes as his own, Toohey calls the architect a "genius."

The government accepts the design supposedly done by Peter Keating. Howard is away on a cruise with Dominique and Gail Wynand as construction starts. When he returns, he goes to take a look at Cortlandt Homes which has not yet been completed. It is his building but with major changes.

Peter practically slobbers in his apology, telling Howard that he just could not prevent other government employees from making alterations. Peter says he will give Howard the fee but Howard is uninterested. The desperate Peter asks what Howard plans and the latter says, "You must leave that up to me now."

Howard visits Dominique. He needs her help because she must distract away the night watchman from Cortlandt Homes on a specified evening to avoid injuring or killing the man. She readily agrees to perform this task.

And the not-quite-finished housing project is dynamited to smithereens. Howard Roark stands by it, ensuring he will be arrested. Gail puts up the funds to bail his friend out of jail.

There is widespread condemnation of this man who destroyed a housing project intended to help the poor. Speculation about his motives included professional jealousy and an alleged resentment that Howard had for a building whose designer appeared to have patterned it, at least to some extent, after his own designs. Ellsworth Toohey rails against the dynamiter in a publication called *New Frontiers*, speculating that this project was destroyed by "One man's Ego against all the concepts of mercy, humanity, and brotherhood" due to "some vague matter of personal vanity." Pickets pace before Howard's office. His commissions are canceled.

For once, Gail Wynand "went against the current." *The Banner* runs editorials telling the public to withhold judgement until all facts are in. It runs photographs of the buildings Howard designed over captions rhetorically asking "Is this the man you want to destroy?" and "Is this the man who has contributed nothing to society?" The circulation of *The Banner* drops, advertisers withdraw, and employees quit. Although Toohey had criticized Howard in *New Frontiers,* Wynand ordered him not to do so in *The Banner* so "One Small Voice" is silent on the matter.

Toohey believes he can discover the truth behind the bombing. He visits Peter Keating. He demands to know who designed Cortlandt. Peter replies that he did. After reminding Peter that he, Ellsworth Toohey, is an expert on architecture, he demands again to know who designed Cortlandt. Again and again Peter says he designed it. The two men go back and forth but Peter realizes that his terrified and defeated manner gives the game away. So he shows Toohey the contract Howard created. Toohey has the evidence he needs.

Gail Wynand is shocked when he opens his newspaper to read "One Small Voice": "This is a test case. What we think of it will determine what we are. In the person of Howard Roark, we must crush the forces of selfishness and antisocial individualism — the curse of our modern world — here shown to us in ultimate consequences. As mentioned at the beginning of this column, the district attorney now has in his possession a piece of evidence — we cannot disclose its nature at this moment — which proves conclusively that Roark is guilty. We, the people, shall now demand justice." Of course, the "piece of evidence" is the contract Toohey got from Peter and passed on to the authorities. Wynand immediately fires Toohey as well as three employees who let the anti-Howard Roark piece get published.

The Banner employees strike, leaving only a few faithful workers behind to help keep the publication going. Strikers set up a picket line. They demand that the fired men be re-hired and that *The Banner* reverse its stance on Howard Roark and the Cortlandt dynamiting.

Dominique returns to work at *The Banner*. She conscientiously works long hours, doing the work of several journalists by herself.

Then it becomes too much. Wynand is trying to put out a newspaper that no one is reading and that is hemorrhaging money. The Board of Directors tells him they see no point in even continuing to put out the paper. They tell Wynand that he must take Toohey and other fired men back plus reverse the newspaper's position on Cortlandt.

Gail Wynand gives in. The men let go are re-hired. *The Banner* runs an editorial denouncing Howard Roark as "a reprehensible character, a dangerous, unprincipled, antisocial type of man. . . . If found guilty, as seems inevitable, Howard Roark must be made to bear the fullest penalty the law can impose on him."

Upset by what she sees as an ultimate betrayal, Dominique stages a kind of dynamiting of her marriage. She spends a night with Howard, then calls police early in the morning to report she lost a ring at his residence. The ring is imaginary; the false report advertises to the public that Gail Wynand's wife has committed adultery, making it socially necessary — this is the 1930s after all — for him to divorce her which was, of course, Dominique's intention.

Close to the novel's end is Howard Roark's trial. The prosecutor asserts that the defendant is "vicious" because he is an "egotist."

Howard acted as his own attorney. Rand writes: "People had whispered that it was a tough-looking jury. . . . Roark had challenged many talisman. He had picked these twelve. The prosecutor had agreed, telling himself that this was what happened when an amateur undertook to handle his own defense; a lawyer would have chosen the gentlest types, those most likely to respond to an appeal for mercy; Roark had chosen the hardest faces."

The prosecution calls witnesses to prove that Howard designed the project and then that he dynamited it.

Howard Roark gave his testimony and summation at the same time. In that testimony/summation, Rand related many of the precepts of her philosophy. Howard started, "Thousands of years ago, the first man discovered how to make fire. He was probably burned at the stake he had taught his brothers to light. . . thereafter men had fire to keep them warm, to cook their food, to light their caves. He had left them a gift they had not conceived and he had lifted darkness off the earth. Centuries later, the first man invented the wheel. He was probably torn on the rack he had taught his brothers to build. . . . thereafter, men could travel past any horizon. He had left them a gift they had not conceived and he had opened the roads of the world. . . . Prometheus was chained to a rock and torn by vultures — because he had stolen the fire of the gods. Adam was condemned to suffer — because he had eaten the fruit of the tree of knowledge. . . Throughout the centuries there were men who took first steps down new roads armed with nothing but their vision. . . . The great creators — the thinkers, the artists, the scientists, the inventors — stood alone against the men of their time. Every great new thought was opposed. Every great new invention was considered impossible." Here we can see why Ayn Rand is popular with teenagers and young adults. Especially if they are intelligent and/or creative, young people often have a sense of "me-against-the-world" that dovetails perfectly with the sentiments just stated.

Howard further asserts, "Altruism is the doctrine which demands that man live for others and place others above self. . . . The man who attempts to live for others is a dependent. He is a parasite in motive and makes parasites of those he serves." Howard later outlines the basic conflict between an egotist or first-hander like himself and the collectivists/second-handers who live for and through other people. "From the beginning of history, the two antagonists have stood face to face; the creator and the second-hander." He further asserts, "The 'common good' of a collective — a race, a class, a state — was the claim and justification of every tyranny ever established over men. Every major horror of history was committed in the name of an altruistic motive." Again we see Rand reacting to the evils of Bolshevism (class collectivism) and Nazism (race collectivism). Howard elaborates, "Now, in our age, collectivism, the rule of the second-hander and second-rater, the ancient monster, has broken loose and is running amuck. . . . It has swallowed most of Europe. It is engulfing our country."

Finally, he ties the philosophy to the specifics of his case: "I designed Cortlandt. I gave it to you. I destroyed it. I destroyed it because I did not choose to let it exist. It was a double monster. In form and in implication. I had to blast both. The form was mutilated by two second-handers who assumed the right to improve upon that which they had not made and could not equal. They were permitted to do it by the general implication that the altruistic purpose of the building superseded all rights and that I had no claim to stand against it. I agreed to design Cortlandt for the purpose of seeing it erected as I designed it and for no other reason. That was the price I set for my work. I was not paid."

The jury takes mere minutes to reach its verdict: Not Guilty.

After the acquittal, the site is purchased by Howard Roark fan Roger Enright. Howard will get to see Cortlandt Homes built as he wanted it built.

Gail Wynand shuts down *The Banner*. He calls Howard to his office to reveal that the money Wynand made from *The Banner* and from other investments will be used to construct a skyscraper, the tallest in the city, called the Wynand building. He offers a contract to Howard to act as the architect. He will have full authority as to how the building is constructed. Howard signs the contract. Wynand says, "Build it as a monument to that spirit which is yours . . . and could have been mine."

Dominique and Howard Roark marry. She visits him at the construction site for the Wynand Building. He is at the top of the structure and she rides the outside hoist up to her husband.

As might be expected of a novel that puts forth a controversial philosophy, *The Fountainhead* received profoundly mixed reviews. Writing for the *Herald-Tribune*, Albert Guerard said its style would "satisfy the most exacting professor" and praised it as "marvelously clever." But he misunderstood Rand when he called Peter Keating "utterly selfish." Rand created this character to epitomize the wrongs of a selfless life.

New York Times critic Orville Prescott called the novel "disastrous" and blasted it for having a "crude cast of characters" who were "grotesquely peculiar." Like Guerard, Prescott badly misconstrued Rand, characterizing Howard Roark as "selfless." Oddly, he praised Rand in suggesting, "Seldom indeed has one first novel shone with so much concentrated intellectual passion." He criticized the length of the novel and misconstrues it when he calls it "a whale of a book about architecture." Of course, architecture is just the backdrop; the novel is about right and wrong ways to live one's life.

Esteemed author Diana Trilling had little esteem for *The Fountainhead*. Trilling called it "a 754-page orgy of glorification of that sternest of arts, architecture." She called Howard Roark "a giant among men, ten feet tall and with flaming hair, Genius on a scale that makes the good old Broadway version of art-in-a-beret look like Fra Angelico." She considered the novel the "curiosity of the year" and, like Prescott, disliked its length saying anyone who likes it "deserves a stern lecture on paper-rationing."

Like Prescott, Lorine Pruette penned a review that was published in *The New York Times*. Pruette noted, "It was the only novel of ideas by an American woman that I can think of." While Prescott found the characters "crude," Pruette found the novel "amazingly literate" and liked its "romanticized, larger-than-life characters as representations of good and evil." Pruette singled out Rand's picture of the villain for praise, calling Ellsworth Toohey "a brilliant personification of a modern devil" who represented "the use of the ideal of altruism to destroy personal integrity" and "the use of sacrifice to enslave." Rand wrote a letter to Pruette in which she said, "You are the only reviewer who had the courage and honesty to state the theme of *The Fountainhead*" and said, "I feel completely helpless to express my gratitude to you for your review of my novel."

Benjamin De Casseres of the *New York Journal-American* described *The Fountainhead* as "the most original and daring book of fiction written in this country." He stated, "Howard Roark towers over any man in the United States." De Casseres showed a true understanding of the novel: "The 'fountainhead' is the ego — your ego, my ego — which is the dynamo of all action and thought whatsoever."

In the *Pittsburgh Press*, Bett Anderson wrote that Rand had "written an allegory, pitting Good against Evil, the individual against the herd. . . . She has written a book that is magnificent and bitter and challenging. Its impact is so terrific that the reader cannot fail to be shaken by its philosophy and its realism." Rand showed appreciation for this five years later when Anderson wrote to the publisher to request a signed copy. Rand wrote a note saying Anderson's review was "one of the only two which I shall always remember. Thank you for giving me hope at a time when I needed it badly."

Marjorie Davis, writing for the *Birmingham News*, displayed a true understanding of Rand's philosophy: "The book is the story of selfishness and unselfishness. It is an argument that the world is destroying itself by its unsselfishness, by its collectivist trend. The premise is that true selfishness, ego, the right of one man to be what his own mind demands, to create, alone, regardless of the pressure of opinion and of usage, is the fountainhead of human progress."

Despite being viewed very negatively by some critics, *The Fountainhead* had a strongly positive effect on Rand's career. It was a best seller and led her to financial success and fame. Although many derided the philosophy expressed, there were also many people who were attracted to it. *The Fountainhead* led to the beginning of Ayn Rand's following as both author and philosopher of a school of thought she named Objectivism.

It also led to the movie version of *The Fountainhead*.

At this point, we will digress to examine special issues about rape raised in *The Fountainhead* novel and later in the movie version of it. We must also briefly examine Rand's general views about women and men.

Ayn Rand, Rape, and Gender Issues

An understanding of *The Fountainhead* as a novel requires a discussion of Ayn Rand's views on gender. Perhaps nowhere do her beliefs about men and women surface in a more troubling manner than they do in the first sex scene between Howard Roark and Dominique Francon in *The Fountainhead*, a scene usually called "the rape scene."

Before going further, this author should probably lay her cards on the table regarding gender beliefs. I used to identify myself as a "feminist" because I perceived "feminists" as wanting to expand choices for women, allow them into professions on an equal basis with men, and end job discrimination against women. I stopped calling myself by this word a few years ago because what it means varies widely from person to person. Individuals called "feminists" often have so little in common with each other as to render the word meaningless. Many people do not link this word to expanding choices and opportunities for women but to hatred and fear of men. Oddly, I have known women who hated and feared men but did not call themselves "feminists." I have heard very anti-male comments from people who do not designate themselves with this word and even express opposition to expanding opportunities for women.

There are puzzling and contradictory elements in this entire area. For example, as noted, some people associate "feminism" with fear and hatred of men. At the same time, "feminism" is linked in the popular mind with abortion legalization. The glaring contradiction is that, save in the rare instance of forcible rape, it would seem obvious that females who fear and hate men would be unlikely to have unplanned pregnancies since they would shun intimacy with men. Man-hating should, logically, lead to that value prized by social conservatives — chastity. In fact, I knew a woman who said,

"I hate men." She was celibate and had not had a relationship in years. A movie made in 1951, *The Lady Says No* starring Joan Caulfield and David Niven, predicted a "feminist" movement pushing sexual abstinence — which makes sense. The 1964 Alfred Hitchcock thriller *Marnie* was about a woman who feared and hated men and was, as a result, celibate. She "couldn't stand" to be touched by a man. A male character talked about how she "was always covering her knees like they were some kind of national treasure." Her man-hating led to modesty, another virtue prized by social conservatives. Both *The Lady Says No* and *Marnie* linked man-hating to abstinence and modesty. However, the women's movement that emerged in the 1970s hardly led to widespread abstinence. Perhaps that is a way in which it failed — at least if one accepts the premise linking it to man-hating.

Back to the scene in Ayn Rand's *The Fountainhead* typically called "the rape scene." This scene led Susan Brownmiller, an author who is often identified as a "radical feminist," to deride Rand as "a traitor to her own sex." In this writer's opinion, the idea of any sort of "treason" to one's sex is foolish since one's gender is not a group to which some sort of ultimate loyalty is owed. There simply is no such thing as a "traitor" to one's sex regardless of whether an individual is male or female.

However, this writer believes Brownmiller is justified in finding fault with the "rape scene" in *The Fountainhead*. Nor are people labeled feminists the only readers who have found this scene troubling. Phyllis Schlafly, a social conservative who shot to fame with a campaign against the Equal Rights Amendment, a law supported by people often identified as feminists, started reading *The Fountainhead* — and stopped reading it when she got to this scene. Schlafly was a stout conservative Republican who, like Rand, enthusiastically and unreservedly supported capitalism. Yet this scene upset her so badly she did not finish reading this fascinating and culturally significant novel.

To understand this troubling scene, we must examine Rand's general views about the sexes. We must also put Rand and those views in the context of her time period.

A single troubling scene in a single novel is not the only problem many people have with Rand's beliefs about gender. They also take exception to her statement asserting "no good woman" would "want" to be president of the United States or chief leader of any country. Some people also dislike her dislike (word repetition deliberate) of certain "collectivist" aspects in the (extraordinarily diffuse) women's movement.

Before I detail the troubling *Fountainhead* scene and its relationship to Rand's gender ideology, it must be noted that there are aspects to Rand's views on the sexes that are remarkably progressive, especially considering the environment in which she was raised. She grew up in an era in which domesticity was widely regarded as the highest and best aspiration for any woman and in which women were expected to behave submissively to men. Yet Rand created heroines in her novels who brashly defied the "feminine mystique." Her heroines are apt to have careers and even careers unusual for females during the time period in which she wrote. Kira Argounova of *We the Living* is an engineering student, Dominique Francon writes a newspaper column on home decorating and architecture, and Dagny Taggart, heroine of *Atlas Shrugged*, runs a railroad.

Rand's support of expanding women's horizons beyond the traditional is underlined in her treatment of engineering student Kira Argounova. A male character named Victor remonstrates with her about her field of study, saying, "I do not believe that engineering is a profession for women." A female character, Lydia, points out, "That will mean dirt, and iron, and rust, and blow-torches, and filthy, sweaty men and no feminine company to help you." Kira asserts, "That's why I like it." Still another female character remonstrates, "It is not at all a cultured profession for a woman." Victor adds, "As a woman, you would be much more useful to society in a more feminine capacity."

Yet Kira is unfazed by sexist assertions of what is proper for women. She wants to be an engineer, knowing her future will be one "of the hardest work and most demanding effort." Even in her early years, she ignored "feminine" ways for her own interests: "She had played with mechanical toys, which were not intended for girls, and had built ships and bridges and towers." Ayn Rand is sympathetic to her heroine's choices and, unlike so many people of the era, believed Kira was right to follow her own interests rather than let them be circumscribed by what other people considered appropriate for her gender.

Dagny Taggart often departs from female stereotypes. Her brother Jim Taggart faults her as among the few people who can "devote their whole lives to metals and engines." His girlfriend, Betty Pope, explicitly criticizes Dagny for defying sex role assumptions: "I think it's disgusting — a woman acting like a grease-monkey and posing around like a big executive. It's so unfeminine." There is a point in the book at which Dagny thinks about the fact that some people might think it unfitting for a female to run a railroad. Describing Dagny's reaction, Rand writes, "To hell with that, she thought — and never worried about it again."

What's more, and perhaps even more startling, in an era in which female chastity was almost universally prized as a virtue, Ayn Rand's heroines were given to sexual adventuring outside of marriage.

In Rand's own life, she defied the expectations for women during her time period in multiple respects. Born into a world in which females were expected to be domestic, Rand devoted herself to intellectual and creative endeavors. Although deeply in love with her husband, Frank O'Connor, she had an affair with a much younger married student, Nathaniel Brandon — albeit with the permission of both their spouses.

Rand does not appear to have been particularly domestic or to have had much in the way of talent or skill in traditional areas of feminine endeavor such as cooking, housecleaning, or needlework. Of course, one would hope that she and Frank between them managed to keep their house clean and tidy but that by itself hardly qualifies Rand as "domestic."

What's more, Ayn Rand was distinctly non-maternal. She never raised a child. It has been suggested that a reason for her not becoming a mother was that she believed she would not be able to adequately care for a child because so much of her time and energy went into her writing. She sometimes told people she was "with book," a play on the expression "with child," and one that emphasized the aforementioned possibility.

It is also quite possible that she believed — realistically — that her talents were not in child-rearing. The number of famous people whose adult children have accused them of abuse or neglect or simply being inadequate parents proves that even people who are gloriously talented in some areas may lack adequate child-rearing abilities. These reports include mothers as well as fathers. Contrary to myth, possessing female sex organs does not automatically mean an individual is a superb caregiver for children. Thus, even had Rand quit her writing career, not replacing it with any other paid career but becoming a full-time housewife, a childless lifestyle might still have been appropriate for her.

It should not be thought that Rand was in any respect "anti-child." Far from disliking children, she wrote of them in glowing terms in her "Requiem for Man" essay: "I will ask you to project the look on a child's face when he grasps the answer to some problem he has been striving to understand. It is a radiant look of joy, of liberation, almost of triumph, which is unself-conscious, yet self-assertive, and its radiance seems to spread in two directions: outward, as an illumination of the world — inward, as the first spark of what is to become the fire of an earned pride. If you have seen this look, or experienced it, you know that if there is such a concept as 'sacred' — meaning: the best, the highest possible to man — this look is the sacred, the not-to-be-betrayed, the not-to-be-sacrificed for anything or anyone."

Of course, this inescapably leads to a disturbing possibility. Contraceptives are imperfect. They were even more apt to fail when Rand was young. How did a woman who passionately loved her husband and, at least for many years, enjoyed a man on the side as well, avoid having a baby by either of them?

Although contraceptives fail, they also may succeed so it is at least possible she never got pregnant because she used contraceptives and they worked. There is also the possibility that a physical issue prevented a pregnancy. Another possibility is that, like a multitude of other women in the early 20th century, she got pregnant and illegally aborted. That abortion was unlawful during her young years was, of course, only a small obstacle to obtaining one. Illegal abortionists did a brisk tax-free business.

When the legality of abortion became a public issue, Rand strongly supported its legality. This was one thing that separated her from many of the conservatives who admired her defenses of capitalism. "Someone who defends rights but objects to the right to have abortions — that's no defender of rights," she said in a speech. She wrote, "An embryo has no rights. Rights do not pertain to a potential, only to an actual, being. A child cannot acquire any rights until it is born. The living take precedence over the not-yet-living (or the unborn). Abortion is a moral right — which should be left to the sole discretion of the woman involved; morally, nothing other than her wish in the matter is to be considered. Who can conceivably have the right to dictate to her what disposition she is to make of the functions of her own body?"

The author of this book is not the only person who has wondered about Rand and pregnancy. In an article entitled "Ayn Rand on Abortion," James Peron writes of his long friendship with Barbara Branden. Peron was interviewing Barbara one day with a tape recorder on. He asked, "Did Ayn have an abortion?" He describes Barbara as "startled" by the question. She requested he turn the tape recorder off, so they could speak "off the record," and he obliged. Barbara asked why he was interested in that question. He said that he believed her statements on abortion sounded "personal" rather than "philosophical." He thought the issue was more to Ayn than just "something to ruminate on at one's leisure." Barbara never answered Peron's question but he writes that he interpreted her non-answer "as a 'yes.'" Later in his essay, Peron writes, "When [Ayn Rand] found herself pregnant in her 20s her husband, Frank O'Connor, borrowed funds from a relative" to pay for an illegal abortion." Peron writes this as fact without citing his source. Thus, the author of this book remains uncertain. Did she have that abortion? If so, was it her only abortion or did she have others?

Yet another possibility presents itself. Rand was never a mother in that she never raised a child, either biological or adopted. But that does not necessarily mean she never gave birth. Women who have placed babies for adoption often keep this matter private. Perhaps Ayn Rand did become a mother — that is, a birthmother to a child adopted by others. Perhaps she dressed for a few months in baggy garments, went into the hospital (possibly telling other people it was to have an ailment treated), and emerged able to bring out the old wardrobe while adoptive parents cooed over the baby she left behind. This is not far-fetched as there are stories about other famous women placing babies for adoption and keeping the matter private. The legendary Marilyn Monroe never had children. She is known to have had multiple illegal abortions. Later in her life, when she was rich in her own right and married to wealthy playwright Arthur Miller, she badly wanted to have a baby. Sadly, she repeatedly got pregnant and miscarried. In most tellings of her story, she never had a baby, However, stories have circulated that she once placed a baby for adoption. There are always things in a person's life that we cannot know for sure.

At any rate, Rand clearly and strongly supported allowing women to branch out from stereotyped roles before it became popular to do so. In her own life, she was far from a feminine stereotype. Rand specifically said she believed men and women were equals and no field of endeavor was specifically male or female. In her own words: "I believe that women are human beings. What is proper for a man is proper for a woman. The basic principles are the same. I would not attempt to prescribe what kind of work a man should do, and I would not attempt it in regard to women. There is no particular work which is specifically feminine. Women can choose their work according to their own purpose and premises in the same manner as men do."

Asked if she believed a woman is "immoral" for choosing to "devote herself to home and family instead of a career," Rand was quick to distance herself from any such anti-housewife stance. "Not immoral — I would say she is impractical because a home cannot be a full-time occupation, except when her children are very young," Rand commented. "However, if she wants a family and wants to make that her career, at least for a while, it would be proper — if she approaches it as a career, that is, if she studies the subject, if she defines the rules and principles by which she wants to bring up her children, if she approaches her task in an intellectual manner. It is a very responsible task and a very important one, but only when treated as a science, not as a mere emotional indulgence." Rand made a very good point in asserting that people who bring up children should first study child psychology. This is common sense not so commonly followed.

Progressive in her views on gender in major ways, holding that women should pursue careers according to their individual talents, skills, and ambition, she drew a line against women entering one position: leader of a country. She did not believe a "good woman" would want to be president. Why would the top job be off-limits to an entire sex? Why would no good woman want to be the nation's chief leader? Rand wrote, "For a woman qua woman, the essence of femininity is hero-worship — the desire to look up to man. 'To look up' does not mean dependence, obedience, or anything implying inferiority. It means an intense kind of admiration and admiration is an emotion that can be experienced only by a person of strong character and independent value-judgments. A 'clinging-vine' type of woman is not an admirer, but an exploiter of men. Hero-worship is a demanding virtue: a woman has to be worthy of it and of the hero she worships. Intellectually and morally, i.e., as a human being, she has to be his equal; then the object of her worship is specifically his masculinity, not any human virtue she might lack." Rand elaborates, "A properly feminine woman does not treat men as if she were their pal, sister, mother — or leader."

This writer believes the whole "hero worship" concept is confused and ambiguous.

As is what is usually called the "rape scene" in *The Fountainhead.* Before describing it, we will first return to Dominique Francon and the overall depiction of her character and sexuality. When Peter Keating first kisses her, he suffers disappointment: "he had not held a woman in his arms; what he had held and kissed had not been alive. Her lips had not moved in answer to his; her arms had not moved to embrace him; it was not revulsion — he could have understood revulsion." It was utter indifference, the tuning out of a woman who just did not care. She tells him she has been kissed before and her reaction was always one of indifference. "I suppose I'm one of those freaks you hear about, an utterly frigid woman," she relates.

Despite this defeat, Peter knows that this is the daughter of his boss and it would help him financially and socially if they married. Peter proposes marriage to the woman who was indifferent to his kiss. He proposes marriage in the full knowledge that the sex that is a usual part of marriage will inevitably be completely one-sided.

"Peter, if I ever want to punish myself for something terrible, if I ever want to punish myself disgustingly — I'll marry you," she states.

Despite the ugliness of that promise, he tells her he will marry her regardless of the reason she has for accepting his proposal. Thus, we know that Peter's desire to please his mother, to please his boss, to advance socially, are such that he would marry a woman who neither loves nor respects him and for whom the consummation of the marriage can never be anything other than a kind of minor surgical procedure.

In much of the novel, Rand underlines the perversity of Dominique's thinking. Returning to the circumstances under which she originally meets Howard allows us to more clearly see that perversity.

During her summer in the previously mentioned Colonial house, she sees no one on most days save an "old caretaker and his wife." The wife cooks and serves Dominique's meals "in unobtrusive silence" and disappears from the house afterward. "The old woman's treatment of Dominique had the same reverent caution with which she handled the pieces of Venetian glass in the drawing-room cabinets," Rand informs readers. Indeed, Dominique's position as daughter of the renowned architect Guy Francon wins her privileged treatment: "the people of the quarry town knew her and bowed to her; she was considered the chatelaine of the countryside."

When Dominique visits the quarry, the sight of the workers makes a visceral impression on her. "They did not look like workers, they looked like a chain gang serving an unspeakable penance for some unspeakable crime," Rand writes. Her own appearance is "an insult to the place below" due to her dress that is "too simple and expensive" and overall mien which "flaunted the fastidious coolness of the gardens and drawing rooms from which she came." Seeing Howard, she feels his gaze like "a slap in the face" and views his face as "the abstraction of strength made visible. . . . she was wondering what he would look like naked."

Elements of sadism/dominance often co-exist with those of masochism/submissiveness. Rand illustrates this co-existence through Dominique. Watching Roark run a drill, "She thought — hopefully — that the vibrations of the drill hurt him, hurt his body, hurt everything inside his body." Then: "She saw the hint of a smile, more insulting than words."

Later, in her Colonial mansion, she dwells on the memory of the quarry worker who attracts her: "She looked at the crystal objects spread before her; they were like sculptures in ice — they proclaimed her own cold, luxurious fragility. . . . she thought of his strained body, of his clothes drenched in dust and sweat, of his hands. She stressed the contrast because it degraded her. . . . She thought of being broken — not by a man she admired, but by a man she loathed. She let her head fall down on her arm; the thought left her weak with pleasure."

When she returns to the quarry, the superintendent tells her that the workers often have criminal records. She asks if the red-haired fellow has such a record but the superintendent does not know. Rand adds, "She hoped he had. She wondered whether they whipped convicts nowadays. She hoped they did."

Her life becomes consumed by the desire to visit the quarry and see the red-haired worker — together with the desire to resist that desire. Rand writes, "She had lost the freedom she loved. She knew that a continuous struggle against the compulsion of a single desire was compulsion also, but it was the form she preferred to accept. . . . She found a dark satisfaction in pain — because that pain came from him." In the company of other affluent people she enjoyed "a vicious thrill" of imagining them knowing "she was thinking of a man in a quarry, thinking of his body with a sharp intimacy as one does not think of another's body but only of one's own." She gets a special satisfaction knowing "that the man in the quarry wanted her." What's more, "She knew the kind of suffering she could impose on him."

One day she thinks, "The house was too safe. She felt a desire to underscore the safety by challenging it." Dominique tries to break a marble slab in front of her bedroom fireplace. She pounds it with a hammer but Dominique is no Wonder Woman and succeeds only "in making a long scratch across the marble." She heads off to the quarry and the red-haired worker. She tells him "there's a bit of a dirty job to be done at my house" and asks if he would like to make some extra money. He would. She requests that he come to her house because a broken marble piece at a fireplace needs to be replaced. Will he remove it and order a new one? Rand writes, "She expected anger and refusal." He asks what time he should be there and they schedule it. She asks what he is paid at the quarry and learns it is less that one dollar an hour. Dominique will pay the same rate for this "dirty job."

Rand continues that Dominique was disappointed because their "secret understanding was lost." However, this is followed by "that feeling of shame and pleasure which he always gave her."

Dominique requested that the old caretaker and his wife remain at the house because their "presence completed the picture of a feudal mansion."

Howard arrives at the place, in his work clothes and carrying a bag of tools, to do the job. She indicates the slab. He sees the scratch. He takes a hammer and wedge, puts the wedge on the scratch, and strikes. He says, "Now it's broken and has to be replaced."

As he works, Dominique gets closer to him and gazes "at the smooth skin on the back of his neck: she could distinguish single threads of his hair." She prods him to talk about something. He tells her he believes the fireplace is "atrocious."

She tells him the house was designed by her father and observes that there is no point in his discussing architecture. He readily agrees. She again prods him to talk about something — anything.

Howard starts talking about the broken marble and the different types of marble, remarking how true marble is produced by heat and pressure: "Pressure is a powerful factor. It leads to consequences which, once started, cannot be controlled." Rand is obviously alluding to the heat and pressure of a powerful sexual attraction. Soon Howard promises to order a new piece and have it delivered to the home.

Dominique estimates that, since he is paid less than a dollar an hour at the quarry and has spent a little less than an hour working on her fireplace shows owe him less than fifty cents. She hands him a dollar bill and adds, "Keep the change."

Rand writes, "She hoped he would throw it back in her face."

He just accepts the dollar.

In the aftermath of the above interactions, Dominique waits for the ordered marble "with the feverish intensity of a sudden mania." The stone arrives. She makes a note stating, "The marble is here. I want it set tonight," hands this epistle to her caretaker, and orders him to give it to the "redheaded workman." After accomplishing this mission, the caretaker returns with a note on a scrap from a paper bag, promising, "You'll have it set tonight."

She is in her bedroom and there is a knock at the door. It is the caretaker's wife and a short fellow in worker's clothing. He tells her, "Red down at the quarry" asked him to fix the fireplace.

Days later Dominique rides on horseback to the quarry, using a tree branch to guide the horse. Not finding "Red," she rides into a wooded area and sees him walking on a path. She demands to know why he did not come to set the marble. He tells her he did not think it would matter who came and adds, "Or did it, Miss Francon?" Feeling this question as a "blow flat against her mouth," she hits him in the face with the branch before riding off.

Three days later, at night, the infamous scene usually called "the rape scene" takes place. It is a remarkable scene that must be quoted at length to be analyzed. Dominique is in her bedroom and preparing for sleep when Howard intrudes.

"He came in. He wore his work clothes, the dirty shirt with rolled sleeves, the trousers smeared with stone dust. He stood looking at her. There was no laughing understanding in his face. His face was drawn, austere in cruelty, ascetic in passion, the cheeks sunken, the lips pulled down, set tight. She jumped to her feet, she stood, her arms thrown back, her fingers spread apart. He didn't move. She saw a vein of his neck, beating, and fall down again.

Then he walked to her. He held her as if his flesh had cut through hers and she felt the bones of his arms on the bones of her ribs, her legs jerked tight against his, his mouth on hers.

She did not know whether the jolt of terror shook her first and she thrust her elbows at his throat, twisting her body to escape, or whether she lay still in his arms, in the first instant, in the shock of feeling his skin against hers, the thing she had thought about, had expected, had never known to be like this, could not have known, because this was not part of living but a thing one could not bear longer than a second.

She tried to tear herself away from him. The effort broke against his arms that had not felt it. Her fists beat against his shoulders, against his face. He moved one hand, took her two wrists, pinned them behind her, under his arm, wrenching her shoulder blades. She twisted her head back. She felt his lips on her breast. She tore herself free.

She fell back against the dressing table, she stood crouching, her hands clasping the edge behind her, her eyes wide, colorless, shapeless in terror."

Interestingly, this entire sex scene — usually called "the rape scene" and also the scene depicting the loss of Dominique's virginity — does not include any speaking. Henry Miller ended a description of a (consensual) sex scene with a character called Ida Verlaine with the sentence, "Not a word spoken." That applies to this scene as well. Kate Millett believed Miller's "not a word spoken" sex scene emblematic of that author's virulent anti-female sexism and put a lengthy quotation from it on the first page of her Ph.D. thesis turned surprise best selling book, *Sexual Politics*.

Howard lifts Dominique in his arms and she bites his hand deeply enough that she tastes "blood on the tip of her tongue." Then he "pulled her head back and he forced her mouth open against his." We are told she "fought like an animal" but "made no sound" and "did not call for help." Is the reader to believe the caretaker and his wife within hearing distance and Dominique is not calling for help because she wants what Howard is doing? Or is she not calling for help because no one is near and it would be futile? That is unclear but we previously read that she prepared for bed in the "vast empty house" which would appear to indicate that the caretaker and his wife are *not* nearby. Rand continues: "She reached for the lamp on the dressing table. He knocked the lamp out of her hand. The crystal burst to pieces in the darkness."

Roark throws Dominique on her bed and she experiences "the blood beating in her throat, in her eyes, the hatred, the helpless terror in her blood." We are told "the sudden pain shot up, through her body, to her throat, and she screamed. Then she lay still."

Here is how Rand describes the first sexual encounter between these two major characters and the first sex Dominique experienced in her life:

"It was an act that could be performed in tenderness, as a seal of love, or in contempt, as a symbol of humiliation and conquest. It could be the act of a lover or of a soldier violating an enemy woman. He did it as an act of scorn. Not as love, but as defilement. And this made her lie still and submit. One gesture of tenderness from him — and she would have remained cold, untouched by the thing done to her body. But the act of a master taking shameful, contemptuous possession of her was the kind of rapture she had wanted. Then she felt him shaking with the agony of a pleasure unbearable even to him, she knew that she had given that to him, that it came from her, from her body, and she bit his lips and she knew what he had wanted her to know."

Howard then takes his leave. She lay in the bed "for a long time" before she "dragged her feet slowly to the door of her bathroom," intending to take a bath. She turns the light on and sees "the purple bruises left on her body by his mouth." She decides against the bath because she "wanted to keep the feeling of his body, the traces of his body on hers." She falls asleep on the bathroom floor.

Meanwhile, we are told that Howard feels the activity of that night was "like a point reached, like a stop in the movement of his life." He knows "they had been united in an understanding beyond the violence, beyond the deliberate obscenity of his action; had she meant less to him, he would not have taken her as he did; had he meant less to her, she would not have fought so desperately. The unrepeatable exaltation was in knowing that they both understood this.

Of Dominique's reaction to the encounter, Rand writes, "She could accept, thought Dominique, and come to forget in time everything that had happened to her, save one memory: that she had found pleasure in the thing which had happened, that he had known it, and more: that he had known it before he came to her and that he would not have come but for that knowledge. She had not given him the one answer that would have saved her: an answer of simple revulsion — she had found joy in her revulsion, in her terror and his strength. That was the degradation she had wanted and she hated him for it."

She later receives a letter from a *Banner* worker, Alvah Scarret, asking her when she is returning to her usual residence and adding, "It will be like the homecoming of an Empress."

Rand writes that Dominique "smiled. She thought, if they knew . . . those people . . . that old life and that awed reverence before her person . . . I've been raped. . . . I've been raped by some red-headed hoodlum from a stone quarry. . . . I, Dominique Francon. . . . Through the fierce sense of humiliation, the words gave her the same kind of pleasure she had felt in his arms." As she goes about her day and people "bowed to her, the chatelaine of the town. She wanted to scream it to the hearing of all." Toward the end of the book, she talks to Gail Wynand, by then her husband, and says of Howard, "He was the first man who had me." She continues, "He didn't ask my consent. He raped me. That's how it began."

Not surprisingly, the first sex scene between Dominique and Howard, plus Dominique's reveling in the thought that she was raped, did not sit well with some activists in the second wave of the women's movement. Susan Brownmiller's attack on Rand for the scene has already been noted. As also noted, people considered feminists are far from the only people to dislike the scene and find it confusing. Revulsion against the terrible crime of rape is widespread among ethical people regardless of their politics or lack of politics.

In a review of Susan Brownmiller's *Against Our Will* published in the right-wing magazine *National Review*, the reviewer made the point I just made that the idea of Rand being "a traitor to her own sex" makes little sense since a person's gender is not a group to which loyalty is owed. However, that reviewer also approvingly described the scene as "Randian man assaults Randian woman who lies back and enjoys it." A letter to the editor by a conservative woman suggested a "wait a minute" to that description. Although the epistle's author disagreed with Brownmiller in many respects, she argued that Brownmiller "was right to criticize that scene" which the letter writer called "just plain kinky." That person quoted someone as saying, "It is precisely because sex is the most intimate of activities that rape is the most insulting."

Indeed, long before the women's movement raised general consciousness about rape, some readers found it difficult to square the idea of Howard Roark as a "moral ideal" with his committing a most immoral — and rightly illegal — act of violence. A fan wrote to Rand about the morality of Howard Roark's action shortly after the novel was first published. Rand replied, "You say you were asked whether 'the rape of Dominique Francon by Howard Roark was a violation of Dominique's freedom, an act of force that was contrary to Objectivist Ethics?' The answer is: of course not. It was not an actual rape, but a symbolic action which Dominique all but invited. This was the action she wanted and Howard Roark knew it. A man who would actually force himself on a woman against her wishes would be committing a dreadful crime." Another time, Rand called it "rape by engraved invitation."

Although these answers give us insight into how Rand felt about this scene, they do not eliminate troubling aspects of it. Rand's answers indicate that the scene is to be read as a kind of consensual sex role playing but she does not show any such role playing being discussed beforehand. What makes it even more troubling is that real-life rapists often rationalize their crimes by saying they believed the victims "wanted it."

Did Ayn Rand condone rape? To answer this question, I believe we must look outside *The Fountainhead.* Discussing the entire subject of what role the government should play in regulating intimacy, Rand declared: "Only one aspect of sex is a legitimate field for legislation: the protection of minors and of un-consenting adults. Apart from criminal actions (such as rape), this aspect includes the need to protect people from being confronted with sights they regard as loathsome. (A corollary of the freedom to see and hear, is the freedom not to look or listen.) Legal restraints on certain types of public displays, such as posters or window displays, are proper." Writing of her profound difference with Sigmund Freud, she contemptuously writes of what she sees as Freud's vision of the archetypal human being: "itching to rape his mother, castrate his father, hoard his excrement."

It is clear that Any Rand knew that forcible rape — the actual, real-life act of forcing sex on an unwilling victim — was a "dreadful crime" that should be legally punished. Thus, the scene in her novel must be understood as a scene in a novel, not an actual act. Rand may have written it as a kind of rape fantasy scene. This would explain Dominique's masochistic reveling in the aftermath of the "rape." It would also her complete lack of concern for a possible consequence of the rape: pregnancy. In an era in which an out-of-wedlock pregnancy meant certain disgrace, Dominique does not give the possibility that she has been impregnated a single thought. She does not wait anxiously for her menstrual period. The author describes no trip to the neighborhood back-alley butcher, no extended vacation at the unwed mother's home, no looking into an adoption agency, no desire for a reputation-saving marriage.

Why did Rand put this violent sex scene in the novel? Why did she make it even possible for a character constructed as a "moral ideal" to be thought by readers to be a rapist?

This author cannot answer those questions. I can speculate that she believed that a certain level of dominance and submission is intrinsic to normal, consensual sexuality and dramatized those concepts through a rape fantasy scene.

But the scene remains troubling.

Years in the story and chapters in the book after their initial sex encounter, Dominique knocks at Howard's door and tells him, "I want to sleep with you, now, tonight, and at any time you may care to call me . . . I want you like an animal, or a cat on a fence, or a whore."

In a later passage: "She tried to demonstrate her power over him. She stayed away from his house; she waited for him to come to her. He spoiled it by coming too soon; by refusing her the satisfaction of knowing that he waited and struggled against his desire; by surrendering at once. She would say, 'Kiss my hand, Roark.' He would kneel and kiss her ankle." Dominique never has any fear of Howard and their marriage at the end of the novel is clearly intended to be part of an overall happy ending.

Ayn Rand believed men and women were intellectual equals. She believed good women hero worshipped, or looked up to, the men in their lives. She created Howard Roark to represent a "moral ideal" and put the possibility of his committing a heinous crime into his story. There are profound inconsistencies here. This author cannot reconcile them. Maybe someone else can. Maybe these inconsistencies are impossible to reconcile.

1945: *You Came Along*

Ayn Rand has been accused of many things but laziness is not among them. Even as she formulated a philosophy and worked on novels, she penned screenplays. Two of her screenplays were made into motion pictures that were released in 1945: *You Came Along* and *Love Letters*.

You Came Along was based on a short story, "Don't Ever Grieve Me," by Robert Smith. Its working title was *Don't Ever Grieve Me* but the title was changed to what studio executives believed was the more movie friendly *You Came Along* before it was released. The original screenplay for the film was also written by Robert Smith. However, producer Hal Wallis was dissatisfied with the script Smith penned and asked Rand to rewrite it.

Movies are, of course, a very different medium from short stories or novels. A film is visual while literature is verbal. There are also differing time constraints in the two mediums. Wallis may have believed that Rand's experience in the film industry would enable her to write a script more in keeping with the specific needs of film.

Rand would say of Smith's screenplay, "It was originally a very cute story — not profound, but clever and appealing." Nevertheless, she agreed with Wallis that the screenplay Smith turned in needed improvement to make a good movie. "I kept whatever was good in the original script and wrote the rest," she recalled. "I got second credit which was fine even though I saved it."

John Farrow directed *You Came Along*. Originally from Australia, Farrow traveled to the United States in the 1920s so he could work in Hollywood, California. Prior to *You Came Along*, he directed films that included *Men in Exile* and *West of Shanghai*, both of which were released in 1937. The famous actress Mia Farrow is among his children.

Starring in *You Came Along* is Robert "Bob" Cummings, a popular actor who had played in comedies like *The Devil and Miss Jones* (1941) and dramas like Alfred Hitchcock's *Saboteur* (1942). After *You Came Along*, he would play in another Hitchcock thriller, *Dial M for Murder* (1954) and eventually have his own TV show, a sitcom entitled *The Bob Cummings Show*. In *You Came Along*, he played United States Air Force Major Bob Collins who returns to America in the company of two fellow Air Force officers who are also his close friends. Don DeFore plays Captain W. Anders, a former schoolteacher nicknamed "Shakespeare." DeFore's first screen appearance was in a bit part in *Reunion* (1936). He started appearing regularly in films in the early 1940s but would become best known in the 1950s as a neighbor of the title characters in the sitcom *The Adventures of Ozzie and Harriet* and even better known in the 1960s for playing the employer of the title character in the sitcom *Hazel*, a series about an outspoken housekeeper played by Shirley Booth. The other Air Force buddy is Lieutenant R. Janoschek, an ex-boxer nicknamed "Handsome." Handsome was played by Charles Drake who never really became a star but would enjoy a busy career in both film and TV. 1945 would see him in both *You Came Along* and *Conflict*, a movie starring Humphrey Bogart.

You Came Along was the film debut for Lizabeth Scott, a beautiful and talented actress who would become most famous for film noir roles. A drop-dead gorgeous woman with silky blonde hair and a sultry voice, her career would take off after *You Came Along*. One of her most renowned movies would be released in 1946 and entitled *The Strange Loves of Martha Ivers*. In that film, she would star with Hollywood heavyweights Barbara Stanwyck, Kirk Douglas, and Van Heflin. She starred or co-starred in many movies, making her last film, *Pulp*, in 1972. However, she had a problem in 1954 when *Confidential*, a popular gossip magazine, ran an article alleging Lizabeth Scott spent much time with "Hollywood's weird society of baritone babes." The article called Scott a "deviate." The article clearly accused the actress of being a lesbian, something widely regarded as horrible in that era. Scott sued for libel. The lawsuit had technical problems due to *Confidential* having its headquarters in New York and Scott filing the suit in her own state of California. This led to the suit being dismissed.

Some writers have said Scott's career was ruined by the *Confidential* article. However, others have said her career was already fading away before the article ran. At any rate, she made musical recordings in the late 1950s and guest starred on TV into the 1960s. As noted, her last film role was in a film released in 1972.

The story of *You Came Along* starts when WWII is still being fought. Bob, Shakespeare, and Handsome are on a War Bond tour. The United States Treasury Department sends a chaperone to accompany them. While waiting for that chaperone, the three answer questions from journalists. Asked what he thinks about when in danger, Bob replies, "I think about my girl." "Which girl?" is the next query. "That's what I'm thinking about — trying to decide which one!" Bob says.

The trio expect to meet a man named I. V. Hotchkiss. They are surprised when a man does not show up but a woman, Ivy Hotchkiss, who is played by Lizabeth Scott. With her lovely blonde hair accented by a black beret, her thick sensuous mouth, sultry voice, and feminine manner, she immediately intrigues the three servicemen. However, they are a bit flummoxed that a female was sent. "The treasury department has no time for sex discrimination," she jauntily explains. Much later in the film, Bob Cummings will make an observation about the female gender: "Women — what a blessing!"

Ivy will soon be warned that the trio are "wolves" but she is confident of her ability to take care of herself. "I don't happen to be Little Red Riding Hood," she asserts.

Bob nicknames Ivy "Hotcha" (this film is rich in nicknames). Bob and Ivy fall in love. This is a movie, after all, and we expect the male lead and most prominent female character to enjoy a romance.

It turns out there is a dark cloud over this couple. There is a scene in which Ivy meets a physician who has treated Bob. From things he says, she concludes (accurately) that the man she loves is terminally ill. Of course she is crushed. Then Ivy's sister Frances (Kim Hunter) marries a pilot named Bill, despite Bill being called to active duty and, therefore, danger. Inspired by this example, Ivy and Bob marry, deciding they will cram all the living they can into the limited time Bob has.

Ivy soon finds herself widowed. After Bob's funeral, Ivy believes she hears Bob speaking from heaven, telling her, "I'm a lucky guy," since, after all, he had her as his wife.

What's this? Ayn Rand, that hard-nosed philosopher, that fanatical ideologue, penned a script as sweet as that of *You Came Along*? How could that advocate for selfishness have written the screenplay of a love story filled with sprightly jokes yet suffused with poignance? How could that atheist and skeptic have ended a screenplay with a character (apparently) communicating from heaven?

There was in fact nothing at all out of character in Rand writing a comedy-romance. Rand was a joyful person who appreciated the more frivolous parts of life. Nor is there anything bizarre in a skeptic writing a script in which a supernatural element appears as skeptics often write science fiction, horror, and fantasy.

Reviews of *You Came Along* recognized the positive qualities of newcomer Lizabeth Scott. The *Hollywood Reporter* noted the distinctive qualities of this young actress, calling her "a blonde girl with a low-pitched and vibrant voice and a fire-beneath-ice personality." However, *New York Times* critic Bosley Crowther found Scott unimpressive, describing her as "clearly inexperienced" — this was her first film after all — and saying she had "little else" except "a fragile and appealingly candid face." Crowther did not think much of the film as a whole. He called it "a sloppy and sentimental patchwork of straight screen stereotypes" without "a shred of distinction in the dialogue or the imagery." Crowther continued that its "sole and profitless purpose seems to be to build up pathos with a whole lot of wistful chit-chat." He found the acting of Cummings "glibly mechanical" and said Don DeFore and Charles Drake are "average cut-ups as his Rover Boyish wolfing-drinking pals."

A *Variety* review had a much more positive take on the movie, calling it "a winner." The critic stated, "It's authentic, rings true, is nicely played, never maudlin, and sound all the way."

More recent critics have also praised *You Came Along*. Reviewer Derek Winnert finds it "interesting and amusing" although "sometimes hard-to-take." Overall, Winnert called it "a watchable entertainment." Winnert elaborated: "It works better as a comedy, in which the laughs are more entertaining than the romance or the sentimentality, though the odd material is generally well handled by both the actors and director." He also stated, "Robert Smith and Ayn Rand provide the smoothly crafted screenplay based on Smith's story. Less cynical audiences might find it very touching."

On the Mystery File website, a reviewer found the story "kind of silly," but concluded, "I'd say you should watch this one for Lizabeth Scott in a role far from the ones her career led her, and for the three buddies she finds herself on the road with. Together they make a very engaging, fun-loving foursome, and like me, you may find yourself enjoying the first half of the film more than the second." A letter to the editor on the website from John Tate said, ""Bob's and Liz's love for each other is one of the most poignant things in movies I think."

A user review on the Internet Movie Database (IMDb) called *You Came Along* "a curious, very memorable, and touching romance." That person continued, "The real star is Ayn Rand's scintillating and well-crafted script that keeps 'sense-of-life as a positive' foremost." Although there is little ideology in the film, another user reviewer asserted, "Ayn Rand's positive and life-affirming views animate the film."

Although not everyone was impressed by Lizabeth Scott's debut performance, she would, as previously mentioned, go on to distinguish herself. Working on this film both launched her career and led to a friendship between Ayn Rand and Lizabeth Scott. In an interview with writer Scott Holleran, Scott remarked, "I loved Ayn Rand." Holleran wrote that Scott considered Rand "one of the few in Hollywood whom she felt understood her ability."

A version of *You Came Along* was broadcast on the radio on January 7, 1946 on *Lux Radio Theatre*, an anthology series that did radio episodes based on stage plays and/or motion pictures. They tried to get the same actors who had played a character in the previous production to do so in the radio episode but that was not always possible. In this case, Lizabeth Scott and Don DeFore reprised their roles. Van Johnson took over the role Cummings had played in the movie. Rand did not write the script for the show. The show's host describes the scriptwriter as "an advertising man" and says this is his first radio script. Although the script was his own, it was obviously strongly influence by Rand's movie script.

In this author's view, *You Came Along* was transferred quite effectively to the medium of radio in this *Lux Radio Theatre* episode. There is an early intimation of "Bob's circumstances when he speaks of his belief in the ancient saying, "Eat, drink, and be merry." It is left to the audience to mentally add, "for tomorrow you may die."

Van Heflin is just as good as Bob Cummings at conveying the pleasant surprise the men experience when they wait for Mr. I.V. Hotchkiss and discover "he" is a "she." Lizabeth Scott is just as sympathetic and believable in audio-only as she was on film in the role of Ivy Hotchkiss. The radio version makes credible the love Bob and Ivy have for each other in the face of their realization that their time together will be short. "Don't ever grieve me, baby," Bob tells her but we know she must grieve him. The episode ends on a note of grief made bearable by the knowledge of time well spent — of a life well spent.

1945: *Love Letters*

Ayn Rand adapted a novel entitled *Pity My Simplicity* by Christopher Massie into a screenplay, giving its plot an inspired spin from the play she most admired, Edmond Rostand's *Cyrano de Bergerac*. That spin led to the movie's title, *Love Letters*. Released in 1945, it was directed by William Dieterle, a German born actor and director who immigrated to America in 1930. In his adopted country, he had directed such films as *The Story of Louis Pasteur* (1936), *The Hunchback of Notre Dame* (1939), and *The Devil and Daniel Webster* (1941). His most renowned picture was probably *The Life of Emile Zola* (1937) which won an Academy Award for Best Picture. *Love Letters* starred two of Hollywood's greatest stars of the era, Jennifer Jones and Joseph Cotten.

Set primarily in England, the story of *Love Letters* tells of British World War II soldiers Roger Morland (Robert Sully) and Alan Quinton (Cotten). Roger is in love with Victoria Morland (Jones) and wants to write letters to her that will impress her and win her heart. Unfortunately, he is not good at writing letters. "I never had any standards, manners, or taste," he candidly admits. Alan, who is naturally articulate and possesses a strongly romantic streak, agrees to write love letters for his pal — as occurred in Rand's favorite play. However, unlike Cyrano, Alan has no extremely big nose or any other feature that would render him unattractive to the ladies.

The letters Alan writes are flowery and passionate. "I think of you, my dearest, as a distant promise of beauty untouched by the world," he writes. In another: "Thank you for seeing life not as a burden or punishment, but as a dream made beautifully real." Such statements might easily strike some people as saccharine. Others will see Rand's idealism in them and her ultimate optimism especially evident in the second statement quoted.

The letters lead Victoria to fall in love with . . . who? She knew Roger only briefly prior to his getting sent overseas with the military. Apparently she found him attractive — he is played by the handsome Robert Sully — and agreeable. Her love started when she was charmed by the letters Alan wrote. Thus, Victoria falls in love with a combination of Roger's appearance and Alan's writing. She falls in love with a non-existent man.

Alan enjoys expressing himself through the letters but suffers a guilty conscience over the deceit. He also develops feelings for her. Although Alan has never met Victoria, or even seen a picture of her, he calls her his "pin-up girl of the spirit."

Alan and Roger are separated when Roger must go to England to be trained as a paratrooper. The military dispatches Alan to the front in Italy where he is wounded. The wound leads to his being discharged from the army.

Freshly freed, he returns home to his lovely blonde fiancée Helen Wentworth (Anita Louise). The couple spend time together but both realize that the feeling necessary for passion in marriage has dissipated between them. They break up on good terms.

Alan discovers Roger has died, not in combat but at home in England. He eventually learns that authorities believe Roger's wife Victoria — the woman with whom Alan corresponded — killed Roger! Alan suffers very confused feelings as he believes his letters were at least partially responsible for their marriage.

At a small party, Alan meets a lovely young single woman who goes by the single name of Singleton (excuse the repetition but this author could not resist).

Haunted by the idea that his letters led to a marriage that led to a murder, Alan starts researching Roger's killing. The official narrative found by the courts was that Victoria stabbed Roger because he hit her. She served a brief sentence before being released.

Later, he again meets Singleton and learns the story behind her name. She is Victoria but does not know she is Victoria.

Extreme trauma led to amnesia. She also has a phobia around letters.

Alan and Singleton soon get the warm fuzzies for each other. They marry. However, Singleton is distressed by information that he may still be in love with a woman named Victoria Morland (she has no idea that she is Victoria). Asked if she wants to ensure he does not meet Victoria, she replies, "I want to give him up!" She loves him so much that she would rather lose him to another woman than keep him in a situation less than optimal for him. There is a clear echo here of Rand's early story "The Husband I Bought."

Love Letters has other secrets and surprises as is true of any mystery. The secrets are all unfolded by the movie's surprising end.

Contemporary critics were not especially impressed by *Love Letters*. *New York Times* reviewer Bosley Crowther wrote, "Whatever reputation as an actress Jennifer Jones may have got for herself in *The Song of Bernadette* is quite likely to suffer a terrible dent as the result of her fatuous performance in *Love Letters*." He continued that Jones could not be entirely blamed for the poor performance as a "worse script or less expert direction has seldom been tossed at an innocent star's head." Crowther denounced the plot as full of "sentimental twaddle" and called Rand's script "a mucky muddle." He also derided Dieterle's direction as "mushy and pretentious."

Reviewing it much more recently, in 2007, Dennis Schwartz gave the film a far more positive review. He wrote that William Dieterie "moodily directs this sentimental love triangle romantic melodrama." Schwartz found its plot "contrived" and believed Jones' performance was "overdone." But he praised the "stunning expressive camerawork of Lee Garmes" and the "haunting score by Victor Young" which would "touch your heart." Still, he wrote that the movie "never managed to stir" Schwartz because it had a "depressing soap opera love story" and a "gooey ending." He gave it a middling grade of "C+."

A review on the "dvdbeaver" website was much more positive, stating "this gripping thriller is an unforgettable romance/murder mystery that both touches the heart and teases the mind." This reviewer, like Schwartz, found the plot "contrived" and found Jones "tiresomely fey." Also like Schwartz, this reviewer was impressed with Lee Garmes "superlative camerawork," concluding "Dieterle's brooding direction makes it a really rather ravishing experience."

The reviewer for a website called Film Fanatic noted that Rand wrote the script but the reviewer was "hard-pressed to see much of her interest or influence here" and adds "this melodramatic romance about amnesia and hidden identities seems to fly in the face of Rand's philosophical approach to life." As noted, many people see Rand as both simpler and more limited than she was. The critic finds it "not a very effectively scripted narrative" as it depends on "other-worldly notions of idealism and transcendent love."

Despite negative contemporary reviews, the public flocked to the movie so it made money at the box office. What's more, Jennifer Jones was nominated for an Academy Award for her performance as Victoria/Singleton. She lost out to Joan Crawford for her performance as the title character in *Mildred Pierce*. Victor Young's musical score was also nominated for an Academy Award.

Love Letters is one of four motion pictures in which Jennifer Jones and Joseph Cotten played. They had previously worked together on *Since You Went Away* (1944) and would go on to co-star in *Duel in the Sun* (1946) and *Portrait of Jennie* (1948).

The film's hit song, *Love Letters*, written by Edward Heyman and sung by Dick Haymes, has been recorded by many musicians including such greats as Nat King Cole, Elvis Presley, and Elton John.

Ann Richards was originally cast to play Victoria/Singleton in *Love Letters* but when Jennifer Jones became available, Richards was re-cast as the protagonist's friend Dilly.

When the film opens and we see Alan writing a love letter, neither the hand nor the handwriting are those of Joseph Cotten. Nor are they those of an understudy or body double. The hand and handwriting belong to studio mogul David O. Selznick. He had not written the screenplay and had neither directed nor produced the film. Rather, he had Joseph Cotten and Jennifer Jones under contract and had loaned them out to Hal Wallace to do *Love Letters.* Selznick asked for, and got, this bit of himself into the film because of the fact that he had so generously provided its stars.

Ayn Rand Testifies Before HUAC

The House Un-American Activities Committee (HUAC) is today notorious as it is automatically associated with "Red baiting," with "seeing a communist under every bed," and, perhaps worst of all, with the blacklisting of movie industry artists for alleged communist sympathies.

In 1947, Ayn Rand was a "friendly witness" before HUAC. That should not be taken to mean that she supported what HUAC was doing. In fact, she is said to have thought its activities "futile."

Ayn Rand was a friendly witness before HUAC because she had no trouble denouncing the land of her birth for its communism, telling the committee that Russia had turned into a "totalitarian" nation in which people generally are "afraid" and "human life is less than nothing." Having grown up under communism, she was understandably repulsed by the tendency of many people to romanticize this political philosophy.

1949: *The Fountainhead* on the silver screen

Six years after *The Fountainhead* hit the best-seller list in 1943, it became a best-seller a second time because the book was given a tremendous boost when the 1949 film version of *The Fountainhead* was released.

It was only shortly after the book came out that Warner Bros. Pictures hired Rand to write a motion picture adaptation of the novel. In an essay entitled, "Adapting *The Fountainhead* to Film," Jeff Brittig writes that the development phase of the screenplay "did not involve Rand alone. Hollywood studios rarely entrusted their film adaptations to the authors of primary works; multiple writers frequently were employed. In addition, studio executives, producers, directors — and censorship boards — contributed to the shaping of final scripts." Producer Henry Blanke supervised the development of the screenplay. Brittig writes that two other writers, Thames Williamson and Harriet Frank, Jr., were hired to write their own screenplay adaptations of the novel. Ultimately, however, Warner Bros. picked Rand's screenplay for the film.

Brittig reports, "Story departments of Hollywood studios evaluated newly published works in order to determine their screen potential." Henry Blanke was "initially unimpressed" with what he had heard of *The Fountainhead*. Esteemed actress Barbara Stanwyck persuaded him to actually read the novel. Once he read *The Fountainhead*, he changed his mind and concluded the book possessed movie potential. Thus, he got a contract with Rand to allow Warner Bros. to make the film with himself as producer. The contract permitted Rand to pen a script but allowed the studio to make changes.

Rand had reservations about how *The Fountainhead* would transfer to cinema. One problem was the 18-year time span of the story told. Another was the psychological and philosophical nature of the novel. Nevertheless, Rand believed the novel could be made into a good movie. As previously noted, many changes are always necessary when a story goes from book to movie as the mediums are quite different. The author, who had, of course, already had experience as a script writer, set out to turn *The Fountainhead* into a film. She felt it vital that the novel's theme of "individualism versus collectivism, not in politics but in man's soul" be dramatized in the movie version. [It should be noted that "man" in this instance does not refer specifically to males but to human beings.] Notes Rand made for the screenplay stated the theme as "man's integrity" and noted that major characters represented both integrity and lack thereof: "Independence — as against obeying the wishes of others, as against the 'social' spirit, which is: Keating, who tried to live by public polls; Wynand, who tried to use the mob; Toohey, who consciously used collectivism for the purpose of gaining power and enslaving mankind." They had to be contrasted with, "Howard Roark, an architect, a man of genius, originality, and complete spiritual independence, [who] holds the truth of his convictions above all things in life. He fights against society for his creative freedom, he refuses to compromise in any way, he builds only as he believes, he will not submit to conventions, traditions, popular taste, money or fame." Discussing Dominique Francon, Rand writes that Dominique "thinks that his fight is hopeless" so she "tries to block his career in order to save him from certain disaster."

About the friendship between Roark and Wynand, Rand observes, "Roark's integrity reaches Wynand's better self, Roark is the ideal that Wynand has betrayed in his ambition for power."

There were also concerns about how the Production Code Administration, popularly called the Hays Office, would react to *The Fountainhead.* In 1943, Rand noted, "Blanke has given me no objections and no restrictions, except on the sex side — we'll have to be careful of the Hays office and treat such scenes as my famous rape scene through tactful fade-outs."

On January 15, 1944, Rand delivered thirty-three pages to her superiors at the studio. She would deliver eight more sets of pages before the final one on May 27, 1944, a first draft of a screenplay 283 pages long.

Brittig states, "From December 1944 to March 22, 1948, the day the studio called her to confirm that she would write the final script — less than four months before the start of filming — the studio's choice of writer remained undecided."

During that time period, the studio was looking over and considering the scripts of the two competing authors. They found that neither Williamson nor Frank was really sympathetic to Rand's philosophy so neither could keep the novel's characters true to the source.

Four years passed and Warner Bros. asked Rand to revise her initial script with the assistance of King Vidor, who had been assigned to direct the film. Rand had always been confident that no other screenwriter could capture the essence of her work, remarking that the studio "didn't know what would ruin it and what would or would not antagonize my readers. That was my great protection."

The first task for Rand was to thoroughly go over her initial script which she had not read in four years. She believed she needed to rewrite several scenes. For many weeks, Rand, Vidor, and Blanke worked closely together to create a good script. Blanke suggested the start be rewritten to give a quick summary of the first major events in the book; Rand followed this advice. He also suggested dropping the Stoddard Temple and subsequent lawsuit; Rand did this as well. Rand moved the introduction of Peter Keating and Dominique to earlier in the story and had them start out as engaged. Gail Wynand was also moved to appear earlier in the story.

The scene in which Howard and Dominique talk about their relationship right after the Enright House opening was pivotal in Rand's opinion. Rand asserted, "Dominique's basic conflict is the violent conflict between her passion for Roark and her despair.

The more she admires him, the more certain she is that he will be destroyed."

Rand, Vidor, and Blanke met on June 12, 1948 to read the script aloud and discuss final changes or cuts. The major concern, Rand later explained, was the summation/testimony Howard gave at his trial: "This is the most difficult thing to write in condensed form, and the most dangerous politically and philosophically, if written carelessly." Rand elaborated, "I had to make every idea crystal clear, cover every possible implication, guard against any chance misunderstanding, avoid any possibility of confusion. I did it — and preserved the dramatic and literary qualities of the speech at the same time." She revised that speech no less than six times. Eight conferences were held to discuss it. Six and a half minutes long, that speech is among the longest in movie history.

Although she had been allowed much freedom in the creation of the film, Rand was disgruntled by some aspects of it.

One major sore spot was the presentation of Howard Roark's architectural style. Rand had written, "It is the style of Frank Lloyd Wright — and only of Frank Lloyd Wright — that ought be taken as a model for Roark's buildings. This is extremely important to us, since we must make the audience admire Roark's buildings." Oddly enough, Frank Lloyd Wright was offered a chance to work on the film and refused it.

The Fountainhead art director Edward Carrere created the designs for Howard Roark's buildings. Carrere did not follow the style of Frank Lloyd Wright. Instead, he patterned Roark's architecture after a branch of modernism called the International Style. Rand disliked the style, saying Carrere modeled Roark's designs after "horrible modernistic buildings" which Rand found "embarrassingly bad."

The trailer for *The Fountainhead* pitched to the individualistic qualities of Howard Roark tied together with the romance of Dominique and Howard. It displayed a copy of the novel and the words onscreen state: "Towering to new dramatic heights come Warner Bros.' proud presentation of a great novel." A voiceover says, "This is Dominique Francon, the kind of woman who could enslave any man — except one. Gail Wynand, molder of destinies. He could rule any man — except one. Ellsworth Toohey, calculating, ruthless, he feared no man — except one." The trailer soon stumbles in its understanding of Rand's work: "Peter Keating, selfish, weak." Of course, he is weak precisely because, as author and screenwriter Ayn Rand created him, he is self*less*. Rand considered Howard Roark the epitome of the healthy selfishness she championed.

Casting a motion picture is always vital. Ayn Rand was a fan of Gary Cooper. She wanted him to play Howard Roark and the studio cast the famous and popular actor in that role. However, despite the fact that Rand wanted it, there is a major problem with that casting. The story in both novel and movie begins with Roark's expulsion from architectural school. Howard Roark was twenty-two. At the time he made *The Fountainhead*, Gary Cooper was forty-eight. He did not look young for his age but had the lines and wrinkles that clearly denote the passing of several decades. Although Cooper was indisputably a great actor, Roark's youthful exuberance was nowhere to be seen in Cooper's portrayal of the hero.

Who should play Dominique Francon? Barbara Stanwyck wanted the role. She was attractive, possessed strong screen presence, and a very skilled actress. She was also forty-two. Female performers of advancing age are rarely cast in femme fatale roles so studio executives wanted a younger actress.

Twenty-three-year-old Patricia Neal, then a relative unknown, auditioned for Dominique. Her career to that point had primarily been on the stage. She acted in a Broadway production of *The Voice of the Turtle*, a comedy by John William Van Druten about the challenges faced by young single New York City people during WWII. Neal won the 1947 Tony Award for Best Featured Actress in a Play for her performance in a 1946 production of Lillian Hellman's *Another Part of the Forest*, a prequel to Hellman's *The Little Foxes* with both plays about a wealthy but troubled southern family named the Hubbards.

Gary Cooper walked on the set while Patricia Neal auditioned for Dominique. He was unimpressed and told Rand her audition was awful. However, as the video "Gary Cooper Collection — *The Fountainhead*" notes, Neal had the "look and the presence that Vidor wanted for Dominique." As a newcomer, she did not command a major star's salary which was also a plus. The day after the audition Cooper criticized, Neal was given the part. Others were soon brought on board with Raymond Massey cast as publisher Gail Wynand, Robert Douglas as villain Ellsworth Toohey, Kent Smith as second-hander Peter Keating, and Henry Hull as aging Roark mentor Henry Cameron.

The black and white film version of *The Fountainhead* told a beautifully dramatic story even as it relayed Rand's individualistic philosophy. The start of the film goes through a series of quick scenes that show us Howard Roark expelled from architectural school for the originality of his designs, Peter Keating telling Howard "I'm going to give the public what it wants" and advising Howard to similarly bow to public opinion, and Henry Cameron scolding Howard as a "fool visionary" but hiring him.

Cut to a scene on a busy city street. "Get your morning *Banner*!" a boy brashly hawks. Henry Cameron is walking down the street and buys a couple of *Banner* issues just to tear them to pieces. Cameron walks in a wavering manner that suggests he is sick. Howard Roark joins Cameron, letting the older man lean against him, and escorts his boss back to the office. "It's no use, Howard!" Cameron says. Then he points out that people are not interested in good, original, modern architecture, saying, "You've done four buildings." He complains that the general public is too backward and philistine to appreciate what either Henry Cameron or Howard Roark has to offer. Cameron rages that what people want is the cliché and scandal filled *Banner*. Overcome by frustration and bitterness, Cameron yells, "I don't want any part of Gail Wynand's city!" He collapses and Howard calls an ambulance. In that ambulance, Cameron complains about how skyscrapers have been built as "mongrels." He elaborates, "The form of a building must follow its function, that new materials demand new forms. One building can't borrow pieces of another's shape just like one man can't borrow pieces of another's soul." Cameron asks Howard to burn his designs and papers. He wants to leave nothing behind for this world. Then he urges Howard to compromise and give the public what it wants. Howard counters that he will be true to his principles. In despair, the dying Cameron declares, "You're on your way into hell!"

Then we go to a scene of Howard Roark acceding to his friend's last wishes and burning Cameron's papers. Who should happen by but Peter Keating? He is wearing an expensive suit and a jaunty bowler hat. He tells Howard that Guy Francon, one of the leading architects in the nation, recently made Peter his partner. "It's Francon and Keating now," he cheerfully relates. Peter notes that the office does not look good and that it is likely Howard will soon have to close it. Howard lets Peter know that things are even worse than Peter assumes. Howard's lighting is being disconnected, he is being evicted, he has less that $15 to his name, and he lacks a watch because he hocked it. Yet he refuses a loan Peter offers, saying, "I neither give nor ask for help." Ayn Rand's ideal person neither gives nor accepts charity.

After Peter leaves, Howard gets a call from a member of a board of directors that is considering his designs.

Cut to a boardroom with aging men in suits. Close to them is a model of a skyscraper that resembles a tall thin box made up of a series of rectangular windows with the whole contraption held up by curved stilts. A happy Howard Roark gazes proudly at the model of the building he designed. "Mr. Roark, the commission is yours!" a board member gushes. The smiling board members note that he will win fame when the building is erected. Three board members are seated while one walks idly around. On a large literal board are some drafting papers and materials. Howard is told that the "brilliant ingenuity" of his plans led to his winning the commission. However, they want one very small compromise. Howard's smile dries up and he asks what it is. All they want is for the building to have an appearance a bit less shocking. They want him to make an adaptation to the façade that will give it a "middle-of-the-road" appearance. Items are put on the façade to illustrate the changes they want.

"If you want my work, you must take it as it is or not at all," Howard asserts. He will not compromise to get the commission. He says, "I'd rather work as a day laborer if necessary." He packs up his materials and leaves the meeting.

The three turn to the man who was wandering around and is now seated and smoking a cigarette in a holder. The man says, "As you know, Mr. Gail Wynand wants buildings that show a classical influence." Board members ask why Howard Roark was asked for a design.

The man explains that suggesting Roark was an "experiment — a very interesting experiment." What to do now? Find another architect. One man says, "Yes, Mr. Toohey." The villain has been introduced. He flamboyantly blows a ring of smoke into the air.

Then we are at the huge office of *The Banner*. Ellsworth Toohey is there to recommend an architect to publisher Gail Wynand. "I'm sure you know I seek nothing for myself," Toohey says. "My only motive is a selfless concern for my fellow man." His advice is "the rising star of the profession, Peter Keating." Toohey is the architectural critic of *The Banner*. He displays photos of a series of buildings Keating designed.

Unimpressed, Wynand comments that they were brilliant when they were first done in the distant past. Toohey says, "Surely you're not in favor of so-called modern architecture . . . It's only the work of a few unbridled individualists. Artistic value is achieved collectively."

Wynand comments that he read that sentiment about artistic value in a recent Toohey column. About Keating, Wynand concludes that he "produces great big marble bromides." He goes on to say that any of the fashionable architects is as inept as another. Wynand decides to ask the opinion of another *Banner* architectural expert, Dominique Francon, who writes a column called "Your House." Her column is something of a rival to Toohey's "One Small Voice." Wynand learns that Dominique has not come into work that day. He decides to pay her a visit to ask her advice on a good architect.

Cut to Dominique at a window of her home, holding a lovely sculpture in her hands. She tosses it out the window, breaking it.

Then she answers the door to find her boss there. Wynand says he needs an architect for a bank building and asks her advice on a worthwhile architect. She answers that she knows of no architect of real ability. Wynand tells her that Toohey supports Peter Keating for the job. "Peter Keating is a third-rate architect," she crisply asserts. Then Wynand reminds her that Keating is her father's partner — and her own fiancé! Yes, she is engaged to marry the fellow she so blithely dismissed as a "third-rate architect." Despite being engaged to Keating, Dominique has not the slightest desire to use her influence to advance his career. Wynand says he wants to meet Peter Keating and invites the couple to dinner at his house. Wynand suggests she could have a greater career herself but she is not interested. She does not appear to be interested in much of anything. She tells him she destroyed a beautiful sculpture because she did not think it belonged in "the world of the mob and of *The Banner*."

We next see a posh dining room. A crystal chandelier hangs from the ceiling and a beautiful painting hangs on the wall. A butler silently goes about serving Dominique, Keating, and Wynand who is at the head of the table. Wynand asks Keating if he really wants this commission.

"I'd sell my soul for it," he merrily answers.

Wynand comments that Keating has made a fine analogy. The price for getting the commission is breaking his engagement to Dominique Francon. Keating is bewildered. He looks to Dominique. She refuses to help Peter by giving her opinion and says he and Wynand can decide it between the two of them.

Keating asks if this is some sort of joke. It is not. Dominique will not beg Keating to keep their engagement. Keating will not sacrifice the commission to marry Dominique. The engagement goes poof!

Wynand tells Keating he might as well go home. He obeys, leaving Wynand and Dominique together. Dominique wonders if Wynand expects her to automatically agree to marry the publisher because of this little trick. He does not. He wanted to show her that people are inevitably corrupt and he is not worse than others. "There is no honest way to deal with people," Wynand proclaims. "We have no choice but to submit or to rule them. I chose to rule."

"A man of integrity would do neither," Dominique avers.

Wynand kisses her but realizes that she cannot respond. "I guess I'm one of those freaks you hear about — a woman completely incapable of feeling," she acknowledges. She touches her fingers to her face and continues that she accepted the marriage proposal of a man she neither loved nor respected because he was safe and unimportant and she knows she can never be in love with anyone. She says if she fell in love it would be like the statue of the Greek god again that she destroyed. Wynand says he accepts that she has no passion. He wants to marry her anyway. She tells him she will marry him if she ever decides to "punish myself for some terrible guilt." Wynand tells her he will wait and wants her as his wife regardless of the reason she might marry him.

Dominique tells him she will spend time at her father's Connecticut residence. She craves "freedom to want nothing."

The film shows us a construction site and a man blasting in it.

Then we see Dominique awakening and stretching in her luxurious bedroom. She visits the quarry her father owns. A woman in expensive and delicate garb, she looks quite out of place among rough and sweaty men performing manual labor. Her eye is caught by a tall gaunt worker who is, of course, Howard Roark. Ah . . . perhaps Dominique is not so freakish, not so incapable of sexual feeling as she believed. Then again, did she believe she was frigid or did she hope she was?

Howard looks at her, she looks at him . . .

The next scene is Dominique in her bedroom brushing her hair. An interpolated film shows us she is thinking of the man drilling. The Freudian symbolism of the drill is obvious. Then we see her back at the quarry, having ridden her horse there. She carries a riding crop. The two banter. She warns him against insolence. He clearly does not take her seriously as he is aware that their attraction is mutual.

When she is again in her room, the sounds of a storm echo the turmoil inside her. She hits a stone before the fireplace repeatedly and summons the tall gaunt fellow from the quarry.

Howard arrives. She informs him that the marble piece is broken and must be replaced. She asks him to remove it.

He takes a look at it and sees it has only been scratched. He hammers it and comments that it is now really broken and must be replaced.

As he works, she laughs. She asks if he wants to discuss anything.

He tells her he thinks the fireplace looks "atrocious." She says the house was designed by her father and says there is no point in his discussing architecture.

None whatsoever, he readily agrees.

He points out the different types of marble and how they are produced by heat and pressure. Again, the references to heat and pressure have strong sexual connotations. Then he promises to order a new piece cut to order. She pays him and he leaves.

Next scene is Dominique again in her bedroom, this time reading. There is a knock at the door. Her maid is there, accompanied by a short stout fellow in a manual laborer's outfit. He explains that the tall man at the quarry said she has a fireplace for him to fix. She tells him to go ahead.

Dominique is soon on her horse. She sees no one at the quarry and rides on until she finds Howard walking on a dirt road. She demands to know why he did not come to her place to set the marble.

"I didn't think it would make any difference to you who came," he answered. "Or did it, Miss Francon?"

She whips him across the face with the riding crop before riding on.

In the evening, she is in her nightgown, seated at her vanity table. Howard Roark shows up in his work clothes. She runs away, hits him, kisses him, runs outside and falls down. He looks down at her and smiles. It is a deliberately shadowy and ambiguous rendition of a "rape scene" that was ambiguous in its source material.

When we see Howard back home, he finds a telegraphed note from Roger Enright who has seen his buildings and wants Howard's services for a special project.

Howard is on his way!

Cut to Dominique at the quarry. She learns the tall gaunt fellow no longer works there. She does not learn his name.

The next scene is in a room in an office of *The Banner*. A man nervously walks back and forth. "I'm at my wit's end!" Alvah Scarrett (Jerome Cowan) exclaims.

"That's not going very far, Alvah," Ellsworth Toohey drolly observes.

Dominique is also there.

Alvah notes the newspaper has crusaded against street car monopolies and canned vegetables and Wall Street. He cannot think of anything else to denounce.

Toohey finds something. He points to plans for a skyscraper to be called the Enright House. Alvah expresses skepticism that anyone would care about a building.

Toohey points out that no one has previously used the structural method so it could be denounced as threatening public safety. Indeed, there are three ways to denounce the building: 1) The architectural conflict of forms with classically designed buildings; 2) The risk of a new structural method; 3) The unfairness of a luxury apartment erected while so many languish in the slums.

Alvah gets on the phone to Wynand who approves the campaign.

Dominique and Toohey leave the room. A dismayed Dominique points out to Toohey that the building is a great architectural accomplishment.

Toohey readily agrees. He is unmoved in his determination to campaign against it.

She demands to know what he wants.

He coyly replies that no one yet knows what he is after but they will eventually learn.

Dominique walks into Wynand's office just as he OKs the campaign against the Enright House. She tells Wynand that the building is great architecture and begs him to dismiss the campaign.

Wynand asks if she is friends with the architect.

Having no clue that an architect would ever have to work in a quarry, she says she has never laid eyes on him and does not care about him personally but is pleading on behalf of greatness.

Wynand will not call it off. Manufactured controversies, scandal mongering, and odes to the trite are the formula that makes *The Banner* popular and Wynand rich and powerful.

Dominique resigns from *The Banner* in protest.

The campaign takes off. Architects sign a petition against the Enright House and letters pour in from various outraged citizens. "We shall win," Toohey says. "Because there are thousands of us —

thousands against one." This little speech encapsulates the whole concept of the evil collective ganging up on the virtuous individual — a concept that Rand saw as the root of much evil.

Enright House is erected despite the public howling. To thumb his nose at the critics, Roger Enright holds a party celebrating the opening of Enright House. At that party, Dominique sees Peter Keating who compliments her on how good she looks. He says he has been taking a poll among the guests about the building. "A poll?" she asks. "So you can find out what you think about it yourself?" He asserts that public opinion must always be considered. She nods as the point has been made about sheep-like people waiting to learn other people's opinions in order to decide their own. We see Roger Enright discussing the building with a guest. "God gave you eyes and a mind, and if you fail to use them, the loss if yours not mine," he comments. The guest asks if he wants to convince her of the building's worth. Enright retorts that her opinion is not his concern. A pause is called for at this point. Atheist Ayn Rand wrote a script in which a character of which she approves says, "God gave you eyes and a mind. If you fail to use them, the loss is yours not mine." How do we explain this bit of dialogue? We could say that Ayn Rand and character Roger Enright do not have the same beliefs. Then again, it could be "God" is meant metaphorically. But whatever the reason for mentioning a deity, the greater point is made that Enright need not convince anyone of the merits of the building or its architectural style.

Also at the party is Ellsworth Toohey. He dislikes geniuses, he informs another guest, because genius by implication insults the ordinary people who constitute the vast majority.

His companion states that he pays little attention to intellectual matters, preferring to play the stock market.

"I play the stock market of the spirit," Toohey declares. "And I sell short."

Then Dominique sees the guest of honor — Howard Roark! She is stunned to discover that the humble quarry worker to whom she was so strongly attracted is in fact the architect who designed the Enright House.

Roger Enright "introduces" them. Enright informs Roark that Dominique resigned her job at *The Banner* in protest of its campaign against the building. Roark tells her he used to read her column. "I admire your work more than anything I've ever seen," Dominique tells him. "You should know that this is not a tie but a gulf between us if you remember what you read in my column."

"I remember every line of it," he says.

Again a pause is appropriate. People do not talk like this. The unrealism of such dialogue is often remarked upon by critics. Rand does not write in a realistic mode so the dialogue inevitably has clunky moments.

Dominique and Howard meet privately in an Enright House room. Dominique reminds him that she did not know his name but he knew hers, yet he failed to try to find her. Roark tells her he wanted her to come to him. She tells him that she loves him "without dignity, without regret." However, she cannot see him again if he continues on the course he is on. She knows he will be crushed because the world cannot appreciate his greatness. The only way they can be together is if he takes a "meaningless job" and they live "only for each other." He cannot accept the offer. He is committed to architecture — and to the architecture he believes is right for his era.

The next scene is Dominique and Wynand on a boat. She accepts his marriage proposal. Wynand tells her he loves her although he realizes that is of no consequence to her.

We see Howard being turned down for a job because, as a business executive explains, the company does not want controversy. Howard looks out a window and sees a newly married bride and groom — Dominique and Gail Wynand.

Howard Roark walks around and sees various buildings going up by other architects. As he strolls by a building constructed by the firm of Francon & Keating, he meets none other than Ellsworth Toohey. Toohey points out that he has been instrumental in closing projects to Howard. Toohey observes that Howard is walking the streets, unable to find work, while old-fashioned copy-the-past architects are doing a bustling business. Toohey takes credit for Howard's failure to find clients. Toohey suggests, "Why don't you tell me what you think of me in any words you wish?"

"But I don't think of you," is our hero's simple and withering answer.

I again remind the reader of who originated this acidic put-down: Frank O'Connor, the husband whom Rand hero worshipped.

Then we see Howard discussing a current project with a client who says he feared Howard would not be interested in designing a humble gas station after designing skyscrapers.

Howard Roark is not a snob. He assures the client that he will design any building providing he is given the freedom to design it as he sees fit. We see a design for a store, farm, residence, office building, factory. We see the design, then the building.

One client marvels that Howard was able to survive a *Banner* smear campaign. Howard says he survived because of people who thought independently.

At his office, Howard learns that someone has called who wants Howard Roark to design a building for him. Who? Gail Wynand.

We soon see Wynand and Howard discussing a building project. It is obvious that Wynand does not remember what his newspaper did to Howard. The publisher cheerfully asks Howard to design a country house for him and his wife. Howard wonders if Mrs. Wynand suggested him as the architect and Wynand says she knows nothing about it. Why does Wynand want Howard for this project? Whenever Wynand especially admired a building, he inquired as to its architect and the answer was always Howard Roark.

Howard readily agrees to design the home even as Wynand explains that he wants the house built as "a temple to Dominique Wynand."

A beaming Wynand returns home to his wife. Dominique comments on how happy he looks. He tells of his plan for a country home. Then he tells her it will be designed by Howard Roark.

Music signifies a sense of crisis. Dominique is clearly distressed and asks her husband if he remembers why she resigned from his newspaper.

Only then does Wynand recall the campaign against the Enright House that Howard designed.

Pacing back and forth, wringing her hands, she reminds him of how *The Banner* smeared Howard Roark, how it threw him to a howling mob just to sell newspapers.

It is Wynand's turn to be shocked because Howard did not remind him of it.

Dominique suggests that the two of them have been wrong in their cynicism. Men of integrity must exist because Howard Roark is one.

Wynand clings to the idea that Howard is no better than anyone else.

We see Wynand and Howard at *The Banner* office. Wynand reminds Howard of the Enright House campaign. Then the publisher offers Howard a contract to design buildings according to traditional principles. Howard says he will accept this offer. Then he sketches a possible design, shows it to Wynand, and asks if it is what the publisher wants.

"Good heavens, no!" Wynand exclaims, as he realizes there is no point in trying to tempt Howard.

Wynand and Howard have dinner with Dominique who goes over the plans for the house she will share with her husband. She tells both men that she appreciates it.

The film has a scene of Keating visiting Toohey. Keating complains that he is getting fewer commissions. Toohey dramatically waves about a cigarette in its holder as he points out that Keating was fashionable but fashions change. The distraught Keating says he thought Toohey was his friend. "I'm a friend of yours," Toohey easily agrees. "I'm everybody's friend. I'm a friend of humanity." Keating begs Toohey to help him secure the Cortlandt Homes housing project. Toohey doubts Keating possesses the talent to design something with the level of structural economy and ingenuity that this project requires but hands Keating the papers linked to it so he can try.

Cut to Keating and Howard. Keating has tried but, just as Toohey suspected, does not have the talent to meet all the necessary specifications. Would Howard do it and let Peter sign his name to it? Howard agrees to let Keating keep all the fees and the glory — providing the building will be erected precisely as he designs it. Keating promises he will ensure no changes.

Then Howard goes off on a vacation with Mr. and Mrs. Wynand. When he returns, he finds that, Cortlandt Homes is close to being finished — but with multiple changes to Howard's design. A deeply apologetic Peter Keating expresses anguish. What will Howard do?

As in the novel, Howard enlists Dominique's assistance so the night watchman will not get hurt when the building is dynamited. Howard waits beside the rubble to get arrested.

Essentially, what happens next is what happened in the novel. The evil dynamiter of a public housing project is denounced by almost every outlet — save *The Banner*. When Ellsworth Toohey denounces Howard, Wynand fires Toohey. Then Toohey's buddies desert *The Banner*. The popular newspaper becomes so unpopular that picketers appear in front of the building with signs like "We Demand the Reinstatement of Ellsworth Monckton Toohey" and "We Demand Reversal of The Banner's Position on Cortlandt." "We Don't Read Wynand" becomes a popular slogan. There is a scene of a cocktail party in which one socialite says to another, "I fired my cook because I caught her reading *The Banner*."

There are, of course, rumors about the dynamiter's motive. Ellsworth Toohey finds Peter Keating and squeezes the truth out of

Peter that the true designer of Cortlandt was Howard Roark. Noting how the anguished man has been reduced to a shivering mass of protoplasm, a satisfied Toohey says, "You are my greatest achievement, Peter, the completely selfless man."

A beleaguered Gail Wynand finally submits to the demands of his board of directors and denounces Howard Roark in *The Banner*. Seeing a newspaper lying on the street with Howard's face and a footprint over it brilliantly dramatizes the way the general public persecutes our hero.

But all is not lost. Howard Roark delivers his six-and-a-half minute long summation/testimony to the jury. It is an introduction of Rand's philosophy of Objectivism as well as an explanation of why he dynamited the building. The defendant tells the jury that he designed Cortlandt — for a price. That price was to see it built precisely as he designed it. When the building was "disfigured," other people in effect stole his work but did not pay him for it. The jury is persuaded and Howard wins his acquittal.

Our hero triumphs. Roger Enright buys the land for the housing project so the true design of Howard Roark will be erected. A scene of Howard in Gail Wynand's office, tells us that Wynand is shutting down *The Banner*. The money will be used to create the Wynand Building that Howard will design. After Howard leaves, Gail Wynand takes a gun out of his drawer and commits suicide. This makes Dominique a widow and free to marry again. She does indeed become Mrs. Roark. The last shot shows her going up a lift on a construction site and Howard at the top of the Wynand building-in-progress.

The Fountainhead as a film retained the basic principle behind *The Fountainhead* as a novel. It successfully transferred to the screen Ayn Rand's concerns with individualism vs. collectivism not politically but psychologically as each person experiences it in his or her own life. Since Ayn Rand was both a novelist and a screenwriter, she understood that different mediums required different tactics and this understanding is reflected in the changes made from book to movie. It was entirely to the benefit of the film that the initial controversy into which the hero was dragged was not about the Stoddard Temple but about the Enright House. The issues about the Stoddard Temple would have been difficult to transfer to film and, in addition, having a controversy about a "religious" building would have acted as a distraction from the real meaning Rand sought to promote.

To appease the Hays Office, Dominique does not divorce either Peter Keating or Gail Wynand as she did in the novel. Having Keating break their engagement to secure a career-enhancing commission works powerfully to underline the flaws in how he lives his life. Having Wynand commit suicide underlines the tragedy of a strong and talented man who took a wrong direction in life.

There are problems with the film version of *The Fountainhead.* Already noted is the casting of Gary Cooper who is just too old to play Howard Roark. At one point, Gail Wynand says he sees "my youth" in Howard. This rings wrong because the architect does not look much younger than the publisher. Another problem is that Gary Cooper, an actor used to playing "action" types in Westerns, is not well-suited to making intellectual points. Cooper himself said he was uncertain about the meaning of what he said during his all-important trial summation.

In this writer's opinion, the other parts are filled quite well. I believe Patricia Ryan was excellent as the glamorous, hoity-toity Dominique who becomes tormented by her own passion. A special kudos should be given to Robert Douglas as Ellsworth Toohey. He is oily, conniving, and perfectly ruthless — one of cinema's most perfectly villainous villains.

Many have faulted Rand for the unbelievability of some scenarios and dialogue. I have already remarked that Dominique's "this is not a tie but a gulf between us" does not sound like anything a person would say in real life.

However, in the film as in the novel, Rand wrote in "romantic realism" in which characterizations are deliberately exaggerated and dialogue is not meant to sound naturalistic but to make a point.

When *The Fountainhead* movie was released, it was not a success either financially or with critics. *New York Times* reviewer Bosley Crowther called it "a long-winded, complicated preachment on the rights of the individual in society" and derided it as "wordy" and "pretentious." He denounced the scenes as "turgid." Like Ayn Rand herself, Bosley Crowther disliked the style of architecture displayed as that of Howard Roark. Crowther denounced the style as "trash." However, like this writer, Crowther was impressed by the acting of Robert Douglas as villain Ellsworth Toohey, writing, "Robert Douglas is elaborately evil." Crowther did not think much of Patricia Neal's performance, calling it "almost funny" because "so affected."

Other reviewers were equally unimpressed with the movie. A review in *The Hollywood Reporter* called the characters "downright weird." Writing for *The New Yorker*, John McCarten called the film "inept."

Despite the negative reviews, the film greatly helped author Ayn Rand because it put the novel once again on the best-seller list. The film may not have made good money but the book once again did. She could have said what Liberace famously said in commenting on a negative review: "I cried all the way to the bank."

Although the film was panned when first released, it has in recent years benefited from critical reappraisal. Critic Dave Kehr asserted, "King Vidor turned Ayn Rand's preposterous 'philosophical' novel into one of his finest and most personal films (1949), mainly by pushing the phallic imagery so hard that it surpasses Rand's rightist diatribes." Kehr elaborated that its "images have a dynamism, a spatial tension" and "the emotions rise and fall in broad, operatic movements that are unmistakably sexual."

Another film critic, Emanuel Levy, writes, "King Vidor took Ayn Rand's didactic and pretentious novel of the same title (inspired by

Frank Lloyd Wright), about individual creativity, power, and compromise, and turned it into a highly enjoyable, juicy Freudian melodrama." Levy also declares, "This highly operatic Greek melodrama is replete with bombastic moralistic speeches and phallic imagery (low angles of horses rising, narrow skyscrapers), but the images are dynamic, and there is tension in the mise en scene of King Vidor, specifically in the way he shoots, frames and edits individuals vis-á-vis their physical space."

The Fountainhead greatly helped Patricia Neal's career. It was also significant for both her and Gary Cooper because they commenced a romantic relationship during the making of the film.

This author is aware that some people have discussed making another motion picture based on *The Fountainhead.* However, nothing has come to fruition as of this writing.

PHOTOS

Photo of Ayn Rand taken by Lester Kraus

Love scene from *The Fountainhead*, Howard Roark (Gary Cooper) holding Dominique Francon (Patricia Neal)

Dmitry Rozental who voiced the male characters in *Red Pawn*

Montage of characters from the animation of *Red Pawn*

The Fountainhead scene of Dominique Francon Wynand (Patricia Neal) and Gail Wynand (Raymond Massey)

Howard Roark (Gary Cooper) and Gail Wynand (Raymond Massey) in *The Fountainhead*

Dearest Resa,

Your work on Ayn Rand has been so marvellous - an incredible help to me building the character - I thank you so much for the choices, for your energy, for your eye and for your imagination. The piece would never have worked so well without you - THANK-YOU Love Helen.

Resa McConaghy was the costume designer for *The Passion of Ayn Rand.* McConaghy received this letter from Helen Mirren

In the made-for-TV movie, *The Passion of Ayn Rand*, Ayn Rand (Helen Mirren) sits with acolyte/boyfriend Nathaniel Brandon (Eric Stoltz)

John Handem Piette played Equality 7-2521 in the 2009 *Anthem*

Jordana Capra played a judge in *Atlas Shrugged Part II: The Strike*

Singleton/Victoria Morland (Jennifer Jones) and Alan Quinton (Joseph Cotten) in a scene from *Love Letters*

Phillipe Coquet played a lead guard in the 2009 *Anthem*

Ryan Rapsys who, along with Scott McRae, composed the musical scores for the animated versions of *Anthem* and *Red Pawn*

From left to right: R. Janoschek (Charles Drake), Bob Collins (Bob Cummings), Ivy Hotchkiss (Lizabeth Scott), W. Anders (Don DeFore)

The Fountainhead: The Rape Scene

There is on YouTube a deliberately goofy video take-off on the previously discussed, and very troubling, "rape scene" of *The Fountainhead*. This short film may have been put up on Oct. 20, 2007 as that date is given under the title. I believe this whimsical short color film should be seen as a take-off on the scene in the novel rather than the film because the latter is more a standard Hollywood passionate kissing scene which may, or may not, go further than kissing when the cameras stop rolling.

The short is entitled *The Fountainhead: The Rape Scene*. The little information this author could gather indicated it was put together by a youth named Gene Zhu for his eleventh grade English class project on "modernism." The short film starts with a handsome young red-haired fellow, a beret on his head, repeatedly swinging a pickax into the ground. There is something nice about the fact that this short was made in color so we get to see Howard Roark's red hair. Then we see a young woman (possibly a man in drag) wearing a pretty dress in the distance. She is leering at the man. "Hel*lo*," she says in a deliberately seductive manner.

Howard comments that it is really hot and begins unbuttoning his shirt.

The woman plays with her hair and tells Howard there is a "dirty job" to be done at her house. She has a fireplace she needs fixed. Would he like to make some extra money?

"Certainly, Miss Francon," he replies.

Dominique asks him to come to fix the fireplace's broken marble part that evening.

Cut to Dominique relaxing on a couch. She is fully dressed and stroking one of her own thighs. The door opens and in comes Howard. He grabs her and rushes her into the bedroom. He pushes her down on the bed and the camera moves toward the ceiling. "Rape! Rape!" Dominique cries — as both Howard's beret and her wig are tossed in the air! Then Howard puts shirt and beret back on and looks back at the woman — who is not on camera. After he leaves, the camera pans to Dominique on the bed with a sheet pulled to her chest, her shoulders bare, her wig back on, and holding a toy panda in her arms.

Then we cut to a man, presumably Gene Zhu, who is seated on a chair reading the book *Why Do Men Have Nipples?* by Billy Goldberg and Mark Leyner. "Hi," he cheerfully says. "This scene from Ayn Rand's novel *The Fountainhead* is a classic example of modernist literature." He talks about authors "breaking away from traditional literature." He remarks, "Ayn Rand in particular used her unique view of Objectivism to show her view on intimacy and the ice-cold ferocity of love." Finally, he opines, "If it was romantic, it would be more like this."

Cut to Dominque and Howard in a field. They run slowly at each other. There is a fade out and the sign "The End."

The comments section for the short is full of praise. "You guys are awesome. Hope you got an A for this" and "LMFAO" and "absolutely amazing . . . way too funny" and "ROFL."

In this author's opinion, *The Fountainhead: The Rape Scene* is a funny, cheeky, delightfully creative little video. Kudos to those who thought it up and those who appeared in it.

1952-1960: Ayn Rand TV Tidbits

In the 1950s and in the year 1960, shows based on Ayn Rand's work appeared on television programs. An hour-long black and white TV anthology series entitled *Broadway Television Theatre* aired an episode entitled "The Night of January Sixteenth" on July 14, 1954. The performers were Neil Hamilton, Stella Andrew, and Virginia Gilmore.

Another TV anthology series, *Lux Video Theatre*, aired two episodes with a Rand link during the 1950s. "Love Letters" was aired on January 20, 1955. Richard Goode directed the episode and Richard P. McDonagh penned a TV screenplay based on Rand's film screenplay. Diana Lynn played Victoria/Singleton, Charles Keane played Roger, and Dan O'Herlihy played Alan.

Lux Radio Theatre aired "The Night of January Sixteenth" on May 10, 1956. Like the film version, this one had a jury of performers. Fred Carney directed the episode. On the Internet Movie Database, Ayn Rand is credited for her play, S. H. Barnett is credited with the "adaptation," and no less than three individuals — Delmer Daves, Eve Greene, and Robert Pirosh — are stated to have had a hand in the "original screenplay." Phyllis Thaxter plays Karen.

ITV Play of the Week aired a production of "Night of January 16th" on January 12, 1960. Michael Currer-Briggs directed it and Norman Ginsbury wrote the episode adaptation. Maxine Audley played Karen Andre.

1957: *Atlas Shrugged*: Ayn Rand's Ultimate Novel

Random House published *Atlas Shrugged* in 1957. It was Rand's longest novel. It was also her fourth, and final, novel. Rand regarded it as her fictional magnum opus and it is regarded as such by her followers. She described its theme as "the role of man's mind in existence." It would be impossible in a synopsis to do justice to this very long and very convoluted story. The following discusses the basic plot of the story and a few highlights.

The story takes place in an unspecified future time period in the United States. It opens with Taggart Transcontinental Vice-President of Operations Dagny Taggart trying to get a broken rail line serving Colorado repaired. The President of the business is her brother, Jim Taggart. They have many disputes that can be viewed as complicated by an element of sibling rivalry. In addition, Dagny is "Randian" in that she is more individualistic, super-capitalistic, and anti-government than Jim.

Dagny is one of a multitude of people confused by a mystery that is plaguing her world. Many top entrepreneurs, intellectuals, and other big shots are mysteriously vanishing. Are they being kidnapped? Murdered? Have they voluntarily skedaddled from a system they oppose?

It is necessary because her finding John Galt and discovering he is more than a catchphrase makes no sense without it. An odd catchphrase has become common. People who cannot answer a question often say, "Who is John Galt?"

Dedicated to the family business, Dagny is working hard to keep good workers on and improve her company's reputation. She also struggles to buy supplies for Taggart Transcontinental. She runs into more problems when the Mexican government nationalizes Taggart

Transcontinental's San Sebastian Line. That line had originally been commissioned to service copper mills belonging to Francisco d'Anconia. However, it turns out that the mills were unproductive anyway so Jim tries to use political clout to undermine d'Anconia's company. Later in the story, Dagny learns from Francisco d'Anconia that he deliberately allowed his copper mills to fail. It should be mentioned that Dagny and Francisco have a romantic history together.

Dedicated to getting Taggart Transcontinental up and going, Dagny works to repair the broken Rio Norte Line. Her original plan was to repair it with Reardon Steel but she agrees to use a recently created alloy called Reardon Metal that Hank Reardon created. This invention, Reardon Metal, plays a major role in the novel's events. It is supposed to be a kind of super-alloy, one that is stronger than steel yet also lighter than it.

The State Science Institute denounces Reardon Metal, causing the stock of Taggart Transcontinental to crash since it has been used on that company's railroads.

Dagny professionally separates from brother Jim and begins her own railway company which turns out to be very successful. Around the same time, she begins a romance with the married Hank Reardon.

The government passes laws that undermine private enterprise. When laws are passed that especially harm companies in Colorado, Dagny cuts train lines in that state.

A famed oil industrialist disappears and there are suggestions that his apparent vanishing has something to do with his having deliberately set fire to his oil rigs as a reaction to nationalization by the government. More movers and shakers "at the top" inexplicably vanish and Dagny suspects some nefarious forces are working to destroy major industries, taking away top people just when they are most urgently needed.

The government hauls Hank Reardon into court for breaking a law that harms industrialists; Reardon defiantly refuses to even participate in the trial. This Randian hero is dedicated to free market capitalism and does not recognize the moral right of Big Government to fetter it.

Wesley Mouch is a lobbyist and politician dedicated to socializing the country. This author cannot help but wonder if Rand chose to give him his name to remind the reader of "weasel" and "moocher." He pressures Reardon to cooperate in the economic changes thought by Mouch and his cronies to be "fair."

Jim Taggart hopes Reardon will help keep Jim's company going. During their association, Jim meets Reardon's wife, Lillian, who is disillusioned with her unfaithful husband and lets Jim know about the affair between Dagny and Hank. Sliding onto the side turning more power over to the government, Jim helps create a patent law that mandates new patents be owned by the government. Hank Reardon eventually signs Reardon Metal over to government ownership.

Understandably exhausted and stressed-out, Dagny Taggart decides to take time off, going to a hideaway in the mountains, to relax and recharge. A huge railway accident occurs, and it's back to work. Learning that a scientist who once assisted her may be in danger, Dagny — who is a pilot — flies her own airplane in the belief that she knows where he is apt to be found. The plane crashes. When Dagny comes back to consciousness, she finds herself in a tiny village — filled with the vanished big shots! Why have they left the "regular" world for their own little mountain hideaway? She is informed that they are on their own special kind of strike.

She learns that John Galt is not just a catchphrase but a person! As noted, Rand's female characters are, like their creator, not averse to non-monogamy so she falls in love with the flesh and blood John Galt. Will she join the strike? Not coincidentally, will she stay with the man for whom she has a first class case of hot pants?

The call of career is strong for this railroad magnate. Dagny returns to work in the normal world — only to discover that, in her absence, the government nationalized her railway. Government leaders demand she publicly support the nationalization. At first she refuses but Lillian Reardon uses knowledge of Dagny's liaison with Hank Reardon to blackmail her into submitting to the dictates of the nationalizing leaders. She even goes on the air to support nationalization — and reveals her non-marital romance with Hank Reardon to the whole world, adding that both she and Reardon were blackmailed into going along with the governmental plan. She warns the people that the government will continue to stifle their freedoms.

Francisco d'Anconia destroys what remains of his copper mines. Then he vanishes. Where could he be? The reader knows the answer. The entire economy appears to be crumbling as politicians stifle businesses and more business leaders vanish.

Eventually John Galt hacks into a radio station and gives a super-long speech that amounts to a summary of the principles of Ayn Rand's Objectivism. He informs that world that he has led a strike of society's greatest minds.

Without those minds, the nation dissolves into shambles. However, Rand ends her story on a note of hope as John Galt tells his fellow strikers it is time to return to the real world and build it back up according to correct capitalist free market principles.

During the course of the novel's events, heroine Dagny Taggert enjoys romances with Francisco d'Anconia, Henry Reardon, and John Galt. It has been reported that Rand was asked why she would create a heroine who would be the object of the lust/love of three different men. "It's my fantasy," Rand replied.

This lengthy and ambitious novel was inspired by a conversation Rand had in 1943 with a close friend, fellow writer and philosopher Isabel Paterson. Paterson told Rand she should write a novel giving a complete explanation of her philosophy.

"What if I went on strike?" Rand replied. "What if all the creative minds of the world went on strike?" This seed blossomed into Atlas Shrugged. Rand said her purpose in the novel was "to show how desperately the world needs prime movers and how viciously it treats them."

Rand started the novel late in 1946. At first, she thought it would be a rather easy project and she could finish it quickly; she soon realized it would take a good chunk of her time — and it sure did.

When Rand finished a few chapters, she read them aloud to her young admirers including Nathaniel and Barbara Branden, Leonard Peikoff, and Alan Greenspan, the economist who would one day chair the Federal Reserve.

By 1953, she had almost the whole novel finished except for Galt's radio speech. It took over two more years for her to write that speech.

Rand had the novel finished in 1956 and began submitting it to publishers.

Unlike previous works that had been submitted to multiple publishers over a long period of time before finding takers, she soon found a publisher for *Atlas Shrugged*. The reason was that the success of her 1943 novel *The Fountainhead* meant that she had a proven track record as a popular writer. Indeed, her contract for *The Fountainhead* gave first dibs on her next book to its publisher, Bobbs-Merrill Company. Their editors reviewed the manuscript and asked her to make cuts and changes in it. Rather like Howard Roark when asked to allow changes to his building designs, Rand insisted her work had to be taken as it was or not at all. Bobbs-Merrill decided they did not want it as it was.

Random House President Bennett Cerf suggested Rand submit the manuscript to multiple publishers to find out which would not only accept the novel but do best in promoting it. Rand liked this idea and talked to a few publishers. Then she decided multiple submissions were unnecessary. She offered it to Random House where it was accepted with Cerf calling it a "great book." However, when Rand looked over the thick manuscript, he asked her to make cuts. She said it would be like cutting the Bible. It was accepted as Rand wanted it.

Objectivism: The Philosophy Ayn Rand Founded

Rand continued her writing career but wrote no more fiction. Instead, she wrote essays and books about her philosophy of Objectivism. She spent much of the 1960s and early 1970s systemizing that philosophy and lecturing about it. From 1962 to 1965 she published *The Objectivist Newsletter*; from 1965 to 1971 she published a much larger periodical entitled *The Objectivist*; and from 1971 to 1976 she published *The Ayn Rand Letter*. Essays in these publications were collected into nine nonfiction books. Among her most influential non-fiction books are *The Virtue of Selfishness* and *Capitalism: The Unknown Ideal.*

Although philosophy is often thought of as something esoteric and otherworldly, Rand held that all human beings are guided by it. The *Encyclopedia Britannica* states, "Rand held that all people, whether they realize it or not, are guided in their thoughts and actions by philosophical principles and assumptions. Philosophy thus has great practical import, and indeed possessing the correct philosophy is essential to leading a successful and happy life. The branches of philosophy that most directly affect everyday life are ethics and political philosophy."

What is this philosophy of Objectivism that Rand formulated? It is a philosophy dismissed by many people. Film critic Roger Ebert cynically summarized it as "I'm on board; pull up the lifeline." A YouTube series called "Why is this still a thing?" called Objectivism a fancy name for "being a selfish asshole." The previously mentioned Susan Brownmiller derided it as "spiritually male," a term that makes zero sense and is obviously sexist. Furthermore, it is especially bizarre that a supposed "feminist" would consider *anything* to "spiritually" have gender. Indeed, it would be odd for a person of any politics to see anything as being "spiritually" limited by gender.

Objectivism holds as a foundational principle that there is a reality that is outside human perception. Humans can accurately perceive that reality through their senses and understand it through their minds.

The highest human virtue, Rand believed, is reason because reason is the human's "basic means of survival." She thought of selfishness as a virtue, rather than a vice, because it meant the rational individual's pursuit of his or her own happiness. Altruism was evil because it meant "the placing of others above self, of their interests above one's own." Basically, what an individual wanted to do was acceptable as long as it did not harm someone else or impinge upon another person's rights. She held that no one "has the right to *initiate* the use of physical force against others." She held this "nonaggression principle" as incompatible with most social programs since they depended on taking from some people through taxes to give to other people. She believed capitalism was the only moral economic system because it was the only one consistent with human nature. "My philosophy, in essence, is the concept of man as a heroic being, with his own happiness as the moral purpose of his life, with productive achievement as his noblest activity, and reason as his only absolute."

Sometime during the 1960s, her relationship with Nathaniel Branden became romantic. Rand wanted to have sex with the much younger man. She was still deeply in love with Frank O'Connor and would not consider divorcing the "king" she found on *The King of Kings*. She was deeply concerned with honesty so she could not deceive her husband to have sex outside her marriage. Thus, Ayn Rand insisted each of them explain to their respective spouses that they planned to engage in a sexual relationship. She further said that both Frank O'Connor and Barbara Branden must consent to the extra-marital dalliance before it could occur. Frank O'Connor was initially appalled and called the arrangement "insanity." However, he eventually decided to go along with what his wife wanted and gave his approval. Barbara Branden was also initially upset at the idea of her husband having sex outside the marriage but she too eventually consented to the arrangement.

Thus, Ayn Rand and Nathaniel Branden started a physical relationship. This relationship lasted for years without jeopardizing either party's marriage. Then disaster struck. Nathaniel Branden had a second affair outside his marriage, an affair with a much younger woman. Rand always knew that he was having sex with his wife as well as with her and accepted his sex life with his wife just as Nathaniel accepted Rand's continuing sex life with her husband. But his second extra-marital dalliance caused her extreme jealousy.

No matter how intellectual an individual is, he or she is not immune to such basic and irrational emotions as jealousy. Infuriated at what Rand viewed as a terrible and wounding betrayal, she banished Nathaniel Branden from her inner circle in 1968.

A longtime heavy smoker, Rand was diagnosed with lung cancer in the mid-1970s. Surgery for the cancer was performed on her in 1974.

In 1976, she stopped publishing *The Ayn Rand Letter* and also cut back on writing and lecturing because Frank O'Connor's health was declining. She was naturally devastated when he died in 1979. She had truly loved him; she had truly "hero worshipped" him. The king she met on *The King of Kings* was gone, leaving Ayn Rand a widow suffering terrible grief. Asked about the possibility of an afterlife, she told the interviewer that she would immediately commit suicide if she believed she could join Frank in death. Not believing in an afterlife, she lived on as she mourned.

Ayn Rand died of heart failure on March 6, 1982.

1975: *La nuit du 16 janvier*

A French TV show called *Theatre Ce Sir* broadcast a version of *Night of January 16th* in 1975 on April 25. Marcel Dubois authored the screenplay and Pierre Sabagh directed the show. Juliette Mills played Karen. This author has never seen the episode nor been able to find much information about it.

As far as this author could find, that 1975 TV episode would be the last Ayn Rand inspired cinematic work to be made, for either the big screen or the small one, for over a decade.

In the 1990s, the cinematic Ayn Rand drought ended — in a manner both flamboyant and humorous.

1992 and 2009: *The Simpsons* Does Ayn Rand

The Simpsons has done two wonderfully comic segments inspired by Ayn Rand's work. The segments were remarkable both for how creatively they skewered Rand's ideals — while at the same time ironically, and probably unintentionally, lending a kind of credence to those ideals.

"A Streetcar Named Marge" first aired on October 1, 1992. Rich Moore directed the episode. Jeff Martin wrote the script; Bill Oakley and Josh Weinstein were story editors. The reason for the title is that Marge gets a part as Blanche DuBois in a community theater production of *Oh! Streetcar*, a Simpsons musical based on the Tennessee Williams classic play *A Streetcar Named Desire*.

The Rand-inspired segment of the episode is a subplot. Marge places little Maggie in a preschool called the Ayn Rand School for Tots. Marge informs a preschool official that Maggie is allergic to strained pears and enjoys a bottle of warm milk before nap time."

"A bottle?" the official incredulously repeats. "Do you know what a baby is saying when she reaches for a bottle? "Baba?" Marge tentatively suggests.

The official insists that a baby asking for a bottle is metaphorically saying, "I am a leach." The official asserts that the goal of the Ayn Rand School for Tots is to "develop the bottle within." When Marge comments that this sounds "harsh," the official brags, "We're the only daycare center in town not currently under investigation by the state."

Maggie is left at the preschool. The official pulls a pacifier from the infant's mouth, asserting, "We don't allow these here." The pacifier pulled out of her mouth is tossed into a locker in which many pacifiers are kept in a tray.

Little Maggie sucks her thumb, a crayon, a block, and then a tiny doll. She is taken to a room in which other babies are napping under Rand-inspired signs proclaiming "A Is A" and "Helping Is Futile."

At this point, a short digression is necessary. "A Is A" is the title of Aristotle's Law of Identity. Rand also cited it often in her own work, while crediting Aristotle as the only philosopher to whom she owed a true debt in forming her own beliefs.

Returning to little Maggie: she soon organizes an infant rebellion, leading the other babies and toddlers to open the locker and liberate its contents. She tosses the pacifiers to the other youngsters.

When Homer arrives to pick up little Maggie, he gasps to see all the members of the Ayn Rand School for Tots happily sucking on pacifiers. He picks up Maggie and says in exasperation, "Babies!

The Rand-influenced preschool official is listed in the credits as Ms. Sinclair. Male actor Jon Levitz voiced Ms. Sinclair.

"A Streetcar Named Marge" was a controversial episode — but the controversy was unrelated to the Rand-linked subplot. Controversy was occasioned because a song in the musical was negative on the city of New Orleans in which the play was set. The song described New Orleans as "home of pirates, drunks, and whores" and "tacky, overpriced souvenir stores."

Writers of *The Simpsons* publicly apologized for slamming the city and the next episode of the series started with Bart writing repeatedly on a blackboard, "I will not defame New Orleans."

An odd aspect of the Ayn Rand School for Tots sub-plot within "A Streetcar Named Marge" is the way it seemed to want to skewer Ayn Rand's philosophy — yet created a heroine very much like the heroes and heroines Rand created. When little Maggie decides that she and the other babies will have their pacifiers, pre-school rules be damned, she showcases the anti-Establishment spirit of Howard Roark. When she liberates the pacifiers from their hiding place, she becomes a cartoon infant version of Dagny Taggart, Hank Reardon, and John Galt. Truly, little cartoon Maggie was the type of heroine who would have warmed Rand's heart.

The second time *The Simpsons* included Ayn Rand inspired material was in the episode "Four Women and a Manicure" that first aired on May 10, 2009. Its title is a take-off on the 1994 motion picture *Four Weddings and a Funeral*. On the Internet Movie Database, Mike B. Anderson is listed as "supervising director" of an episode directed by Raymond S. Persi. The episode was written by Valentina Garza.

Our story begins in a salon with female characters getting manicures. A discussion starts about whether or not women can be traditionally attractive and feminine as well as intelligent and accomplished. This leads to fantasies about four female characters, one who actually lived and three fictional: Queen Elizabeth I, Snow White, Lady MacBeth, and Maggie Roark. The last segment, of course, is based on Ayn Rand's *The Fountainhead* with Maggie a feminized version of hero Howard Roark.

Like the previous lampooning of Ayn Roark, this one is also set in a pre-school. Jodie Foster supplies the voice of toddler Maggie and Hank Azaria voices teacher Ellsworth Toohey.

It is told as a story-within-a-story with Marge Simpson holding Maggie as she tells the story of "Maggie Roark" who is also her daughter. Marge relates that Maggie Roark was "an architect who refused to compromise."

Mediocri-Tots Daycare Center is the setting for the majority of this story. A group of babies and toddlers are assembled and their teacher, Ellsworth Toohey, tells the kids they will be playing with blocks before the blocks spill from a locker and cover the kids.

When Mr. Toohey examines the work products of the children, he likes the ordinary productions. Carrying a pen along with paper on a clipboard, he approvingly notes, "Banal . . . very banal . . . wonderfully pedestrian." Then he happens upon Maggie's beautiful block building. He is outraged: "Maggie, dancers must not kick too high and buildings must not reach the sky." He kicks the project over. He notes the rubble is still high so he stomps on it. "Welcome to the real world, baby," he tells Maggie. She crafts other projects and teacher Toohey ruins all of them, boasting, "Mediocrity rules!"

Parent-teacher day rolls around and Mr. Toohey says, "I want everyone to see how un-creative and beaten down you've become." He tells the parents, "See what your children have done. Don't brace yourselves. You will believe your eyes."

After opening the door, Mr. Toohey gasps when he sees the brilliant block creation little Maggie Roark has crafted. Maggie holds up a block and points to the letter "U" and then points to her pacifier-filled mouth. The caption translates: "You suck." The outraged Ellsworth Toohey proclaims, "You will be tried as a toddler." She is tried before a jury of her fellow pre-schoolers. "The child's crime was to remind the rest of us that we are merely ordinary," Toohey declares before recommending a sentence of "Nine time-outs to be served consecutively."

Like Howard Roark before his jury in both the novel and film versions of *The Fountainhead*, little Maggie Roark eloquently defends herself. "Throughout the ages, the finger painter, the Play-Doh sculptor, the Lincoln logger, stood alone against the daycare teacher of her time," Maggie confidently asserted. "She did not live to earn approval stickers. She lived for herself, that she might achieve the things that are the glory of all humanity. These are my terms. I do not care to play by any others. And now, if the jury will allow me, it's nap time."

We learn that little Maggie Roark grew up to become a brilliant and successful architect. We see her holding a briefcase as she goes toward a skyscraper we are to assume she designed and that Marge calls "one of the wonders of the world." We see a poster advertising a play that will be staged in the building in which Homer Simpson plays MacBeth. At the top of the building is a daycare center — one in which "every child is free to follow their dream."

Then we switch to the present day in which Marge remonstrates with her little Maggie who has painted a version of Vincent Van Gogh's famous *The Starry Night* on the salon wall with fingernail polishes. "Bad baby!" Marge exclaims. In total, it was an entertaining segment, one best appreciated by those who had read *The Fountainhead*, regardless of whether or not they supported the philosophical ideals it espoused.

In her fiction, Ayn Rand often created larger-than-life, even cartoon-like characters. Thus, it is strikingly appropriate that those characters served as inspirations for the writers of a popular cartoon series.

1998: *Ayn Rand: A Sense of Life*

In 1998, a documentary on Rand's life was released entitled *Ayn Rand: A Sense of Life*. Michael Paxton wrote and directed the film and Sharon Gless narrated it. The movie runs for two hours and twenty-five minutes. It includes a potpourri of stock footage, clips from productions associated with Rand, "talking head" interviews with Rand herself and those who knew her, and other material about this unique author and philosopher. Most of the motion picture is in color but there are sections in black and white.

The director of cinematography on *Ayn Rand: A Sense of Life* was Alik Sakharov. It had an additional director of photography and that was Jeffrey M. Hoffman. "Michael Paxton was a good friend of mine and he knew that I shared a philosophical interest in Ayn Rand and Objectivism," Hoffman recalled in an interview with the author of this book. "We both had a friend, Objectivist philosopher Ron Pisaturo, who introduced us."

As director of photography, Hoffman "worked with the director to set up interviews. I set up lighting so we could film people who appeared in the documentary. I shot a number of interviews."

Hoffman very much enjoyed working on the film. "I'm a big fan of Ayn Rand and Objectivism and it was a chance to get something out there to audiences who aren't familiar with her or Objectivism or might have false ideas about her," he commented.

The documentary begins with Sharon Gless quoting Rand that the theme of her life was "individualism" and noting the irony that she was born into the anti-individualistic society of Russia. The quote includes Rand's realization that she had to make the United States her home as it was a place in which she would be "fully free to write."

Ayn Rand: A Sense of Life shows early on a 1959 interview in which journalist Mike Wallace notes that the application of Rand's philosophy could "revolutionize our lives" and in which Rand instructs him that her ethics are "based on objective reality" and are a "rational morality." Then the film returns to Rand's early life story from her birth in 1905 in St. Petersburg, Russia. It covers all the Rand basics. She was born in Czarist Russia, a tyranny under a monarch and a culture steeped in the mysticism of the Russian Orthodox version of Christianity. The film discusses her rejection of mysticism even as a child since she decided she was an atheist at the tender age of nine years old and never wavered from that position. The documentary discusses how she grew up one of three sisters with a father who brought them into the middle class through his pharmacy and a mother who believed herself an intellectual and stimulated the minds of her children. Viewers learn of the growing young woman's love for ideas, motion pictures, and the lighthearted turn of the century popular tunes she was to nickname "tiddlywink music." The film tells the story of her emigration to America, her years of poverty and struggle, her meeting and marrying Frank O'Connor, and her successful years as author and philosopher. The film talks about how her acolytes formed the group that first Rand, and then all its members, humorously called "the Collective," and how she and Nathaniel Brandon engaged in a sexual relationship with the knowledge and consent of their respective spouses. There are several cuts from her TV appearances in which she was interviewed by various talk show hosts. One was done after she was widowed. The host asked if she would not really want to believe that Frank O'Connor was in some sense still in existence? Wouldn't that idea bring her comfort? "If I thought that, I would immediately commit suicide to be with him," she answered.

One of the most powerful scenes in the documentary is a brief filmed portion of a scene from a theatrical production of Ayn Rand's play *Ideal*. Like the documentary that showcased it, the production was directed by Michael Paxton. Janne Peters starred as actress Kay Gonda. Garbed in a black dress, Peters-as-Gonda appears positively transfixed when she recalls how impressed she was by a particular man's appearance. Gazing into the distance, she says that once she saw a man standing on a mountain and he seemed like "a string tumbling to a note of ecstasy no man had ever heard." His visage made her think that "this is what life should be" and elaborates, "I can't forget the man on the rock."

Since an excerpt from a stage production of *Ideal* was included in the documentary, this author interviewed Janne Peters about her work in the play and views on Rand.

How was she cast in the role of Kay Gonda? After moving to California from Manhattan in the fall of 1988, she joined the Gateway Theater in Los Angeles. "We were a collaborative group of professional actors, directors, and writers presenting scenes each week to hone our craft with the goal of creating projects together," she disclosed. "I'd been there several weeks when director Michael Paxton approached me to do a cold reading of *Ideal* by Ayn Rand. I wasn't familiar with the play, but was intrigued by Kay Gonda and her journey. Afterwards, Michael decided to mount a production of *Ideal* in Los Angeles. I was honored that Michael offered me the role! I knew Gonda would be one of the most challenging roles I would ever do!"

Like many people, she made an acquaintanceship in her youth with Ayn Rand. "I became aware of Ayn Rand's *Atlas Shrugged* in college," she told the author of this book. "I loved old movies and had seen *The Fountainhead* with Gary Cooper and Patricia Neal. I was drawn to Ayn Rand's strong female characters. They were intelligent, passionate woman who were independent. I didn't know anything about Ayn Rand's philosophy but respected her writing."

This author asked how Janne Peters prepared specifically for the scene excerpted from *Ideal* that appeared in *Ayn Rand: A Sense of Life*. "I had to see 'the man on the rock' so vividly in my mind that his being spoke to my heart and soul through Ayn Rand's words."

What did the actress enjoy most about doing this scene? "It was the 'ideal' that Gonda was striving for and a 'sense of life' that she wanted others to to realize was possible," Peters answered. "I believe that journey is our destiny as human beings."

The documentary later discusses the void left in her when her husband passed away. As a widow, she still wrote and worked. The documentary shows an aged and widowed Rand saying, "I've had my time. I can't complain." It describes her 1985 death at the age of 77 and her legacy.

Michael Paxton, in an interview with the author of this book, revealed the reasons he was intrigued and impressed by *Ideal*. "*Ideal* was written in 1934 at a time when Ayn Rand was working at a day job in Hollywood while working on her novels," Paxton stated. "Thematically, it is about how people don't live up to their professed ideals. It is about how they betray themselves and those around them by not having the courage of their convictions or commitment to their own lives and integrity. The play, mostly through the character of Johnny Dawes, also shows how difficult it is to have a benevolent sense of life in a society that is riddled with weak and dishonest people. Although Ayn did not discuss what career Johnny was pursuing, I saw him as an artist struggling to make sense of the world and his place in it. This was not a foreign struggle to me, as I was in a similar situation when I first discovered Ayn Rand's works. I felt I understood Johnny on a very deep level and what Kay Gonda meant to him; it often paralleled my own feelings about life and certainly reflected what Ayn Rand meant to me personally."

Michael Paxton's background led him to want to craft a documentary about Ayn Rand. "I was brought up in a household where the Catholic religion was considered the philosophy of life," he recalled. "I was taught all the usual 'turn the other cheek' and altruistic values. At the same time, my parents were born and bred hard-working middle-class Americans who believe in honesty, earning their keep and providing much love to all of us in the family. These were the values that were instilled in me despite what I heard at church every Sunday. Even at the age of seven, I didn't think that what was said on the pulpit Sundays made much sense. Mostly, this was a metaphysical issue for me, that is the concept of 'God' and man's relationship to 'him.' Still, I saw the earmarks of altruism everywhere around me and struggled to integrate those into my own life. For many reasons, which I can't go into here, it was impossible to do this. Suffice it to say, I was pretty lost and felt hopeless about my purpose as a human being and about existence in general. Fortunately, when I was really struggling in middle school, I found *We the Living* in a bookstore and was exposed to Ayn Rand's point of view. Reading her ideas about individualism, rational self-interest, and the role of reason in human life, I 'felt the earth move,' as they say."

It took off from there, Paxton continued. "The next decade was filled with reading and delving into philosophy as my college major," he disclosed. "After changing my career path to filmmaking, philosophical themes in the movies became my focus. Not surprisingly, I had thought about making a documentary about Ayn Rand's life and ideas when I was at NYU film school around the time that she passed away in 1982. Since Ayn Rand's work and ideas had truly changed my life, I wanted to pay homage to her in some way through my filmmaking. However, since my focus was on narrative film, I filed that idea away in the back of my mind as I forged my way into the film industry. When I moved to Los Angeles, and after I had directed Ayn Rand's *Ideal* and *Anthem* for the stage, I had a good professional relationship with Leonard Peikoff, the heir of Ayn Rand's estate. At the same time, I was approached by an investor who was willing to fund the making of a documentary on Ayn Rand. The stage was finally set for me to not just pay homage to Ayn Rand but to project her point of view — her sense of life — to the world on movie screens."

What aspects of Rand's life did Paxton try to emphasize in the documentary? "As the title suggests, I decided to focus on Ayn

Rand's 'sense of life' — what she described as 'a subconscious view of the universe and man's place in it . . . a person's most personal, emotional response to existence.' To do this, I knew that I had to give proper context to how she grew up and formed her ideas. Therefore, I focused on two parallel tracks: her external circumstances and her reactions to them. What was the world like around her as she moved through life and how did she perceive and deal with them to create her art and philosophy. That being the goal, I knew that art (novels, painting, theater, movies, etc.) was essential to her development and that it should hold a prominent place in the telling of her story. Not only how the art she loved influenced her as an artist, but also how it changed the course of her working life from being an extra in DeMille's *The King of Kings*, writing scripts for Hal Wallis *(Love Letters, You Came Along)* to adapting her own novel of *The Fountainhead* to the screen."

What were the major challenges in creating *Ayn Rand: A Sense of Life*? "As with most documentaries, there were budgetary constraints," he replied. "In my case, the biggest challenge was licensing for all the images, music, and television/movie clips. These were the most expensive elements that took up a third of the overall budget. In addition, I had decided to film dramatic sequences from *Ideal* to run parallel to Ayn's biographical story to be integrated throughout the film. This meant that I was also doing a narrative film within a documentary. Having a small budget, it was a challenging shoot; basically, an hour-long movie shot over a period of five days. But I was fortunate that the actors were wonderful to work with and my crew worked feverishly to create something quite special under the circumstances. Unfortunately, due to the length of the completed documentary, most of these scenes were excised because of time constraints. Only one short but poignant scene was left in the film. This was what I termed the 'Man of the Rock' speech that Kay Gonda delivers in the play. It is Ayn Rand describing the ideal man. The good news is, I was able to combine that scene and all the remaining scenes together to create a separate narrative film. I raised the money to cut the negative of this material, and am now working on integrating it into a new feature-length dramatic film called *Gonda: A Hollywood Story*."

Paxton found one part of making the documentary something of a breeze. "Oddly enough, the easiest part of the documentary was writing the narration and editing the film," Paxton revealed. "I knew the story I wanted to tell and had written a script that proved to be a good blueprint for the film. Things seemed to fall into place nicely for the editors and it was like filling out an enjoyable crossword puzzle; you get stumped here and there, but overall you have a steady sense of accomplishment as the 'holes' get filled in until the puzzle is completed. It's a good feeling when you're done!"

Ultimately, directing this documentary was a lot of fun for the director. "For me, the most enjoyable part of directing *Ayn Rand: A Sense of Life* was being able to juggle all the audio/visual elements at my disposal to tell the story I wanted to tell," he stated. "As many documentary filmmakers will tell you, documentaries are often 'made' in the editing room. It's that period of the production when you have most or all of the pieces of the 'puzzle' before you and you can finally put them together so that they 'fit' the way that best tells the story. It's a marvelous feeling to do that on a daily basis. I would hardly call it work, and it's what makes filmmaking such a joy as an art form and as a craft. The other enjoyable part was working with the actors on the *Ideal* segments. First there was Janne Peters who originated the role of Kay Gonda in the stage version of *Ideal*. She was the centerpiece of those sections and embodied Ayn Rand's heroine beautifully. I also loved working with one of my favorite actresses, Sharon Gless, who recorded the narration. Such a professional, down to earth, and talented actor. Then I had the opportunity to interview such luminaries as Mike Wallace. I also had phone conversations with Patricia Neal and Ayn Rand's housekeeper but neither of them was able to be interviewed for the film. Still, it was great to have conversations with these extraordinary people."

Ayn Rand: A Sense of Life was nominated for the 1998 Academy Award for Best Documentary Feature but did not win. It won the 1999 Satellite Award for Best Motion Picture, Documentary.

Reviews of *Ayn Rand: A Sense of Life* were mixed. Writing for *The New York Times*, Janet Maslin said the documentary "does little beyond appreciating its subject as unwaveringly as possible" and called it "dutiful in outlook and utterly conventional in format."

Reviewer Mick LaSalle of the *San Francisco Chronicle* observed "with communism no longer perceived as a threat or a tenable system, much of the urgency surrounding the reading of Rand has receded." Writing specifically about the documentary, LaSalle wrote, "It just assumes her importance and goes about telling her story." Then he acknowledged, "It's quite a story" and that the documentary portrays her as the "woman of enormous courage, tenacity and fire" that she assuredly was.

In *The Austin Chronicle*, Marc Savlov stated, "Paxton reveals a woman ahead of her time, neither feminist nor shrinking violent, and above all stridently passionate."

1999: *The Passion of Ayn Rand*

An earlier section of this book briefly discussed Rand's personal relationships including that with acolyte Barbara Branden and acolyte-turned-lover Nathaniel Branden. Barbara Branden wrote a book entitled *The Passion of Ayn Rand* that was the basis for a made-for-TV-movie entitled *The Passion of Ayn Rand* that first aired in 1999.

Christopher Menaul directed the film. The script for the motion picture was co-authored by Mary Gallagher and Howard Korder — and there is a story behind that co-authorship that will soon be discussed. The movie boasted a line-up of respected actors: Helen Mirren played Rand, Peter Fonda played Frank O'Connor, Eric Stoltz played Nathaniel Branden, and Julie Delpy played Barbara Branden.

The film starts with an overview of a city at night. Then we see people holding a sign proclaiming, "John Galt Lives." We hear a female saying, "On March 8, 1982, a line formed outside a funeral parlor in New York City." The voice tells us that the deceased was denounced by some as a "leader of a cult" and "threat to public morality" and praised by others for having "changed their lives for the better." She adds: "Her name was Ayn Rand and I loved her."

A security guard (Robert Thomas) explains to those in line that they can view the deceased but "in the interests of others, we ask that you limit your time." Someone (Katharine Trowell) quips, "In the interests of others — I don't think she would have liked that!"

Cut to Los Angeles, 1951. Inside a mansion Frank O'Connor (Peter Fonda) is arranging flowers. The doorbell rings. He answers the door to find two attractive young people Nathaniel Blumenthal (Eric Stoltz) and Barbara Weidman (Julie Delpy). "Are you Mr. Rand?" Nathaniel inquires.

"I suppose I am," Frank diffidently replies before revealing his name is O'Connor.

In walks Ayn Rand (Helen Mirren). Mirren looks remarkably like Rand with bobbed hair, tight-fitting velvet pantsuit, and her cigarette elegantly held in a cigarette holder.

Nathaniel and Barbara have been very impressed by *The Fountainhead* and want to learn more about its author.

"Tell me your principles," Rand demands.

"To think for myself," Barbara replies.

Rand is impressed.

On their way home, it is obvious Nathaniel and Barbara are even more impressed with Rand now that they have met her. The couple kiss.

In another scene, Rand and Barbara discuss the latter's feelings for Nathaniel. Rand believes Nathaniel is the right man for Barbara; Barbara is uncertain.

At a gathering, Rand discusses the novel she has recently begun, *Atlas Shrugged.* Alfred (Don McKellar) speculates that he might write a screenplay for the novel when it is finished but Rand is turned off when he talks about how something left him "wracked with guilt."

There is a scene of Nathaniel and Barbara making love followed by their wedding. Ayn and Nathaniel dance; Barbara and Frank dance. Ayn tells Nathaniel he has been selected to continue her work.

In another scene, we see a discussion between Ayn and Frank. Ayn says she wants to live in New York. "Near Nathaniel and Barbara," Frank observes. Ayn acknowledges they will be there. Frank says he loves where they are but it appears a move to New York is in the offing. Ayn and Frank begin making love. Ayn says, "Not so gently! Must you always ask my permission?" Frank obligingly rips her dress. This echoes the famous "rape scene" in *The Fountainhead* with its implication that Ayn liked rough sex.

Scenes follow in which Ayn expounds on her beliefs, making statements the real Ayn famously made as when she shuns the conservative label to say she and her followers are "radicals for capitalism" and that people can become "heroic beings." In discussing gender relations, she declares, "The man must have the woman who reflects the deepest vision of himself."

As also happened in real life, Ayn wittily played on her own championing of individualism and deriding of "the collective" by suggesting her followers routinely get together and the group be called "The Collective."

Ayn holds meetings and her followers listen raptly as she expounds. They also question her and are questioned by her, often admitting to faults because they cannot live up to her precepts.

A depressed Frank O'Connor has a heart-to-heart conversation with Barbara. He fears he is not the heroic being of his wife's philosophy. Barbara assures him he is very talented. "I have a gift for flowers and painting," he acknowledges. "Not much like Howard Roark."

Soon after this Barbara notices that the teacher-student relationship between Ayn and Nathaniel is becoming romantic.

At the Rand/O'Connor home, both couples meet. Ayn wants permission from both her husband and Barbara for Ayn and Nathaniel to have a sexual relationship. This might not fly with "lesser people," the philosopher acknowledges but declares, "We are not lesser people."

Frank is adamant, "No!" He calls the plan "insanity." However, after mulling it over, he gives consent to the plan. In a conversation with Barbara, Frank recalls how he and Ayn met as extras on *The King of Kings* and Ayn called him her "ideal man." However, the fact is that, as a famous author, she brings in far more money than he does. His standard of living would drop if he divorced her. Of course, he still has the option of just putting his foot down and demanding fidelity. The film suggests that his love for Ayn is such that he agrees to the affair in part because he believes she may draw inspiration from it for her art. Finally, there is a sense in the film, as in real life, that Frank O'Connor always knew that no one could take his wife away from him. Her sexual dalliance did not threaten the marriage.

Ayn and Nathaniel embark on an affair that she promises will "last one year" and consist of "one afternoon and one evening per week."

Steamy lovemaking scenes alternate with scenes of Ayn at her typewriter, conscientiously sweating it out over her magnum opus.

Barbara finds herself increasingly confused and stressed-out. In an anxiety attack, she calls Ayn and starts talking about her fears and asks if they could meet.

But she has called when Ayn is with Nathaniel.

Rand reacts with fury: "How dare you! Do you think only of yourself? . . . This is our time! You are not to dream of coming here!" That the self-professed philosopher of selfishness derided a disciple for "thinking only of yourself" underlines how philosophical principles erode when confronted with messy human realities.

A dizzy and sick Barbara allows trumpet player Richard Folger (Tom McCamus) to take her home. Nathaniel is dismayed to find the man with his sick wife.

The film shows scenes in which Nathaniel, as a psychologist, is treating another Rand acolyte named Caroline (Sybil Darrow).

There is a scene in which Ayn tells Frank, "I finished the book. After twelve years, I finished the book!" Frank displays a painting that Rand decides is perfect for the cover.

Frank arranges a surprise party to honor Ayn for completing *Atlas Shrugged*. Sourly she states, "I don't like surprises." It is hard to remain grumpy when people have gathered to celebrate your achievement and Rand warms to the party. As she is given tributes, she gives her own tributes, "My husband, Frank, my good friend, Barbara, and my intellectual heir, Nathaniel."

The audience expects Nathaniel to have a romance with Caroline and Barbara to have a romance with Richard: sure enough, both affairs occur.

Ayn makes the talk show rounds, holds seminars, delivers speeches. She explains how *Atlas Shrugged* shows what happens when the movers and shakers quit the world and "the motor stops." She praises "reason" and "heroism." She defends herself against accusations that she promotes Fascism and counters that she is "fighting dictatorship."

At one speech, a smart-aleck in the audience challenges Ayn to state the "essence of your philosophy standing on one leg."

The aging author actually stands on one leg and says, "Metaphysics — objective reality. Epistemology — reason. Ethics — self-interest. Politics — capitalism."

Inevitably, Ayn Rand discovers that the married man with whom she is having an affair is having another affair. Nathaniel is in the middle of giving a speech when he is informed that Ayn demands to see him.

Frank and Barbara are present as Ayn jealously rails at her lover. The degree to which ideology permeated her thinking is underlined when, during her jealous rage, she says, "You said I was your highest value!" She vows to exile him from her movement and ruin him professionally. Then she slaps him repeatedly, causing a nosebleed. During this tirade — and physical assault — Frank and Barbara silently watch.

There is a telling scene after this in which Rand is shown taking questions and answers after a speech. Asked her favorite TV show, she cheerfully answers, *Charlie's Angels*. What does she think of President Reagan? "I liked him in *King's Row* but, in the White House, not so much," she answers.

A questioner asks, "What is the nature of love?"

Rand is stunned. She is looking at Nathaniel Brandon. But then her vision clears; it is not Nathaniel. "Love is the command to rise to one's highest potential," she states.

The film takes us back to right after its beginning. Ayn has died. We see the gravesite of Frank O'Connor and Ayn Rand. Barbara leaves a bouquet of flowers on Ayn's grave and the movie ends.

There are a couple of anachronisms in the movie. In a scene set in the 1950s, Frank O'Connor says he and his wife met on *The King of Kings* that was "the silent version." At the time this conversation supposedly occurred, it was the *only* version as the talkie was not made until 1961. In another scene, Alfred tells Nathaniel that Rand is working on *Atlas Shrugged.* Its working title was actually *The Strike.* Rand renamed it shortly before its publication because she liked the title Frank suggested.

The late Barbara Branden had a major hand in the made-for-TV movie based on her book called *The Passion of Ayn Rand.* She commented on the film in a lengthy letter written in 1998 to her friend, philosopher John Hospers. She called the script "excellent" and added she was asked to give her input into it. She was pleased with the actors, calling Merrin's performance "superb" and both Stoltz and Delpy "very, very good." Branden was especially impressed by Peter Fonda's depiction of Frank O'Conner. She wrote, "He doesn't act Frank; he is Frank. He has me in tears almost every time he's on camera." She added that Mirren "often does too."

However, Barbara Branden acknowledged "disappointment" in the depiction of Caroline. Branden called the actress who played Caroline, Sybil Temchen, "a fine young actress" but said the depiction was "not at all like" the real life person "in her personality, her psychology, or her character."

Branden wrote that Helen Mirren thoroughly researched Ayn Rand before playing her: "She read my book, watched interview tapes of Ayn, read a lot of her work, and came away convinced that Ayn was a great woman, great in intellect and in passion." Mirren told Branden, "I will not let her down. I will not let her be diminished." Branden asserts that Mirren "kept her word."

Branden added dialogue to the film so she was able to put "ideas into the script that I had badly wanted to get in — such as: No man has the right to initiate the use of force."

The original writing for one scene made Barbara Branden "unhappy." That was scene during which a jealous Ayn slaps Nathaniel. Barbara Branden complained, "Her words in this scene were weak, not psychologically true." She suggested the filmmakers "go to my book for the dialogue." She continued that only "a couple of days before that scene was to be shot, Helen came up to me with a sheet of paper on which she had rewritten her dialogue for that scene." Mirren believed that the scene as previously written made Rand appear "petty" when "she should be shown as an erupting volcano." Mirren went to Branden's book for her words and "chose almost exactly the lines I would have chosen — and she had the clout to get them accepted by the director."

Overall, Barbara Branden found working on the film "an incredible experience."

In 2000, Branden added a "note" to her letter. She said she wrote it before viewing "the final, edited version." She said she had "no input" in the editing and was to some degree disappointed by it. She believed that the editing made a film that was "unjust" to Nathaniel and failed to show his "brilliance, his dynamism, and his unwavering dedication to Objectivism." She was also disappointed because the film showed Nathaniel having a romance with a woman named Caroline which the filmmakers had invented rather than the actual romance he had with Patrecia Wynand (later his wife Patrecia Branden) which ruptured Nathaniel's relationship with Ayn. How did Barbara feel about her own character as depicted? She thought it made her appear a "wimp" and failed to accurately depict her as "more aggressive and forthright." She placed no fault on Stoltz and Delpy but only on the editing. The final film was fair to Frank O'Connor in Branden's estimation: "I did not feel I was watching an actor but that I was watching Frank O'Connor, whom I had deeply loved."

Although Barbara Branden wished "more of Ayn Rand's ideas [had been] presented in the film" she elaborated "enough was presented to intrigue people." She was especially happy when people saw the movie and told Barbara Branden that they now intended reading Rand's books and/or Branden's biography.

This book's author did an extensive interview with screenplay co-writer Mary Gallagher. She was an experienced screenplay writer when she started work on *The Passion of Ayn Rand.* "Producers optioned Barbara Branden's book," Gallagher remarked. "She was involved in all the meetings and had a say in the script. She wanted to tell her story. It's very interesting reading." What, in Gallagher's opinion, made Branden's book so interesting? "I think the absolutist way of thinking that Rand had was an attraction for many people, especially young people," Gallagher avers. "It gave Barbara Branden and others a kind of firm footing. She and Nathaniel were not in love when they met Ayn Rand. They were brought together by their uncertainty and by reading Rand. In the course of the long trajectory that the book covers, Barbara fell in love with Rand in a platonic sense and as a parent-figure. She and Nathaniel went to Rand in a kind of pilgrimage. They believed in Rand's philosophy, in how the gifted person should be the person who decides how things go."

Gallagher found Rand a fascinating and contradictory figure. The screenwriter believes Rand's "tumultuous and traumatic experiences in what was becoming communist Russia" shaped her thinking. Gallagher continues, "When Rand first lived in America, her goal was to be a screenwriter but she wasn't artistically gifted, at least in my opinion." The limitations of Rand's thinking were themselves a draw, Gallagher feels. "It was her tunnel vision that made people fall in love with her thinking," Gallagher speculates. "Howard Roark was her, John Galt was her, she saw herself as having that kind of manifest destiny. When people are uncertain, they fall in love with this person who seems to have all the answers. A sort of semi-parental relationship evolved between Rand and Barbara and

Nathaniel that was upended when Ayn persuaded Nathaniel that they should have a sexual relationship."

Barbara Branden's memoir of her life with Ayn Rand is a very long book. "I took this enormous book of Barbara's and broke it down," Gallagher said.

Plans altered several times before the movie was made. "The producers wanted us to do a mini-series starting with Rand's life in Russia but we couldn't get a station to agree to do the mini-series which would have been extremely expensive. We persuaded Showtime to give us the development money to pay me to write this script. It took at least a year to write a script." The process of writing a screenplay is complicated. "You write a screenplay in stages," she noted. "You send it to producers and you and the producers discuss it until you get on the same page. Then it goes to network executives and then we go back and forth. They have questions and suggestions for changes."

According to Gallagher, "I turned the script in but Showtime wanted only a few changes. At a certain point, Showtime was really happy with the script. We needed to find a person to star in it. A network won't give the green light until you have a star. We had meetings with Angelica Huston who is a wonderful actress but she wouldn't go for it."

Showtime's choice to play Ayn Rand did not go over with Gallagher. "They wanted Diane Keaton," Gallagher recalled. "I thought that was a terrible idea. She's mostly a comedic actress and this wasn't a comedic part. I demanded a meeting with Diane Keaton so I would know what she was looking for from this project."

Diane Keaton met with Gallagher and network executives at the Four Seasons Hotel in Los Angeles. "I asked her what she wanted the film to be like," Gallagher said. The actress said she wanted to play a "neurotic person." Keaton elaborated, "I don't usually get to play a character like that. I want to show something I haven't gotten before.'" However, Keaton said, "I'm not going to do the accent."

Gallagher was disappointed because she knew that Rand's English was heavily accented and coaches work with actors to make accents sound authentic. Gallagher remarked to this writer that actors like to play characters drastically different from their previous parts. "Often they get an Oscar or an Emmy as a game changer," Gallagher asserted. "We knew that if Diane Keaton agreed to do it, then Showtime would do it. So it was about six months later [after the Four Seasons meeting] and we had a polished draft and sent it to Showtime and they sent it to Diane. I was in New York and these producers called me. Then I heard: 'Are you sitting down? She wants Ayn Rand to be funnier.' She wanted Rand to be someone funny, kind of like Martha in *Who's Afraid of Virginia Woolf?*"

Gallagher believed such a portrayal would grossly distort its subject. "Ayn Rand had no sense of humor," Gallagher asserted. "I couldn't do that. We did another draft and it was sent to Diane. Showtime was willing to do it but Diane wouldn't do it. Showtime stopped employing me — with great regret because they liked what I had done — because Diane wouldn't take my script."

Although Mary Gallagher did no further work on the script for the movie based on Barbara Branden's memoirs, it was hardly a wasted effort: "Screenwriters are legally protected. I had to be paid off because it was the standard complete deal and I had a great agent and a good track record. They paid me for the initial work, the first draft and the revised first draft. They have to pay you even if they let you go. But you don't get the bonus you get if they make the movie."

Howard Korder was then hired to revise Gallagher's script. "He's a good writer," she readily acknowledges. "He did a draft and one or two polishes. The revised script was my script with mostly just some dialogue revised by him."

The script, done for the most part by Mary Gallagher with some dialogue and other tweaking by Howard Korder, was presented to Diane Keaton. "She turned down Howard's script," Gallagher related. "She had other projects and decided she just didn't want to make the movie." Gallagher is glad Keaton ultimately bowed out. "She's not a dramatic actress that could pull off Ayn Rand," Gallagher said. "She doesn't have the chops to do a complicated dramatic role like that of a woman who came to the United States from another country when she was very young."

Only a few structural changes were made in the script by Korder. "In my version, the night Barbara and Nathaniel first make love is the night when they first go to the Oscars," she noted. "In Howard's version, they have just become like kids to Ayn Rand and they make love." Gallagher continued that Korder put in the aforementioned scene in which admirers surprise Rand with a party in her honor and she brusquely states, "I do not like surprises." Gallagher believes, "It was probably a good decision to put that in. It shows the audience what they should already know about Rand."

Even after Gallagher was no longer working on the screenplay, she would occasionally call a producer to ask questions about it. When she called to ask who would star as Ayn, a producer said, "Mary, are you sitting down?"

The producer said Helen Mirren would play Ayn. Gallagher was overjoyed. "I was so happy because she's such a great actress, she's not going to change the character, she will become the character," Gallagher informed this author.

Generally speaking, a screenwriter is not usually on set when the movie is filmed. However, producer Linda Curran Wexelblatt told Gallagher, "You've got to come on the set." Thus, Gallagher was often on set when *The Passion of Ayn Rand* was filmed.

Just as Gallagher was delighted to see Helen Mirren play Rand, the screenwriter was also happy to know that Menaul would be the director. "He directed Helen in episodes of the TV series *Prime Suspect*," Gallagher stated. "We also got Peter Fonda and he plays Frank O'Connor as following in Rand's wake and very few top male actors would do that, would play a character who is powerless, who is weak, who is basically along for the ride."

Being on set was fascinating for Gallagher even though she had put so much into the script. "I didn't know the sequence that the director would shoot a scene," she stated. "Menaul would shoot a scene over and over, five or sex times, and sometimes moved in closer and sometimes changed the angle a little bit." When the camera was closer, Gallagher observed, "Helen would get a little smaller, that is, her voice would be a little softer and her face would be a little less expressive and I recognized this as her acting technique. Peter Fonda was always the same." After one scene, Menaul asked Gallagher, "Is that one of your scenes or one of Korder's?" "They're all my scenes," she replied. "He just re-wrote them." Gallagher told this author, "Some lines were changed on the set."

The main actors helped greatly in producing an effective film. "They were all in the same movie," Gallagher said. "That's an expression in the business — all in the same movie — to describe how the acting of different performers comes together to make a harmonious whole. In the end, I thought the film was a truthful depiction of a complex character. That's good because my name is on it."

She also liked what happened when the filming finished. "We went to the Sundance Film Festival," she said. "We were selected and it was a huge thing. We went to the Sundance Film Festival and we had a blast. You see all these films, meet all these interesting people, and it was fabulous and we had a great time."

Resa McConaghy was the costume designer for *The Passion of Ayn Rand*. How was she selected for that job? "Dufferin Gate Productions was an established service company for films/TV," she told this author. "Their clients included Showtime and Paramount. DGP would supply a roster of talent for department keys on a given project. I had done several movies for DGP and one (A House Divided) had been a period piece for Showtime. I was presented along with other Costume Designers for the director, Chris Menaul, to interview."

McConaghy knew it was important to familiarize herself with the subject of the film to know what costumes would be appropriate for the film. "The Internet was young and there was not much information available," she elaborated. "I spent two days at the Toronto Research Library looking into the life of Ayn Rand. Books, magazines, promotions, and newspaper articles are not allowed out of this library. However, they had Xerox machines. I had to pay to use them, and use them I did. I found a lot of information and a slew of photographs."

Preparing for her return interview for the costume designer job meant crafting a dramatic display. "I bought some Bristol board and glued the photos in a timeline that was in accordance with the script based on Barbara Brandon's book," McConaghy told this writer. "There was a ledge, a moulding running around the interview room. It was a very old building. I placed the boards in order along it. Then I ran through the boards as they pertained to the story's timeline." Her display was a winner. "Chris later told me that it was the presentation that convinced him that I was the Costume Designer."

McConaghy believed what was most important in designing appropriate costumes for this film was "working with Helen and Barbara to get the character, Ayn, right. We had a lot of research so I had copies of actual garments made. The rest was an extrapolation."

Barbara Branden helped McConaghy create appropriate clothing for this movie. "Barbara gave me a photo of Ayn in a cape she wore a lot in New York City," McConaghy recalled. "She always wore it with a silver pin that was a dollar sign." That dollar sign silver pin is prominent in the film. As McConaghy points out, "Ayn wears the dollar sign pin several times including at the beginning of the movie, when she is in her coffin."

The preparation McConaghy did for the costuming in *The Passion of Ayn Rand* was extensive. "I made a huge closet of builds and rentals from the actual periods the story passed through," she commented. "Once we began shooting, Helen was in command of the character and had a special feel for what Ayn would wear that day in the story. I always made sure there was lots to choose from in her trailer. It usually worked out, in the sense that something I chose was on the money. On the rare occasion that she didn't feel there was something there, she'd pop down to the wardrobe truck, in character. It was always a joy to see her. She was totally welcome and I was honored to work with her. After that, working with the other main actors to get their characters right was of utmost importance. We had amazing actors on this movie. All of the opinions mattered to me."

There were challenges in costume designing for *The Passion of Ayn Rand*. "The look of all of the time periods were a challenge for more reasons than staying on budget," McConaghy explained. "Each era needed its own costumes. We went from 1949 through to sometime in the early 1970s. Footwear was an issue as was underpinnings for the women. There were a lot of wide and full shots that included feet. Men's shoes, basic oxfords, was not so much of a problem. However, women's shoes and boots had not remained classic like men's shoes. Where was I going to get high heels from 1950 through the 1960s? Luckily, I found some high heels at a local designer shoe shop. The designer was recreating those periods, in an ISH way. I bought a lot of shoes there." What does she mean by "in an ISH way"? "They were not perfect copies of the period but one couldn't tell unless looking up close," she replied. "Perhaps a high heel was a tad thicker, or the colors were not of the era. In that case, we just bought white or tan shoes and had the shoe dyed to be the color we wanted."

McConaghy pointed out that she had to take into consideration major differences in women's apparel between eras. "In the 1950s women's boots fit over the shoes," she stated. "I found some boots at a rental place that were in good shape. They were only needed for the lead women, so that was fortunate. Women wore pointy bras, girdles, wisps to achieve wasp waists and/or longlines to achieve the silhouette of the era. There were still some girdles around although the waists weren't as tiny. So, we also made some waist wisps."

Difficulty arose in finding a particular undergarment. "I was looking for a current bra that might be able to be altered into the time's shape but not having any luck," she remarked. "One day I was walking, looking for a shop I'd heard about that had lots of old/old style fabrics. I passed a deserted store front. There was a grimy display window. Oh my, there was one item behind it and it was a Maidenform bra box. The style of bra on the box was what I needed. There was nothing, nor anyone, in the store. I knocked loudly, for a while, just in case. Someone came out of a door at the back of the store. I inquired about the Maidenform box. The person told me this had been a women's undergarments shop, but was not in business anymore. Turned out the person had leftover stock in storage, and could bring it in for me. A couple of days later I returned and bought all of the bras. They were old but all new and unworn. YAY!"

Attention to detail is vital to any film set in the past, even the recent past, this costume designer points out. "It's not so noticeable on the background but leads need to set the look and tone of the era," she asserted. "Julie Delpy was a gem in this regard. She wore it all, and we achieved fabulous silhouettes for the '50s and '60s."

Were there costumes that were especially enjoyable to design? "Yes!" McConaghy answered. "It was a joy to design the costumes for the 'Wedding of Barbara and Nathaniel Brandon.' There were photos [of the real event] available and I was able to recreate Barbara's wedding dress and veil. We had a palette for the California years. At the actual wedding, Ayn wore a black satin and crepe formal length dress and the men wore black tuxedos. It was Helen that suggested grey for the black. So I had Ayn's dress recreated in mid-grey satin and crepe. The men had mid-tone grey tuxedos built by a tailor here in Toronto. I rented the dresses for the background guests. I found a lot of vintage 3/4 length, full skirted 1950s cocktail/party dresses that were still in great shape. They are the kind of dresses that get worn once or twice, so they survived the passing of time. The silks, satins, laces, and netting were all in colors true from the period. It made a beautiful look for the wedding as the guests danced around and passed by the leads."

McConaghy found another scene almost as fascinating and satisfying to costume. "The '*Atlas Shrugged*' congratulatory dinner party was a wonderful experience," she asserted. "I had bumped into a collection of mostly clip style hats in black. Each hat was unique but all were embellished in black, whether veiled, beaded, or sequined. I had also collected a large assortment of jewelry sets from the period. The sets all had a necklace and matching earrings. Some had a matching bracelet or pin. The sets all had faux diamonds, rubies, emeralds, or sapphires. The producers, director, director of photography, etc. had just returned from a location scout, and it was time to make my presentation. As we were doing the New York segment, black was totally cool. I pitched all black cocktail dresses, with the black hats and colorful jewels on the women and all black tuxes for the men. There was a silence and someone said, 'We need a different location for these costumes.' It's the only time in my career as a costume designer that I am aware of where the costumes influenced the look of the set. The scene looks gorgeous! I'm quite proud of it."

McConaghy told this author about two unusual situations that occurred during the making of *The Passion of Ayn Rand.* "They were calling for actors on the set," she remembered. "Eric stopped by the wardrobe truck on the way, and showed me his tie. The thin part of the tie was hanging lower than the wider front part. Eric had done up the tie, so that the front ended at the perfect spot. There was no time to select another tie and change ties. I grabbed my scissors and cut the long skinny part. The tie looked perfect. There was a cool-funny second between Eric and myself, then they took him to the set."

Another incident occurred on the day the wedding scene was shot. "Everything was set and the camera had rolled," she said. "I could never eat when a big scene was going up, until the first shots were in the can. At that point I would go to the Craft Truck and make my usual avocado, tomato, and onion sandwich. I was slicing the onion, and the craft person began to loudly lecture me that onions made bad breath, the fact that I was the costume designer, that I worked close to the stars, what about the day players, extras, and my crew? During the lecture, I could see Helen walking toward the Craft Truck so I was sure she could hear the lecture. As she entered the truck, the craft person shut up. Helen complimented the look of the wedding, grabbed a couple slices of onion, and ate them there and then. She grabbed what she came for, and headed back to the set."

Interviewed by this book's author, Lindsey Hermer-Bell described her job as a production designer. "In designing sets for film and television productions, I evoke the atmosphere and set the stage for the action," she related. "I have to know everything about the characters to breathe life into them, show you how they live, and uncover their dreams, hopes, and aspirations. This has to appear effortless, subliminal, and unconscious. I have to draw the audience in. The artifice must be hidden but must reveal the characters as natural extensions of their environments. I convey their worlds to you in moments. I give you brief glimpses of the characters by showing you their surroundings and possessions visually. I have to understand every aspect of the lives and personalities to accurately convey their worlds."

How was she hired as production designer for *The Passion of Ayn Rand*? "I was interviewed and had to present an approach to the design of the project," she replied. "This was not difficult as I have always been a big fan of Ayn Rand. I have read all her books and in fact chose my career as an architect partially because I read *The Fountainhead* which made a huge impression on me as a young student. I was an architect and then moved into the film industry. Hence my delight at being selected to work on the Ayn Rand project." Experience was also a major plus in landing this gig. "I had also designed many period shows," she explained.

Challenges are part of any major undertaking. "Challenges were most importantly designing spaces the actors would feel comfortable acting in and which were consistent with their understanding of the characters," Hermer-Bell remarks. "Especially Helen Mirren, who is always very in touch with her environments and characters. She is also very, very vocal if she does not feel comfortable with the sets. I had worked with her on a previous project and knew of her complete understanding of her characters she portrays so I had to be mindful of this. I chose an Art Deco design feel to her environments as I wanted her to feel contemporary and [also] ahead of her time. Her house was very mid-century modern [as] this was a location I had found, and her New York apartment also had some Art Deco details. This was a darker feel in keeping with New York. Her house was lighter in feel in keeping with L. A. It was also shot in the dead of winter in Toronto so we had to find a clever way of introducing tropical plants to evoke the feeling of California. The house had internal courtyards which helped with this. I think this may have been the biggest challenge. Any exterior shooting in winter would show a mist when speaking so internal courtyards were the best solution. Finding the perfect solution was a challenge. There was also a challenge in making Toronto look like New York, particularly as it was not the present day. Adding awnings to buildings, changing and hiding street signs, making sure we had period cars and taxis to create the ambiance of the period."

The production designer elaborated that her goal in working on this film was "to properly portray the complicated character of Ayn Rand visually, creating a timeless vision of this timeless woman. I did not want the feel of the show to be old-fashioned and obviously 1930. This is the reason behind the Art Deco sensibility."

Hermer-Bell found that director Christopher Menaul had a bit of a temper. "The director was a very interesting man," she commented. "He had directed Helen Mirren in the first *Prime Suspect.* He was an Englishman. The biggest danger was pissing him off. Not something anyone wanted to do. Luckily, we got along but he was demanding." She was surprised by the actor depicting Frank O'Conner. "Peter Fonda was unexpected," she recalled. "A wonderful, kind, caring, and humble man."

The experience of doing production design for *The Passion of Ayn Rand* was very positive for Hermer-Bell. "The whole experience for me was remarkable," she asserted. "I loved Ayn Rand and what her ideals were, and of course was (and still am), in awe of Helen Mirren who is a true master of her craft. I felt honored to be working with such a talented cast and crew and director."

David Martin was the film editor for *The Passion of Ayn Rand.* Martin described film editing to the author of this book. "The process of film editing looks fairly straightforward — cutting out all the bad bits and editing the actions shots into an exciting sequence," Martin explained. "This can be rewarding for the editor, but it's not entirely what the 'art' is all about. What drives editors is story and structure, creating moments by seeing and feeling how two shots go together, and in which order they should be, and in which order action in a scene should develop, and then in which order the scenes are arranged so as to deliver the strongest emotional moments however slight they may appear; the difference between a cut in a scene of just two frames can make the moment happy/sad/frightening, or something that just falls flat. It's a very precise business. This is, of course, the fundamental process of filmmaking; the director has a vision, creates it (hopefully) with the cameraman, but that vision doesn't fall out of the camera already edited. Editors come in many shapes and sizes, all bringing their individual emotional bags and baggage, but in my experience all good editors share a passion for their work. Through the process, which can be many months, the editor 'owns' the film and guards it like a mother would a child. In the case of a feature film, it's a very long process."

Martin observes that, for a film editor, "'Getting the gig' can be anything from having worked with the director before, to just being in the right place at the right time! In this case, although I knew of the director and his work, I hadn't worked with him before but the film's producers approached my agent and arranged a meeting when he and I just hit it off. I liked the script and we knew we could work together."

The Passion of Ayn Rand had already been filmed before the film editor worked on it. "The film was shot in and around Toronto and was 'in the can' before I saw a single frame," he stated. "Normally I would be on the film from day one but in this case, they wanted to bring the editing to London. The first assembly is normally left entirely in the hands of the editor, and my job is to put the film together as scripted and to advise the director and producer if I feel extra material is needed — at this stage, I am the one offering them my thoughts. Ideas about making changes to refine the film will come later when we will have many hours of discussion, hopefully amicably, as it was in this case because the director did a great job and the producers were both constructive and supportive."

What were David Martin's goals in editing this movie? "My goal on any film is not to mess up!" he cheekily answered. "Seriously, my goal in any film is to get the very best out of the actors' performances. In this case, the cast was excellent, there was no weakness anywhere with no one needing a little help. This is very much down to the director who, in the end, creates the on set ambiance that allows a cast of this caliber to deliver such powerful performances. The cinematography and production design created a strong period feel, there was nothing weak in any department, so to me the film is a great success and I'm proud to have been a part of it."

The subject was, of course, a very controversial individual. "Ayn Rand is deep water," Martin observed. "I'm afraid I have seen very little of her work on the screen beyond *The Fountainhead*. I think our film is a beautifully crafted piece of work that also serves on every level as a metaphor for her philosophy."

Reviewing the film in *New York* magazine, John Leonard called it "as delicious as it is dumbfounding, as mirthful as it is misbegotten." Leonard derides the actual figures, Ayn Rand and Nathaniel Branden, as "self-indulgent" and "self-justifying" but was impressed by the way the film's star played her subject. Leonard commented, "[Mirren] darkens her eyes and hair, waves her cigarette holder like a wizard's wand, and coarsens her whole body to burrow into intimate chats like a white mole into a potato bin." He elaborates that she is "the shameless marvel: sacred monster, dippy diva, Serpent of the Volga, Invisible Hand of the Erotics Trade." He concludes that Rand comes off as "risible" in the film and wonders if the filmmakers "know how much subversive fun" they have made of her. Critic John Carmen, writing in *SFGate*, asserted that Mirren's performance of Rand was a "direct hit." He continued that Mirren's was "one of four astonishing performances in the year's best made-for-TV movies" with the other three being Fonda, Stoltz, and Delpy. Carmen elaborates, "Based on a book by Barbara Brandon, the movie lifts the curtain that surrounds Rand, peeking at her inner circle and private life." He calls *The Passion of Ayn Rand* "an unabashedly adult movie with plenty of sexual sizzle." (Author's note: Of course, "adult" does not mean pornography in this case but a film best understood by mature people.) He compliments Delpy who "wins sympathy as a scorned woman who breaks down under the tug-of-war between her intellectual and emotional lives." Carmen also states that the film "benefits from a big-screen visual texture and a jazzy score, by Jeff Beal, that fits the movie snugly."

Helen Mirren won an Emmy for Outstanding Lead Actress in a Miniseries or Movie for her performance in *The Passion of Ayn Rand* and Peter Fonda was nominated for Outstanding Supporting Actor in a Miniseries or a Movie for his performance. The Golden

Globes reversed matters: Peter Fonda won its award for Best Performance by an Actor in a Supporting Role in a Series, Miniseries or Motion Picture Made for Television and Hellen Mirren was nominated for its Best Performance by an Actor in a Supporting Role in a Series, Miniseries or Motion Picture Made for Television.

2009: *Anthem*

A short color film, only seven minutes long, came out in 2009 entitled *Anthem*. Galen Carter-Jeffrey directed the film and wrote its screenplay. He also edited the film. Alison C. Wroblewski produced it, Andrew Dollerson supplied the music and Charles C. Nwahukwu was the cinematographer.

John Handem Piette played Equality 7-2521. Phillipe Coquet played the "Lead Guard" while Mark Holiday and Angelique Naylor played other guards. T. K. Henderson played "Head Scholar" and Hope Carpenter played another scholar

It begins with a man seen from behind running down a long corridor. The screen momentarily goes white. We see a man turning over in his hand an item, possibly a light bulb, that is broken. His thoughts are heard: "It is a sin to think this. It is a sin to think beyond what we all think. And we know that there is no sin darker than to think what others do not." The camera pulls back and we see that he is behind bars, apparently in jail. We hear a voice in the background, something like a distant radio, warning against what will happen to "violators" of certain rules. The jailed man seems to have flashbacks of himself running down a corridor.

Then we see the protagonist out of doors, white clouds against a fair blue sky, opening up what could be a cellar door. This is followed by the same man in darkness lighting up a match. He holds a candle. For the first time, we see a name tag on his shirt: Equality 7-2521. He examines an old typewriter. We hear his thoughts again: "We question the way the world works. And questions give us no rest. We ask: why must we know? But it has no answer." Another, older man enters the cell. Still another man is behind him.

"Tell us where you've been," the older man orders.

"No," Equality 7-2521 replies.

"If you will not, then you leave us no choice."

Equality gets up and tries to flee but is easily caught and repeatedly shoved against the floor. A group of jailers beat him.

A female voiceover states: "What is not done collectively cannot be good."

Equality is holding a light bulb and linked apparatus on a wooden board. He says, "We give you the key to the earth. Take it. Let's harness this power."

We see three people, a woman flanked by men, in front of Equality. They berate him for the light bulb and say it would ruin the "Department of Candles."

A voiceover tells us, "There is one single word which is not in the language of men but had been."

Equality is seen back in jail and he lights the light bulb. A jailer comes to him. He falls and Equality escapes, running in his white jail suit. Now the audience sees the one word that will set humanity free: "I." The "I" turns into a "T" of the word ANTHEM. The film ends.

Galen Carter-Jeffrey informed this book's writer that he did not make this short film out of any dedication to Rand's philosophy. "I'm not really a believer in her philosophy and pretty much consider it a joke," he acknowledged. "I couldn't even get through *Atlas Shrugged*, it was so boring."

He may have struggled with Rand's longest novel but Carter-Jeffrey had no problem getting through *Anthem*. "When I was in college, I picked up a copy of the book and thought it was an interesting read," he revealed. "I've always enjoyed dystopian novels and ideas. When I graduated from college, I wanted to keep making short films, and I wanted to try adapting something and this was something that I thought was doable."

What was his biggest challenge? "The biggest challenge is just planning and keeping people motivated. Nobody will ever care about your projects as much as you do, so it's a constant battle to get people motivated to spend their time doing something for free."

This version of *Anthem* was cast with a combination of friends of the filmmaker and volunteers from Craigslist. "One location we ended up using was an old power plant downtown," he said. "It has since been converted to a Trader Joe's which is kind of funny."

About $1,000 was spent on filming Carter-Jeffrey's *Anthem.* "It was more of a learning experience than anything else," he concluded.

In an interview with this book's author, John Handem Piette recalled how he got the part of Equality 7-2521. "I was in film school at the time at the University of Texas and a fellow film student friend of mine, Galen Carter-Jeffrey, asked me to star in his short film," Piette revealed. "I had been in a few of his previous films and it's always a pretty collaborative process acting in fellow filmmakers' films."

How long did it take to make this short? "Galen had been writing the short film based on the book for a few months," Piette said. "I believe the short was about four days total and we spent another few weeks editing. So it was probably six months total from inception and writing through post-production."

Piette believes that his life experience helped him in the rougher aspects of playing Equality 7-2521. "It was a relatively stoic straightforward role that wasn't too challenging until the scenes where Equality is being berated and then beaten," he commented. "Just psychologically as a black man in America, to portray that scene obviously has its loaded emotional heft that I didn't really have to fake in the scene." However, the consequences of those scenes frightened someone near and dear to Piette. "I remember when I was home at my parents house for the weekend and my mom noticed some bruising on my arm from some of the man-handling and beating from the scenes we'd shot the day before and she absolutely freaked out and made me promise I wouldn't act in scenes where I'm getting beaten up anymore," he stated. "I had a good laugh about it because those 'beating' scenes didn't actually hurt at all in the moment but anyone who's shot a fight scene in a movie knows that the sheer repetition and number of takes create a bruising by attrition sort of thing. I wore the bruises as a badge of honor for my commitment to the craft."

How familiar was Piette with Ayn Rand and Objectivism before working on *Anthem*? "I wasn't actually too familiar until my film school buddy Galen started working on the script and telling me more and more about the plot and the ideas at the crux of the story," he replied. "We were both sort of default raging liberals at the time, the outset of the Obama era."

Phillipe Coquet found playing the Lead Guard demanding. "The most challenging thing for me was to be so violent, especially to whip a black man!" he informed this author. "It made me feel all kinds of gross. I am normally a very gentle person, and have been actively anti-racist my whole life. I guess even playing a prison guard was also uncomfortable but, I am an actor, and it's what we do."

What did Coquet like most about playing in *Anthem*? "It must have been the sets and that it felt somewhat futuristic," he answered. "And I enjoyed the folks on set, particularly the lead actor [Hamden] as I remember."

An element in Coquet's life attracted him to the film. "I had fairly recently left a 25 year experience of being in a cult," he remembered. "So I think I was drawn to the subject matter in relation to me really finding my own identity for the first time in many years. It felt personal to me to be involved in the story."

2011: *Ayn Rand & the Prophecy of Atlas Shrugged*

In 2011, a feature length documentary was released entitled *Ayn Rand & the Prophecy Of Atlas Shrugged*. Emmy award winning writer and producer Chris Mortensen was producer and director of the documentary. The executive producer was John Corry and the associate producer was Fawaz Al-Matrouk.

The documentary gives the outlines of Ayn Rand's life, summaries of her major novels with a special emphasis on *Atlas Shrugged*, and points to parallels between that novel and real life. Much of the movie consists of photographs and film of Rand herself, stock footage of relevant matters such as Bolshevik soldiers marching and the Statue of Liberty, and a series of talking heads. Those talking heads include Rand friend and philosopher Harry Binswanger, hedge fund manager and co-founder of AQR (Applied Quantitative Research) Capital Management Clifford Asness, *Ayn Rand and the World She Made* author Anne C. Heller, *Goddess of the Market* author Jennifer Burns, *Rules for Radical Conservatives* author Michael Walsh (also known as David Kahane), *The Capitalist Manifesto* author Andrew Bernstein, and *Letters of Ayn Rand* editor Mike Berliner. Some interviewees make interesting observations. Anne C. Heller astutely comments on the background that led Rand to shudder at communism or anything that might lead to it. "Her father's business was taken away," Heller stated. "Red soldiers marched in and closed the shop and he never worked again. What she saw as a twelve-year-old girl was that the people who had worked the hardest and achieved the most were punished." Binswanger intelligently discusses Rand's disappointment with the critical reception of *Atlas Shrugged*: "She thought there would be a minority, but a vocal minority, of intellectuals who would recognize what a philosophical achievement she had done with *Atlas Shrugged*. But it didn't happen."

In an interview with this author, Andrew Bernstein, an Objectivist who frequently writes and lectures on Rand, recalled how he got into the documentary. "Chris Mortensen approached me," he said. "He's seen me lecture on Rand's novels and philosophy." The met at the hotel called Sofitel New York. "I think it was late in January 2011," Bernstein related. "He asked a bunch of questions and then we filmed it." There were no rehearsals or multiple takes as far as Bernstein could remember. "We just sat down and did the interview and it was filmed. He asked questions which I answered. It was a friendly discussion."

Ayn Rand & the Prophecy Of Atlas Shrugged adequately summarizes Rand's life, her struggles, her triumphs, and her frustrations. It also does a reasonable job of pointing out that she may have foreseen negative trends in her work. The documentary does not balance praise with criticism or interview any author who addresses flaws in her world-view. Thus, it's appeal is apt to be limited to people who already admire Rand.

A "user reviewer" on the Internet Movie Database called it "by fans for fans" and "a good introduction for new converts." Another wrote, "This film is a must-see for any Rand fan and/or anyone who's ever been affected by her novels. Also recommended for anyone who has not read Rand but wondered what all the fuss was about." Still another derided the documentary as "hagiography" and deplored its lack of balance. A critical user review asserted, "A mediocre philosophy gets a mediocre documentary" and added, "I became quite bored watching a parade of cheerleaders whooping it up for Ayn." A more positive review called it an "easy-to-watch summary of Ayn Rand's philosophical views" and found it "an inspiring and enjoyable introduction to Ayn Rand's life." This author agrees with the last assessment quoted.

2011, 2012, 2014: The *Atlas Shrugged* Trilogy

A motion picture series, released in three parts, was made as *Atlas Shrugged: Part I* (2011), *Atlas Shrugged: Part II* (2012), and *Atlas Shrugged: Part III* (2014). The second in the trilogy is sometimes entitled *Atlas Shrugged II: The Strike.* The third and last in the series is sometimes depicted with the words *Who Is John Galt?* in its subtitle.

In 1972, Canadian-American movie and television producer Albert S. Ruddy approached Rand about making her magnum opus into a motion picture. Rand was open to this possibility but wanted final script approval. Ruddy did not want to grant her that approval so nothing was done.

In 1978, Henry and Michael Jaffe made a deal with Rand for an *Atlas Shrugged* TV miniseries for NBC. Screenwriter Stirling Siliphant was hired to write a script. He showed it to Rand who approved it. In 1979, Fred Silverman became NBC President. Soon afterward, the project was dropped.

Ayn Rand decided that no one could write a better script of her masterpiece than she could so she set about writing an *Atlas Shrugged* screenplay. When she died in 1982, she had completed about one-third of that screenplay. Her estate was left to Leonard Peikoff who got the film rights to *Atlas Shrugged* as part of that estate. Peikoff sold an option to Michael Jaffe and Ed Snider. They wrote a script but Peikoff would not approve it; that deal collapsed.

The moving spirit behind the making of all three parts of the *Atlas Shrugged* trilogy that actually appeared in the theaters is entrepreneur and movie producer John Aglialoro. A longtime Rand admirer and committed Objectivist, Aglialoro is a trustee of The Atlas Society, an organization promoting her philosophy.

In 1992, Aglialoro paid Peikoff over a million dollars for an option to buy the film rights that included complete creative discretion. In 1999, Aglialoro sponsored Ruddy to agree to make a TV series of *Atlas Shrugged* with Turner Network Television. However, the project ended after the AOL and Time Warner merger.

Years of hit and miss negotiations followed, with deals suggested but never made. Then Aglialoro and Harmon Kaslow got together to act as co-producers for *Part 1* of *Atlas Shrugged*, making this motion picture as an independent production. Aglialoro and Kaslow would act as producers for all three of the *Atlas Shrugged* trilogy. Jeff Freilich would help produce the second film. Aglialoro was a screenwriter in all films in the trilogy with Brian Patrick O'Toole the co-writer of the first film.

In an interview, Aglialoro spoke of the frustration he suffered when he spent years trying to get the film made. "Year after year passed, and it got to the point where I had to make a decision to finance it myself — and to arrange for the casting and get it done — or lose the movie rights altogether," he recalled.

Letting the project just slip away was not an option for Aglialoro. "I had made a kind of commitment to Ayn Rand herself," he recalled. "I didn't make it to her one-on-one personally." He had seen her in person only once and that was in 1981 when she gave her last speech at the Ford Hall Forum. "Making the movie was something that I felt as an Objectivist I could carry out one way or another. I wanted to be able to visit Ayn Rand's grave in New York and say, 'We got it done.'"

2011: *Atlas Shrugged: Part 1*

The lease Aglialoro had on the movie was set to expire June 15, 2010. It was near expiring when he approached estate owner Leonard Pekoe and requested an extension. Peikoff refused. Aglialoro suffered "sleepless nights." He *had* to make a movie of *Atlas Shrugged.* "My wife pointed out that if I didn't do it, it would haunt me for the rest of my life," he stated.

Aglialoro remembered reading "six or seven" different screenplay treatments of the novel throughout the years. In 2006, a contract was signed with Lionsgate and they asked Randall Wallace to write a script. Aglialoro was impressed by Wallace's screenplay but believed it would require a movie longer than what was reasonable. He decided making a single motion picture out of the novel was not practical. "The idea for a trilogy came from the talk of a miniseries which Ayn Rand herself at one point said would be a good idea." Aglialoro was unable to find a TV station backing a miniseries. A single huge-budget film would have required a studio. Since the novel *Atlas Shrugged* is divided into three parts, Aglialoro decided on a trilogy of films that followed that three part structure.

At one point, it appeared Angelina Jolie might play Dagny Taggart. However, Jolie found other projects.

Many people, including many in the entertainment industry, admire Rand. According to Aglialoro, that was a plus in restraining expenses. "Many of these actors came on at minimum rate just because they wanted to be associated with the project," he stated. Some of them were hired at a rate "perhaps 25% of what they normally make."

Producer Harmon Kaslow said, "John and I and the rest of the production team recognized at the outset the enormous task that we would have of making a movie based on something treasured by so many people."

American born Canadian actor and director Paul Johansson both directed the film and played John Galt who is heard but only seen in shadow. Taylor Schilling was cast in the pivotal role of Dagny Taggart. With her slender blonde fashion model good looks, she was certainly an appropriate choice from a physical viewpoint. Aglialoro observed, "She's got that tall, thin look with a tight-lipped smile that's very beautiful." Of course, her prominence was also a draw. As Aglialoro elaborated, "She's a big talent."

The role of James Taggart was filled by Matthew Marsden. Grant Bowler played Henry "Hank" Rearden. Into the well-heeled shoes of Lillian Reardon slipped Rebecca Wisocky. Jsu Garcia was cast as Francisco D'Anconia.

While Rand wisely did not specify a year for the future in which her novel was set, the 2011 first part of the film trilogy was set in the year 2016.

The movie starts with news reports depicting an America in crisis. Dow Jones stock average has sharply dipped. There are severe oil and gas shortages. Turmoil in the Middle East cuts off oil imports. A major oil spill occurs. Due to these various problems, rail travel has re-emerged as the only affordable long-range travel means. Crises have led to the proposal of a law making it illegal to fire employees from profitable companies. A moratorium has been placed on wage increases. The "Fair Price Bill" restricts price increases on goods and services. A headline states pirate Ragnar Danneskjold has struck again. Crime and violence are skyrocketing. We see a train derailing.

Cut to a rainy urban outdoors scene. A shabbily dressed man (Frank Cassavetes) walks into a diner.

Then we see a TV studio and talk show in progress. Taggart Transcontinental Railroad CEO James Taggart and noted lobbyist Wesley Mouch (Michael Lerner) are in-studio guests. Ellis Wyatt

(Graham Beckel), identified as an oil and gas entrepreneur "responsible for the current economic boom in Colorado," is being interviewed remotely.

Back to the fellow in the diner. He gazes at the TV talk show hanging from the wall. The talk show host asks James Taggart about the "dozens of derailments" on his line. Ellis Wyatt grumpily advises that railroads like those of James Taggart ought to fix their railways instead of adding new ones.

The server asks, "What happened to you?" The man replies, "Who is John Galt?"

An expensively dressed man enters the diner and picks up a packaged order. We learn his surname is Mulligan. Exiting the diner, he walks into the rain. A man in shadow shouts, "Midas Mulligan?"

Mulligan replies, "Who's asking?"

"Someone who knows what it's like to work for himself and not let others feed off the profits of his energy!"

"That's funny," Midas Mulligan muses. "Exactly what I've been thinking."

Midas asks who the speaker is.

Scene freezes sans answer. Words on the screen report:

Missing: Michael 'Midas' Mulligan

Banking CO

Vanished: September 2, 2016

For the first time, we see the title of the movie *Atlas Shrugged.*

A phone rings in a luxurious home. Dagny Taggart picks it up. She sees a TV news report that a Taggart Transcontinental train has once again crashed and derailed.

Dagny heads for work, attired in a standard female-style dress-for-success business suit.

Huge shiny skyscrapers of the sort Howard Roark might have designed are seen. Then we are in James Taggart's office. Eddie Willers (Edi Gathegi) plops a stack of papers on the desk, explaining that they are cancellations. Willers points out that another railroad company's line, the Phoenix/Durango "has cut deeply into our business." He says Ellis Wyatt, head of Wyatt Oil, is giving his business to competitors.

Dagny Taggart enters the office. Eddie exits. Dagny informs James she has ordered replacement rails from Reardon Steel. James protests that they have a contract with Orren Boyle. She tells him she canceled that contract. She points that it is a main priority to get Ellis Wyatt's business. James accuses her of catering to monopolies. She replies that Wyatt's business is necessary for Taggart Transcontinental.

They discuss Rearden Metal. Dagny believes the alloy is good. Taggart Transcontinental will use it. James reminds her that metallurgical authorities are skeptical about it. Dagny is confident in her own estimation of it because she studied engineering in college. She goes by her own judgement and says Rearden Metal is "tougher, cheaper, lighter than steel and will outlast any metal in existence." He points out that no one has used Rearden Metal. Why should Taggart Transcontinental be first? She believes it will save the company. She takes responsibility. The Rio Norte Line will be fixed with Rearden Metal; she has an appointment to finalize the deal with Hank Reardon.

James Taggart makes a general statement about his sister's personality: "Other people are human. They're sensitive. They can't just dedicate their whole lives to metals and engines. You've never had any feelings. I don't think you've ever felt a thing."

"I guess I've never felt anything at all," she agrees.

This author is going to stop the story to point out a problem in this exchange. There are no people without emotions as emotions are motivators. It would be difficult, perhaps impossible, to create a character without emotions. Mr. Spock of *Star Trek* was presented as emotionless — but he never was. Mr. Spock was motivated by emotions like curiosity, loyalty, and pride. Dagny Taggart has those emotions plus ambition and greed which, to her creator, are virtues.

We see a train moving. The word "Philadelphia" appears on the screen. Dagny buys a newspaper, a headline of which announces: "Dagnar the Pirate Strikes Again."

On to Henry Rearden watching work in his metal factory through a window. A female worker presents him with a jewelry case. He opens it and pronounces the contents, "Beautiful." The worker tells him the names of those who have sent messages. "File it," he repeatedly says. That is his code for "discard." This reminded this author of a high school teacher who referred to a trashcan as "the circular file."

Henry meets with Dagny to discuss the deal. She suggests he wants the new metal on the Rio Norte Line because "it will be its first showcase." They both acknowledge they are taking a risk on the metal. The Rio Norte Line must be completely re-railed within about nine months or the company will, in Dagny's word, "crash." He notes problems caused by other people; she says she does not get angry "with people like my brother and his friends in Washington" but gets busy fixing the damage.

Home at his mansion, Hank sees people are there with wife Lillian. She mentions a special event in a few months to celebrate the anniversary of their wedding. Henry hands Lillian the jewelry box. It contains a bracelet crafted from the first pour of Reardon Metal. Lillian believes it is "the chain by which he holds us all in bondage."

Then he goes into another room and talks with his brother Phillip who works for Friends of Global Awareness. Henry says he will authorize a gift of $100,000 to the organization. Henry does not care about the less privileged but will authorize the funds for his brother's sake. (No Rand hero or heroine is charitable since Rand disliked charity.)

In the next scene, Paul Larkin tells Henry he should not have given that money to Phillip's group. Then he declares Reardon Metal "terrific." Paul points out, "You're not very popular, Hank." Henry says his customers do not complain. Paul tells him that people think his only goal is to make money. "My only goal *is* to make money," Henry readily agrees. Paul answers, "But you shouldn't *say* it." Paul has nothing against greed but knows the general public may not trust a greedy person. It is mentioned that Wesley Mouch (Michael Lerner) is Henry's "man in Washington." As the conversation continues, Paul points out that some questions are useless like "How high is the sky?" or "Who is John Galt?"

A scene takes place in a restaurant with Paul, James, Wesley, and Orren Boyle (Jon Polito). Orren believes Taggart Transcontinental is inviting disaster by making use of Henry Reardon's invention. Wesley mentions that a group of metallurgists issued a report against Reardon Metal. The approval with which he mentions this signals us that the "man in Washington" might not be loyal to Henry. Orren discusses a bill called "The Equalization of Opportunity Bill" that limits the number of businesses owned by any individual to one.

The foursome spots a trio, one man with a woman on either side of him. The ladies' man is identified as Francisco D'Anconia. The four did a deal with him concerning an ore mine in Mexico. Paul, Wesley, and Orren excuse themselves from the table. James stares at Francisco and his girlfriends.

The next scene is Dagny and James in an office. Dagny tells her brother she just found a contractor for the rebuilding of the Rio Norte Line. James expresses concern about what the company has in Mexico: one passenger train per day on the line and a single freight every other night. How can the Mexicans develop that area with only a single passenger train running once a day? They will *not*. Dagny moved everything else of value that Taggart possessed in that country out of Mexico. She did not want to leave anything for "the looters" because Mexico is apt to nationalize rail lines. "That Mexican line was helping those destitute people get back in the game," James observes. It was also good public relations for Taggart Transcontinental. Dagny saw no reason to build business in that region. James believes she took good services from "people who need our help." He leaves.

Owen Kellogg (Ethan Cohn) enters. He is resigning for personal reasons. Nothing Dagny can offer will make him budge. She pushes him for a reason. "Who is John Galt?" he asks.

The audience sees the message:

Missing: Owen Kellogg

Taggart Executive

Vanished: October 15, 2016.

As the movie progresses, Dagny and Hank fall in love, more top business people vanish, and laws are passed putting more restrictions on businesses. Reardon Metal is tested on a Taggart Transcontinental run. The two make a discovery about an engine that never got past prototype stage and whose inventor they try to find. Altruism and charity are denounced and get what you can capitalism is praised. Events draw to a close that is meant to suggest that there must be another movie to answer questions raised but unanswered in this one.

Atlas Shrugged Part 1 script co-author Brian Patrick O'Toole believed the story has a special meaning for females and that it was important the screenplay communicate that meaning. "It is a very empowering movie for women," he asserted. "It is about a woman who takes on a lot of forces that are against her." O'Toole continued, "I wanted to tell Dagny's story and to do that I had to introduce her world." He took a look at the first part of the book and "tried to find the basis of it." He searched for a "skeleton" on which to flesh out what the film would say. "To me, this was the underdog's story," O'Toole asserted. O'Toole saw Dagny as a risk-taker — albeit a very informed risk-taker. She believes Rearden Metal will work and she gambles that it will save her company. When she and Rearden join forces to prove Rearden Metal's value, O'Toole notes, "It pisses off everyone who has been against them all along." O'Toole believes the movie is based on the most fundamental principles in existence.

"The whole theme of the story is really human evil," he contends. "And human evil spawns from good intentions. I mean, the government isn't malicious. They think what they are doing is right. They don't realize the consequences: that's human evil. And that to me is what the government in this book was doing."

Interviewed for the Hans G. Schantz website, O'Toole said he did not read any other treatment before collaborating with Aglialoro on a screenplay. He followed a practice previously used to craft the script for this movie. "I have previously adapted other novels for film adaptations so I approached *Atlas Shrugged* the same way, which was to start by breaking down each chapter into scene headings and then highlighting important directions and dialogue under each heading," O'Toole stated. "Then John and I discussed each part and talked about what needed to stay as written or what could be changed for a more cinematic experience."

Time constraints meant scenes from the book had to be left out and even important characters given less space. "The most difficult aspect to capture is what is inherently difficult in all book-to-film adaptations and that is deciding what must stay, what must be added to enhance the cinematic version, and what can go from the source material," O'Toole commented. He makes a whimsical analogy to a drawing of a bear: "I look at writing an adaptation as if it were a bear and everyone involved in the development process was asked to draw a picture of a bear. I guarantee you that everyone would draw a different picture of a bear. Some would be cartoony. Some would be realistic. Some would be fierce-looking. Some would be gentle. And so on. Now, the screenwriter's job is to take those pictures and create one bear that represents the most common aspects of all those other ideas/drawings (along with the original source material) and hope that it incumbencies most of the vision of everyone involved."

Aglialoro noted in an interview for *Reason TV* that it would not be possible to please all fans of the novel. "With the density of this book, no matter how hard you try, there is no way not to disappoint some people because you have to make some edits." Aglialoro has noted in another interview that there was a scene in the novel that he personally liked but did not include in the film: "The scene with Phillip Rearden and his mother going to Hank Reardon's office to ask for a job for Phillip. I thought that would have made a fabulous little two-minute scene. But we were trying to do so much already that various circumstances kept us from doing everything we would have liked." What is the movie ultimately about? "It's about what's best in all people," he concluded. "It's about the responsibility of the individual, that you are responsible for your own decisions. . . . It's all about individuality."

Atlas Shrugged: Part 1 was shot in a little less than six weeks. "There was not a lot of rehearsal time," Aglialoro observed. "Normally actors get weeks or months to study the nuances of their characters but for this project time was very short."

Elia Cmiral was music composer for *Part I* and *Part III* of the *Atlas Shrugged* trilogy. "I knew a post-supervisor and I knew Ayn Rand's books, so I asked him to introduce me to the producers," Cmiral informed this author. "I played them some of my scores and expressed a great enthusiasm to write a score for this project." [A post-supervisor is defined by backstage.com as "responsible for supervising the post-production process."]

Cmiral wrote all the underscore music. "Working on the *Atlas* project I didn't have any other challenges than I did when working on any project," he said. "Meaning I had to come up with good thematic material right for the movie characters and support the director's and producer's ideas." He clearly enjoyed working on the *Atlas* films. "The producers were greatly supportive, we were a great creative team, and I loved to work with them," he asserted.

Did anything unusual occur while Cmiral worked on this motion picture? "When I was done with writing the whole score for *Part I*, still inspired by the film and Ayn Rand's book, I got an idea and wrote a piece of music I called *John Galt Theme*," he replied. "Producers loved it and, since there was not a place for it in the movie since the whole score was done already, we recorded it anyway and used it as an End Title. This theme was later developed and used extensively in *Part III*."

In 2011, *Atlas Shrugged Part 1* made it to the screen and was seen in theaters. Aglialoro praised Johansson as a director, saying, "Paul is a hands-on, take-charge kind of guy and he worked very well with the actors." The time for the project was limited and Aglialoro as director was "able to get [the performers] focused on their roles right away."

What did actor Grant Bowler think about his *Atlas Shrugged: Part 1* character? "Henry Reardon is incredibly intelligent, incredibly decisive," Bowler asserted. "He's an exceptional businessman. Self-directed. He doesn't really need input, advice, support. He doesn't need to cry on anybody's shoulder. He's almost that Randian perfect man. Probably the only thing that holds him back from her idea of his full evolution is guilt. He has a sense of responsibility to those around him. Or at least he deigns to carry them. So there is a conflict there. He's not complete. He can't just drive forward in his passion and be at one with that." Would people who love Ayn Rand love the way Grant Bowler plays Reardon? "Maybe," Bowler equivocated. "People are always going to look different as to how they look in your head when they read the novel. It's really none of my business. My business is to tell the story as well as I possibly can." Bowler believed it was natural circumstances would draw characters like Hank Reardon and Dagny Taggart into a romance. "Impassioned people seem to be drawn to each other if they share drive," the actor noted.

Grant Bowler is very aware of the big differences between a novel and a movie made of that novel. "It's difficult at times to know what to pull out and what to keep in because a novel is always going to have so much more density than a film. In a film, you've got to pick out two hours and you've got to cut, you've got to cull."

Prior to working on *Atlas Shrugged Part 1*, Jsu Garcia has known its casting director, Ronnie Yeskel. "I knew her because I had cast her daughter in the film called *The Wayshower* that Dr. John-Roger and I produced and directed together," Garcia told this author. She, Ronnie, came up to *The Wayshower* film set and saw what we were doing. We hit it off."

Thus, when Ronnie Yeskel worked as casting director on *Atlas Shrugged Part 1*, she phoned Garcia and asked him to audition. How much of Ayn Rand had he read? "I was familiar with Ayn Rand but hadn't read *Atlas Shrugged*," he revealed. He continued that he had not been much of a reader in his youth. "I only read three books when I was sixteen to nineteen years of age," Garcia stated. Those three? "*The Godfather*, *The Fountainhead*, and *The Once and Future King*," he stated. All three books profoundly affected Garcia. "My life would change from the mystical in *The Once and Future King* to the realist in *The Fountainhead*," he explained. "From *The Godfather* I learned family, honor, and loyalty."

Garcia has mixed feelings about Rand and her work. "Many times since the age of sixteen I was influenced by *The Fountainhead*," he stated. "I listened to her interviews. I'm not a follower of hers. I am more spiritual in my thinking and my way of being but some of her language and philosophy is pretty good. These are my words and interpretations of her work. I follow my teacher Dr. John-Roger's motto: take care of yourself first so you can take care of others. Ayn was about the individual and optimizing the individual and I like that. We are all God's children so we optimize the world and I love how individual men or women can inspire and we need those people in the world. Group and mob rule doesn't always work."

Garcia's audition for *Atlas Shrugged Part 1* went well. "Paul Johansson, the director, liked my audition," Garcia remembered. "Johansson was an inclusive and kind director. I got the role of

Francisco D'Anconia and I loved it and I prepared for it. I read that giant thick book *Atlas Shrugged* — what an amazing experience!"

What was most challenging about playing Francisco D'Anconia? "Nothing!" Garcia emphatically replied. "I was perfect for the part. Actors know what this means. It fit me like a glove. I loved the part and when you really love the part, it's easy." Garcia elaborated that he believed he should "not make the part political." Why? "The actor's role is to play the part and if you get political, you lose the compass of the character. Bias can get in the way; you could color the role with bias. I would try to find the dimensions in Francisco D'Anconia."

Garcia enjoyed trying to bring all the levels of his character's personality to the surface. "It is a trap to think that he's a womanizer," Garcia asserted. "He's not. He's very ethical, he loves the energy, and he's also playing a part so that he can ultimately make his move so he's a very interesting guy, a guy with a plan. John Galt is his friend so they've all talked about it to make their new world plan and he would do what he can to deceive and make that plan come true so he's a chameleon."

Some of the settings of the film very much impressed Garcia. "The interesting things were the art deco buildings we were shooting in downtown LA," he commented. "The director was amazing. I was taken care of very much. Production wise it was amazing to see the film shot in Red Camera technology. My part was very limited in the first Part 1 and it's with the girl and meeting at art deco type areas in downtown LA and you can almost feel Ayn Rand from New York City with the art deco scene. The director had to update the story to today's timeline." The period in which the film was created made for special challenges. "We were shooting in the middle of the elections and that's where it gets sticky," Garcia said.

Garcia told this writer he did not know why the casts were replaced in the other parts of the *Atlas Shrugged* trilogy. "It is a great story to tell while other actors replace each other," he noted.

"It's funny, it's like Hans Solo/Harrison Ford in the Star Wars trilogy was replaced by Richard Dreyfuss and Robert Redford. It is an actor's wish to complete the ROLE. I don't recommend this process of splitting up the role but one through line in which continuity is clear. It is a great book but fragmented performances are hard to follow." However, he is not terribly disappointed by the actors who followed him in playing Francisco D'Anconia, "My two favorite actors Esai Morales and Joaquim de Almeidia. How can I be upset? The three amigos!

John Mott was production designer for *Atlas Shrugged: Part 1*. What does a production designer do? Prospects website states, "Production designers are responsible for the visual concept of a film, television, theatre production. They identify a design style for sets, locations, graphics, props, lighting, camera angles and costumes, while working closely with the director and producer." I read this description to Mott and he found it an accurate description of the duties of a production designer. "I basically tell people I'm in charge of the look and feel of the show," he told this author.

When this writer inquired as to his major goal in designing for *Atlas Shrugged: Part I*, he replied, "I felt the show was really taking place in another gilded age. They were living in this gilded world which I through was parallel with our current age. There was a robber barons gilded age awhile back and the *Atlas Shrugged* guys were living in a similar world that is parallel to our own time."

What was the major challenge in *Atlas Shrugged: Part II* production designing? "Probably the budget," he replies. "They didn't have a lot of money so we didn't have much money to build sets or build the train. It's basically about this new metal, Rearden Metal. We had to find a lot of locations that sold the idea without building sets. We found the fancy houses, we found Rearden's office — they were real places that we modified. For example, we put more metal in Rearden's office. We modified an office already mostly steel and metal to make it more so in order to give it the feel it has in the show. We built the cab of the train. We based it on the Acela Train, a real high-speed train on the east coast. We build a similar cab and modified it to make it seem a little different from the Acela Train on which it was based."

Places in real existence were often used. "We tried to pick places that helped us in the story we wanted to tell," Mott told this writer. "We used an actual house for Hank Rearden's house but made some changes like putting up paintings and adding some greenery outside." The final scene had to both be climatic and a cliffhanger since sequels were planned. "We built a large hill of dirt for the final sequence," he disclosed. "I think we had an actual fire that was small and controllable but most of the fire was special effects."

Is there anything that especially benefitted from the production design? "I think Hank Rearden's office was good and the train bridge was my design but all digital, done as a special effect," he said. "I wanted a thin and long bridge, impossibly beautiful, and they produced the digital model seen in the film."

Joe Dea was not a storyboard artist by profession when he was hired to work in that capacity on *Atlas Shrugged: Part I*. "I was a TV director for most of my life," he told this writer. "I sometimes did storyboards for myself and I had done some for a couple of other directors. I was between jobs when I looked through the trades and saw that the makers of this film were looking for a storyboard artist." He applied, showed his previous work, and was hired.

"I did designs for special effects," he remembered. "They gave me the script and I designed what the special effects would look like. The primary special effects were about the train. I did one for the bridge. I'm a digital artist. I did electronic renderings. I did it all digitally, using photographs and photoshop and a tool called SketchUp." Regarding his storyboard art on this film, he elaborated, "When they shot special effects with real people in the shot, I designed how they should shoot it and how they should look."

In our conversation, Dea recalled an incident that might have been linked to digital cameras being "still new at the time." He said, "They shot at least an hour's worth of acting with that digital camera. Then the technician said it was not recorded! They had to do it all again."

What did he especially like about doing the storyboard art for this film? "I liked working with the director," he answered. "Paul is very smart and very open to my ideas. He knew I'd have a director's sensibility in designing."

Natalie Contreras was assistant property master for *Atlas Shrugged: Part I*. "I had worked on a TV show prior to *Atlas Shrugged* with set director Lori Mazuer of *Atlas Shrugged*," she informed the author of this book. "She hired me as her buyer in the beginning of the project which is when I met the prop master who hired me on as his assistant for the run of filming."

Contreras had several duties as assistant property master. "My responsibilities were to prep whatever the scene called for with the property master: set up the directors chairs for company, prep food scenes if there were food scenes, make sure Dagny had her bracelet (that was VERY important), prop the actors with their props for the scene such as wedding rings, cellphones and ear pieces, watches, eyewear, files, coffee cups, briefcases, etc," she stated. "Once everyone was ready for the camera, I then watched the monitor for continuity to make sure that every time the actor did something with the props it matched every take or when the camera moves in for a close-up that it all matched to the prior scene. Everything has to match per take so when the editor goes in to edit the project, it all matches."

What were her major challenges? "The most challenging part of my job during this film shoot was that it moved very, very fast," she disclosed. "They had a lot of driving shots and sometimes moved locations multiple times in one day. So for me, aside from watching the scene for continuity, I also had to make sure they were prepped and ready to move when company moved to head to the next scene and set up. Prepping for the next scene, wrapping the scene you are walling away from all the while watching the monitors for continuity, you have to be able to think quickly and anticipate everything. When you're working on a film shoot that is 100% locations, that can be quite challenging. One relies heavily on the first and second assistant directors, the script supervisor, and the on-set dresser. When we filmed larger press scenes or cocktail events, etc., our prop master John Brunot would bring in additional crew to assist with background actors. I always kept to the principal talent."

When this writer inquired as to what was the most unusual thing she did in her capacity as assistant property master, Contreras answered, "In our industry, everything has its own set of challenges. So nothing to me would seem unusual. To me, that's the best part about our industry! Whether it's locations you've never been to before, scenes that have something surprising or interesting happen, requests that would come up often that weren't necessarily scripted, script changes that would cause us to be flexible, it is all part of the job. So I can't think of anything that was particularly unusual."

However, something did take place worthy of special mention: "One thing that sticks out in my mind that was probably the funniest, maybe not so funny at the time, moment of filming was when we were out in Piru, CA. We were filming a dinner scene at Ellis Wyatt's house (played by the brilliant Graham Beckel) with Henry and Dagny. We had to have been on our 11th hour trying to get this scene. All of a sudden, a bat flew right over their heads. Of course the whole shooting crew were standing by (what we refer to as 'lock it up') waiting to roll, but the bat kept flying over their heads every time the Director Paul Johannson would call 'action.' It was one of those moments where you just can't help but laugh while trying to get this bat out of the house. We were quickly becoming unstitched. Come to find out, there were a few bats taking up residency in the attic of this amazing Victorian house they were filming in. That was a long night. But if you watch the scene in the film, they are happily eating and drinking and ended it all with a toast."

The movie did poorly at the box office. It took $20 million to make the film. It made only $4.6 million at the box office.

Atlas Shrugged: Part 1, also received mostly negative reviews. Writing for *Slate*, David Weigel contended "the movie doesn't work as drama" but added "as allegory, it works about as well as the Randians could want it to." Weigel said he believed the novel *Atlas Shrugged* "worked as a thought experiment" and that the movie "sort of works as a thought experiment" but "it's an incomplete thought." Weigel concluded, "Rand's gospel of selfishness works better on the page than on film."

Film critic Roger Ebert was harsher in his panning of *Atlas Shrugged, Part 1*. Ebert called it "the most anticlimactic non-event since Geraldo Rivera broke into Al Capone's vault." [If anyone is unfamiliar with the Al Capone vault debacle, it was a much-hyped media event. There was widespread speculation that bodies, by then skeletons, would be found in that vault or that vast amounts of money would be discovered. When the vault was finally opened, there were a few empty bottles, a stop sign, and a whole lot of dirt.] Ebert wrote that the film is basically "a series of business meetings in luxurious retro leather-and-brass board rooms and offices, and restaurants and bedrooms that look borrowed from a hotel no doubt known as the Robber Baron Arms." He stated that many discussions are hard to decipher as "dialogue seems to have been ripped throbbing with passion from the pages of *Investors' Business Daily*." He commented on how "breathless urgency" is shown in this movie about "the laying of new railroad track." Ebert concluded that even Rand's hardcore fans will "get a letdown" from the movie because it portrays her beliefs in "an incoherent and murky fashion."

Writing about *Atlas Shrugged, Part 1* for *Variety*, Peter Debruge asserted, "A monument of American literature is shaved down to a spindly toothpick of a movie." He speculated, "This hasty, low-budget adaptation would have Ayn Rand spinning in her grave." Debruge described the "decidedly un-cinematic economic scenario" in which government regulators "undermine the progress of society's most successful entrepreneurs with anti-competition and spread-the-wealth statues." He disliked the casting of Taylor Schilling as "tough-as-nails railroad tycoon" Dagny Taggart, faulting Schilling for playing her "unassertively." He grants the production a few positive points in the "key railroad-rebuilding exteriors" and says they "wisely commission visual effects for the new line's virgin run" and a "climactic oil-well fires" scene. However, he concluded that the audience has little reason to care about the answer to "Who is John Galt?"

Casey Broadwater reviewed *Atlas Shrugged: Part 1* for *Blu-ray Review*. He called it "a depressingly low-rent adaptation that's stilted and poorly scripted and completely devoid of entertainment value." Broadwater elaborated, "Most of the film consists of filthy rich characters sitting in plush rooms having awkwardly worded conversations about how the industrious business class is being stilted by regulation and fed upon by the parasitic non-contributors of society. You might say this is a film for the 1%. It's tiring in its pseudo-profound wordiness and non-stop sloganeering."

The film even got a negative review in *Reason*, a pro-libertarian organ with the slogan "Free Minds and Free Markets." Reviewer Kurt Loder stated, "It's a blessing, I suppose, that Ayn Rand, who loved the movies, and actually worked extensively in the industry, isn't alive to see what's been made of her most influential novel. The new, long-awaited film version of *Atlas Shrugged* is a mess, full of embalmed talk, enervated performances, impoverished effects, and cinematography that would barely pass muster in a TV show. Sitting through this picture is like watching early rehearsals of a stage play that's clearly doomed." Loder allowed, "The film was obviously a labor of love for producer John Aglialoro, a multimillionaire Randian who held movie rights to the book for 18 years, and made every effort to set it up as a professional production." Loder states that viewers are apt to be "intrigued' by the question "Who is John Galt?" Then Loder writes that we only see John Galt "togged out in a trench coat and a rain-soaked fedora like a film-noir flatfoot who's wandered into an epoch far away from his own."

In The Atlasphere, a website for Rand fans, Hans Gregory Schantz gave the film a very positive review, calling it "an outstanding movie." He found "the dialogue and acting" to be "remarkably solid, even brilliant, at times." He liked the way Taylor Schilling played Dagny as "cold and unemotional" when in conflict with her brother while she "relaxes with, warms to, and ultimately allows herself to be seduced by, Grant Bowler's Hank Rearden." Schantz was especially impressed by "Grant Bowler's flinty portrayal of steel tycoon Hank Rearden," finding "Bowler's Rearden is as eminently heroic as he is tragically flawed. The power of Bowler's acting is enhanced further by Rebecca Wisocky's amazing performance as his wife, Lillian. Wisocky's Lillian is as beautifully elegant as she is viciously vile. Wow!" This critic believed "many challenging aspects of the plot" were "carried off flawlessly due to the excellent script and strong acting." Schantz stated, "Another pillar of the film is Graham Beckel's Ellis Wyatt. He is an elemental force of nature barreling into Dagny's office, yet becomes warmly gregarious as he recognizes kindred spirits in Dagny and Hank. Despite having tragically little screen time, Jsu Garcia makes mysterious playboy Francisco D'Anconia come to life. I can't wait to see more of him in part two. Edi Gathegi's Eddie Willers and Nikki Klecha's Gwen Ives also delivered solid support." He faulted the film for some dialogue that amounted to "technobabble" but, overall, the critic believed the film to be an "exciting, fast paced, and breathtaking romp."

An IMDb user review stated "I was prepared to cringe at this *Atlas Shrugged*, universally panned by the critics for its low budget and no-name cast. Instead, I was pretty impressed. The story was faithful to the book, and the message and narrative clear, with the producers wisely sidestepping most of Rand's stilted polemics." That same reviewer continued, "The cast, and especially Taylor Shilling, who played Dagny, and Grant Bowler (Rearden) did a great job."

Another Internet Movie Database writer commented, "I was convinced *Atlas Shrugged* could not be put on film, but this movie proved me wrong. It has a contemporary look and feel, while retaining the Art Deco elegance of Rand's novel. The acting is superb, particularly Taylor Schilling as Dagny Taggart and Grant Bowler as Hank Rearden. Bowler manages to cram more meaning into a half-cocked eyebrow than most actors in a dozen lines of dialogue, and Shilling captures the sleek, cold elegance of Dagny, while giving just a hint of the passion simmering beneath the surface. Indeed, all the performances are impeccable." That person went on to praise the film for "sets, locations, and costumes that are both gorgeous and convincing." The reviewer "wanted to stand up and cheer" at a pivotal scene.

2012: *Atlas Shrugged Part II: The Strike*

Atlas Shrugged Part II: The Strike was released in October 2012. It had a new director, John Putch, the son of actress Jean Stapleton who became famous for playing Edith Bunker in the groundbreaking sitcom *All In The Family.* Brian Patrick O'Toole was back to write the script but the others on the screenplay were new, Duke Sandefur and Duncan Scott.

The cast was new. Samantha Mathis played Dagny Taggart, Patrick Fabian played James Taggart, Jason Beghe played Henry Rearden, and Kim Rhodes played Lillian Rearden. As Jsu Garcia said in his interview with this writer, Esai Morales played Francisco D'Anconia.

Producers originally intended to use profits from the first *Atlas Shrugged* to finance *Part II*. However, that was impossible as *Part I* lost money. Still, they were able to make the movie with a budget of $10 million.

Atlas Shrugged II: The Strike starts with information flashed across the screen: "Sometime in the near future . . . Railroads have re-emerged as the only affordable means of transportation. Excessively high energy prices have greatly reduced automobile and commercial air travel . . ."

Then we see two airplanes flying past mountains. One plane appears to be following the other. A close-up reveals Dagny Taggart piloting one. There is a close-up of a bracelet that those familiar with the story (through either novel or *Atlas Shrugged: Part I)* will recognize as the bracelet crafted from the first pour of Rearden Metal. Dagny starts having trouble with the plane and asks herself, "Who is John Galt?" *Crash!* The plane slams into a mountain.

"9 Months Earlier" appears onscreen. Dagny and Dr. Robert Stadler (Robert Picardo) are in a train tunnel discussing the motor prototype she and Hank Rearden discovered in an abandoned car factory of the defunct Twentieth Century Motor Company. Dagny takes him to the motor. The scientist is impressed but notes that it is missing a necessary element to function. Dr. Stadler and Dagny have a negative history. She reminds him that he and his State Science Institute colleagues declared Rearden Metal "unsafe" in an effort to prevent Dagny from building the John Galt Line. "But you built it anyway," he says with obvious admiration. She prods him as to who could have designed the motor and who could make it work. Dr. Stadler does not know. He observes that finding great minds "has become difficult since the disappearances." Does he have the brilliance needed to make it work? He does not. "I haven't disappeared," he explains.

The next scene is at the Taggart Midtown Station in New York City. A group of demonstrators wave signs with messages like "We Are The 99.9%. Where's my FAIR SHARE?"

Dagny is approached by Eddie Willers (Richard T. Jones). They discuss recent losses to the company.

News reports inform the public that the "Fair Share" law passed. It requires companies to supply goods equally to all customers. The news also reports that many businesses are failing due to shortages of raw materials. The face of Director of Economic Development Wesley Mouch (Paul McCrane) appears onscreen. The newscaster quotes Mouch calling economic troubles "a temporary setback."

Cut to Eddie and Dagny in the back of a limo. She mentions how Ellis Wyatt was dedicated to his work but walked away from it. Before doing so, he set fire to his oil field and storage facilities.

"It's like some destroyer is sweeping up everybody who could dig us out of this mess," Dagny observes.

"Who is John Galt?" Eddie desultorily replies.

Dagny tells him she hates that expression.

In a meeting with underlings, a depressed Dagny learns of how bad things are getting for the business. "This railroad doesn't function as a charity, Eddie," she declares. She orders that a line be dropped.

A TV talk show appears. Well-known conservative commentator Sean Hannity has a cameo as himself. "Henry Rearden is a hero," he avers. "He's a job creator. He's an innovator. His metal is a cheaper metal. This is capitalism 101. The Fair Share Law is more big government."

The next scene starts with a close-up of yellow metal being poured. Then we see Henry Rearden (Jason Beghe) at his desk. A government officer, Leonard Small (Bug Hall) visits Henry. He has a government order for rights to Rearden Metal. The government will compensate.

"I've never met a looter with your kind of dedication and endurance," Henry observes.

"I'm not a looter," the man objects. The two of them do not come to agreement.

In another scene, James Taggart (Patrick Fabian) is in a store, searching for a tie.

A starstruck cashier, Cherryl Brooks (Larisa Oleynik), approaches him. "You built the John Galt Line," she says. "You're my hero."

"And now you're mine," he replies. He invites her to ride in his limo to a concert at which a top pianist will play. Pianist Richard Halley gives an outstanding performance. The audience gives him a standing ovation. There is a break. The curtain rises but the pianist is absent. A card is on the piano and on it is written "Who is John Galt?"

Plot machinations include the examination of the motor by scientist Quinton Daniels (Diedrich Bader), a soap opera-style confrontation between Hank and Lillian about his extramarital affair, and the wedding of James Taggart and Lillian Brooks. That wedding reception has fascinating dialogue lifted straight from Rand's novel. Cherryl says, "I'm the woman in the family now." Dagny retorts, "That's quite all right. I'm the man."

The Head of State (this future has substituted this office for President) imposes directives promoting government control of the economy, the economy continues deteriorating, and Hank Rearden is dragged into court for violating the Fair Share Law. Also charged is entrepreneur Ken Danagger (Arye Gross) who must be tried in absentia. The trial is before a panel of judges. They find Rearden guilty but avoid actually punishing him for fear of creating a martyr.

Eventually we get back to the plane crash beginning and . . . John Galt!

He is a flesh and blood person, not just a catchphrase.

Samantha Mathis has discussed playing Dagny Taggart in interviews. "It was a daunting prospect to play such a beloved character from fiction that so many people have an affinity for," she said. At the time *Part II* opens, she noted Dagny was "having a tough time" because "the government are continuously interjecting themselves into all businesses and many of the great minds who are her contemporaries are disappearing" which makes it "harder and harder for her to do her job." How did Mathis prepare to play this pivotal and unique character? "The book was a great resource for me in terms of building a backstory for Dagny, particularly because she has this long-ago history with Francisco that we don't really address per se in the second installment but that is definitely an undercurrent — their childhood friendship that developed into a romance. The book was really helpful to me in terms of me utilizing all that to sort of create my own memories. The same is true for the backstory of Dagny and Hank." Mathis saw "several driving arcs" in the story. One is the repeated question, "Who is John Galt?" Another of those "driving arcs" is "Where are all the great minds disappearing to? Is there some 'disappear-er' who is taking all these minds or are they choosing to go because they've lost faith in the system?" Mathis: "She's still trying to hold onto the company faith in the world that things can still work even though things look so bleak." Mathis says there is a special tension between Dagny and Francisco: "She still wants to fight the good fight and she feels he has given up." Thus, Mathis notes, the former lovers "are at cross purposes." Others have seen Dagny Taggart as an emancipated woman and example for females of what women can accomplish. Does Mathis believe this is true? "Too often strong women are labeled a word I won't say and strong men are just labeled strong," Mathis observes. "I certainly was attracted to the material and to playing Dagny because of her strength. She can be perceived as off-putting at times. But she believes in what she believes in and I think that's an admirable quality."

How did Jason Beghe view Hank Rearden? "I guess if there is a word that would describe him or that is integral to who he is, that word is integrity," Beghe asserted. "Along with that is honor. When you look at someone's personal ethic, it may not make sense to you, and that's why it's a personal ethic. . . . Somewhere in that personal moral code is the idea that if I made a commitment, which I did when I put the ring on her finger, then I am not going to renege on that responsibility." He believes that Hank Rearden "wants to make it as easy as possible for Lillian to end it" but he cannot end it because of the marriage contract. How does the actor believe Rearden reacts when Lillian discovers Dagny is his bedmate? "The way I understand it, he's not embarrassed or ashamed . . . within the confines of the contract he has with Lillian, because of Lillian's own duplicitous behavior, that's how she found out, he didn't throw it in her face. There's no need to lie . . . . I think he's a very honest person."

Patrick Fabian found his character, James Taggart, to be a kind of "hollow man." Fabian asserted that James Taggart is "not a villain" but is "misunderstood." He observed, "I don't think James necessarily creates anything and that includes his own thoughts. I think he has to be told what to think. It depends on whose sphere of influence he happens to be in at the moment. When Wesley is giving the orders, it is 'yes, Wesley, yes Wesley,' I will mouth this. And when he's working with Dagny, I think he has a sense of brotherly shame and also abdication of the family business. She really is running it even though he presents it. He has to have a shame about that. When he's in his own workplace, they all know it, too. He is hollow leadership in his own bed basically . . . . The only time he feels his plumage is working is when he's out with Wesley and the rest of the guys." The actor sees James Taggart as a man who does not even "know what he believes." The absence of principle and firmness in the character of James Taggart is reflected in his choice of wife. "He can never have the Dagny level woman," Fabian states. Thus, he turns to Cherryl, "A woman he can help rescue." However, "He also has contempt for her because she's so beneath him." Thus, he rescues but also "punishes" her for being "from the station that she is from." Fabian believes the character is "sympathetic" because he says things that people will automatically agree with but "don't think it through." He also believes people identify with James: "Their hopes and dreams are that they are like Dagny. The reality is that they are like James." Does he consider the film to be a love story? He found it about "love for freedom."

The actress who played cashier/James Taggart love interest Cherryl, Larisa Oleynik, has praised Ayn Rand. "For me there's no doubt that she was an incredibly intelligent woman whose philosophy was based on her own life experience and what she witnessed of the failures of communism," Oleynik stated.

Kim Rhodes, who played Lillian Reardon, believes Rand remains relevant to the present day and will be relevant in the future. "The fundamentals of freedom I think everyone can agree with," Rhodes remarked. "It's just how it's implemented that people disagree on. I think this is a wonderful philosophy and there are amazing ways that it could be implemented." In a video broadcast on YouTube, David Kelley, founder of The Atlas Society, asked Rhodes about the trial scene in the film. "Did you want Hank to win?" he inquired.

"Who are you asking — Kim or Lillian?" was her reply question.

"I'm asking Lillian," he revealed.

She slipped into character. "No, because he's an embarrassment," Kim Rhodes-as-Lillian Rearden declared. "Absolutely just shut up, go away, do your job, you're making a scene and you're costing me money." Commenting on the overall feeling of this socially conscious socialite, Rhodes speculated, "I think the mortification of just being there was just astounding. That's her low point in life, having to be in there because of her husband who clearly doesn't know his place and has the audacity to have ideas."

How did Esai Morales feel about what his character, Francisco D'Anconia, did in the story? "He's a character study," Morales commented. "He's throwing them little bits and pieces to see if they chew or if they gag or if they swallow whole. He's baiting people, he's testing them." Morales believed the character was "kind of like a CIA operative who has to get the mission done but can't afford to risk the ire of people who don't understand. He can't give it away before it is time. He has to play, he has to be very careful and basically rely on his instincts." Morales said he himself sometimes tells people "too much" whereas Francisco must "let people wonder."

Costume designer for *Atlas Shrugged Part II: The Strike* Bonnie Stauch was interviewed by this author. How was she hired for this job? "For one thing, I am a costumer designer," she replied. "For another, I knew the director and had worked on other movies for him. I came in, I presented my ideas, and I got hired."

Backgrounding was vital to her work in the movie. "The first thing I wanted to do was read the novel again," she explained.

Bonnie Stauch had strong ideas about costuming for the film. "I wanted Dagny subtly associated with the railroad," Stauch disclosed. "After I was hired, I searched and found all sorts of different jewelry, dresses, and suits reminiscent of railroads and box ties. I found a necklace that had two to three inch cylindrical pieces of different colors that reminded me of a line of boxcars and that necklace went on Dagny. Anything similar to a railroad went on Dagny. She was dressed with strong angles like shoulder pads and her waist was nipped in a skirt to give it a dramatic 1940s look even though it was set in 2016. Her clothes showed her as a force to be reckoned with and the same was true with Henry." Since Henry made his living with metal, Stauch sought to dress him in "a cool palette made of all the different colors of metal."

While Stauch wanted Dagny to appear "a force to be reckoned with," she sought a different look for compromise prone James. "He couldn't be sloppy but I wanted him less defined, less sharply dressed. His shoulders were less strong and the colors less saturated." His wife Cherryl was dressed in costumes that contrasted with those Stauch crafted for Dagny. "She was much softer," Stauch related. "Her wedding gown had several layers and was very fluffy, an extravagant gown to show her as arm candy." For the country's leader, or Head of State, Stauch sought "a very dramatic look with a lot of contrast." Overall, what was it like to be costume designer on this picture? "I have to say it was really, really tough because we had many costumes, at least several hundred."

Jordana Capra played one of the judges, Judge Glesie, on the panel before which Rearden was tried. "The casting director, Jeff Gerrard, has brought me in to audition for ages and had booked me into different gigs over the years," Capra informed the author of this book. "I had also known the director for quite awhile from the TV commercial world. John Putch was one of the busiest actors in commercials (on top of his film and TV acting work), so I was very happy to see that he was broadening his talents to include directing. I was originally asked to audition for a TV news announcer, and was delighted to be told that they were offering me the role of Judge Glesie. And no, no one ever referred to my character by name, I think mostly because no one was sure how to pronounce it! Gleee-see? Glay-sigh? Gluch-sight-ee? Gleh-see-aye?"

What did Capra seek to emphasize in playing the jurist? "The point of this scene serves to emphasize the government's greedy and lazy position that any invention of value should be shared, i.e., given, to the world (read: government) at no cost, so that the world (again read: the powers that be) can profit from said invention with zero effort or investment of time, knowledge, or money. Fortunately, I had two of the most wonderful actors, Kip Gilman as my fellow jurist and Jason Beghe to play off me. Jason was so good in the role of the brilliant inventor and Kip has such a grounded approach, they both made my experience onset and my job as an actor easy and gratifying."

Capra found few challenges in playing a judge in this film. "Short of the drive to Long Beach, California, this was a dream gig!" she cheerfully declared.

Working on this motion picture led to a rekindled relationship for Jordan Capra. "Years before, in 1993, I was fortunate to be cast in a film called *Watch It!* that was shot in Chicago, and the makeup artist, Felicia Linksy, and I became friends," she stated. "When someone spends an hour or more quite literally 'in your face,' touching you and then touching you up throughout the day, it's a very intimate relationship. She and I had remained in contact for years after she moved to Los Angeles. But, as is often the case, she moved and we lost touch. I had checked the makeup department on EVERY call-sheet for every project that I worked on for years to see if I was going to get to work with her again . . . no luck. The call-sheet for *Atlas Shrugged Part II: The Strike* was the first call-sheet that I didn't check. When I stepped into the makeup trailer that morning, there she was — you can imagine the squeals of delight and hugging that ensued!"

Vito Trotta worked as assistant department head for hair on *Atlas Shrugged Part II: The Strike*. "I was friends with the other department head, Kimberly Carlson, and also with the director, John Putch," he said to this writer when asked how he was hired.

Trotta described his duties as "designing looks for the cast, and implementing those looks every day that certain cast members worked. In conjunction with the actors and the directors, I designed looks for their hairstyles."

How were hairstyles selected for particular characters? "It starts with reading the script, what I envision, I take it to actor and director and we go from there," he answered.

Atlas Shrugged Part II: The Strike was not screened for film critics prior to its release because producer John Aglialoro was skeptical about "the integrity of the critics." However, it was screened for two right-wing political and social organizations, the conservative Heritage Foundation and the libertarian Cato Institute.

Atlas Shrugged II: The Strike was very positively reviewed by John Tamny in a *Forbes* website. He praised it as "a must see because it in a very handsome way described the world in which we live today whereby the achievers are being shackled by the moochers."

However, most reviews were negative. In the *New York Post*, Kyle Smith derided it as possessing "production values from a 1986 porno" and having "special effects like something your nephew cooked up on his Mac." Moreover, Smith disliked the ideological thrust of the film, finding its "'Yay, money!' zingers" to be "just a big bag of sad."

Jim Lane in the *Sacramento News & Review* gave the film a mixed review. Lane wrote that it was "a respectable effort" but found it "hampered less by its limited budget than by the dogmatic contrivances of Rand's plot and the straw-man polemics of her wooden, declamatory dialogue."

Like its predecessor, this film did not draw many people into the theaters and failed to make money.

2014: *Atlas Shrugged III: Who Is John Galt?*

Atlas Shrugged Part III was released in 2014. It often has *Who Is John Galt?* as its subtitle.

J. James Manera was the director and contributed to the screenplay along with John Aglialoro, who contributed to Part I. Harmon Kaslow also contributed to the screenplay. In an interview, Kaslow commented on how Ayn Rand found America consistent with her ideals when she first came here. "Here's this woman who had that moment that really none of us have had," he commented. "She steps off the boat and sees the Manhattan skyline, she sees the Statue of Liberty, and she says to herself, 'I've come to the land of opportunity.'"

Cast line-up: Laura Regan as Dagny Taggart, Greg Germann as James Taggart, Rob Morrow as Henry "Hank" Rearden, Joaquim de Almeida as Francisco D'Anconia, Peter Mackenzie is Head of State Thompson, and Kristoffer Polaha as John Galt.

Atlas Shrugged Part III starts with a meeting at the Twentieth Century Motor Company. It is announced that everyone will work their regular time but be paid according to "need."

"I don't accept it!" young John Galt shouts. "I'm going to put a stop to this! I'll stop the motor of the world!"

Flash to a series of reports of how factories are closing, the seas are unsafe, and cargo cannot reach their destinations because of a pirate. Regulations strangle the coal, gas, and nuclear power industries. There are rampant power outages.

Taggart Transcontinental is one of the few major industries still robustly operating.

Cut to a mountainous area. In the last film, Dagny had just crashed her airplane into it. In this film, the man who found her, John Galt, takes her in his arms and brings her to the little hidden village he has established.

As John Galt holds the wounded Dagny in his arms and carries her, the audience cannot fail to observe that the bracelet made from the first pour of Rearden Metal adorns one of her wrists. She learns that Galt is leading a "strike of minds." Various big shots have abandoned a world they believed was against them.

The film goes back and forth between the strikers and the real world they left behind. John Galt tells Dagny of the vow the strikers take: "I swear by my life and my love of it that I will never live for another man nor ask another man to live for me."

The most ferocious conflicts occur when John Galt takes his message of Objectivist ethics back to the real world and faces the persecution of the nationalizing and socializing forces that have overtaken America.

John Galt and Dagny fall in love. The bigwigs try to corrupt and persuade Galt. Unable to change him, they brutally persecute him. Will he break? Any Ayn Rand fan can guess the answer to that question as the filmmakers are true to her vision.

Kristoffer Polaha felt he had a firm grasp of Rand's message in his playing John Galt. "I think the most important message that Ayn Rand was trying to get out there is that individuals are always going to be the most productive part of any society," he asserted in an interview at the film premiere. "I think that's something that anybody along any party line is going to agree with. If you talk to Stephen Spielberg, he's an individual who is extremely creative making films, producing things." What was Polaha's greatest challenge in playing one of the most iconic literary character? "Basically not to F it up!" he cheerfully replied. "You don't want to be the guy that has people say, 'That's *not* who John Galt is'

When asked why the works of Rand have survived so well in the decades since they were first published, Laura Regan answered, "I think there's a universality, a timelessness to her ideas, to believing in oneself, to working hard for something you believe in, for standing up for your own right to do hard work and be rewarded for it. They're very American ideals." What does she believe the most important message is that viewers should take away from this movie? "I think the most important message is that if you have something that you really believe in, don't be afraid to buck the trend of the world," she asserted. "Don't be afraid to swim against the current and stand up for you ideas, your thoughts, what you really believe in."

As previously noted, Elia Cmiral composed the music for the first and third films of the trilogy. Were there special challenges in creating the music for *III*? "Not really," he told this author. "The main goal I was working with in *Part III* was to connect the first and third part thematically together and develop the material accordingly. That was a great challenge and I enjoyed it a lot."

The third of the *Atlas Shrugged* trilogy resembled the first two in both poor box office receipts and dismal reviews. *Variety* critic Dennis Harvey noted the "prior installments weren't very good movies" and called this final installment "the worst of the lot." Harvey said it has "the feel of a low-grade TV soap opera, with acting to match."

Writing for *The Village Voice*, Alan Scherstuhl called it "the last and least of the cheapjack adaptations" of the novel. Scherstuhl continued that the romantic interlude between Dagny and Galt was a mere "30 seconds of close-ups of backs and bras and lips" and noted that it cuts from the lovemaking to a railroad worker using a lantern to guide a train into its tunnel." Scherstuhl found the juxtaposition "hilarious." He said the "slipshod" movie causes him to "almost feel for Rand."

Ignatiy Vishnevetsky wrote a review for *A. V. Club* that noted how Ayn Rand, a heterosexual woman, possessed a "fixation on trains, skyscrapers, and other idealized symbols of phallic power." Vishnevetsky found the movie "cut-rate to the point of incoherence." The reviewer asserted, "People talk like malfunctioning robots trying to pass for human" called the film "Z-grade" and concluded "it's a screed about capitalism and government that seems to have no clue as to how either works." On that last point, Vishnevetsky said it was "also a problem of the source material."

An *Austin Chronicle* critic complimented Ayn Rand: "At her very best in *The Fountainhead* and the first three quarters of *Atlas Shrugged*, Rand is a master storyteller." The critic stated that this film "substitutes the most knee-jerk Tea Party beliefs for Rand's far more ambitious and complex philosophy. This is brought home by having Sean Hannity, Glenn Beck, and Ron Paul presented as voices of moral authority and political wisdom." The reviewer derided the movie as "stylistically mundane" and afflicted by "leaden storytelling." The reviewer concluded, "In 1949, when Warner Bros. filmed *The Fountainhead*, Rand threatened to burn down the studio if they compromised her novel. I'd like to think that if she were alive she'd be looking for lighter fluid for this one."

All three attempts to transfer *Atlas Shrugged* from novel to movie failed to generate a profit at the box office. All three received more negative than positive reviews. Writing specifically about the middle film of the three, reviewer Scott Tobias noted: "The irony of *Part II*'s existence is rich enough: The free market is a religion for Rand acolytes, and it emphatically rejected *Part I*." That free market also rejected P*arts II* and *III*.

It is this writer's opinion that not every book translates well from novel to screen. *Atlas Shrugged* has never gone out of print and is beloved by many. It is also a super-lengthy novel in which characters and situations exist primarily to dramatize the author's philosophy and political opinions. Perhaps this is a book that cannot be successfully translated into film.

2015: *Anthem*

In 2015, a Solebury School Production of *Anthem* was made. It is in color, 13 minutes long, and can be viewed on YouTube. The short film opens with a candle surrounded by blackness. The voiceover states: "It is a sin to write this. It is a sin to think words others do not think. We have broken the laws . . . . May we be forgiven." Then we see the word "Anthem" on the screen. Following this, we see two youths sitting across from each other at a table. There is a candle on that table as well. One youth says, "No, no, NO! You shouldn't decide on a job for yourself. That wouldn't benefit the people at large." He tells the other youth that he must not be a scholar but a street sweeper: "For the greater good . . . your moral duty."

Cut to the youth sweeping the streets along with other sweepers. One sweeper remonstrates with him about the sweeping technique our protagonist uses. He is ordered to keep using the particular technique he was taught.

When we next see him, he is in the dark at a table by a candle and reading. He thinks, "I could be sentenced to ten years in prison if these words are discovered." He tells us his name is Equality 7-2521, that he is 18 years old, and that he feels he was born cursed.

Equality finds a tunnel underground. He goes into the tunnel and discovers a light bulb! He looks through a book where he discovers an unfamiliar word: "I." He tells himself that he must report the discovery of the light bulb to the City Council. He believes he is kin to Prometheus, who stole fire from the deities of ancient Greek mythology to give to humanity.

There is a scene in which Equality is before three figures in masks. "Throw away torches and candles!" one says. "Do you think yourself a messiah?" another asks.

The film ends with Equality stating, "I am, I think, I will. I will live for myself." He carves from a rock what he calls the sacred word: "EGO."

The film ends with a snippet of Tom Brokaw interviewing Ayn Rand about how she says people "are attacked for their success."

This short was directed by Ian Berwick who also wrote the script and played Equality 7-2521. Joshua Reinsten played Fraternity 2-5503 and Connor Ott played The Guard. Credits show George O'Connor as International 4-8818/City Council Member #3, Joshua Reinstein as Fraternity 2-5503/City Council Member #1, and Sean McLaughlin as City Council Member #2.

George O'Connor was interviewed by the author of this book. Except for Equality, the names of the characters are not stated within the film. "I was the council member furthest from the audience's left," he said. "I'm the shortest one. As International, I was one of Equality's friends who's there when he discovers the underground room." O'Connor's contributions to this short went beyond acting. "I was the cinematographer on several scenes," he said.

Asked how he was cast, O'Connor disclosed, "There wasn't a formal casting process. There were only six people in our class, so whoever wasn't already behind the camera ended up in front of it. All six of us (except my friend Vivi, who didn't like acting) appear in *Anthem*. My friend Josh and I each played two roles. The only 'guest star' was our friend Sean, who played the middle council member. Sean had transferred to a different school that year but was still able to come back and help out for a day." O'Connor did cinematography, he elaborated "because I always enjoyed cinematography and volunteered to shoot *Anthem*."

For the then-high schooler, shooting this short meant branching out from previous film projects. "We had never done anything like *Anthem* before," he commented. "Most films we made in our class were silly comedies, so a dystopian drama was new to us. But

Ian had a very clear vision and a lot of passion for the source material, which is why the film turned out as well as it did."

Participating in the making of this film was very satisfying for O'Connor. "I felt *Anthem* was the best film our class had produced that year," he said. "It even swept most of the awards at a student film festival held at another nearby high school. I think what made it so effective was Ian's vision, direction, performance, and overall passion. I remember being very moved at his final speech when I first saw it."

How does O'Connor feel about the fact that a film he participated in making as a high school project is still on YouTube? "I think the fact that a film I made years ago can live on and find a new audience is something special," he replied.

O'Connor said Ian Berwick's appreciation of Ian Rand led to the short film's creation. "Ian was a big fan of Ayn Rand, and quoted her in the yearbook," O'Connor recalled. "As to why he chose *Anthem* specifically, I'm not sure. I can only guess it was because its themes resonated with Ian and because it's a public domain work."

What does O'Connor think of Rand and her philosophy? "I had never heard of Ayn Rand before making *Anthem*, and I didn't look into her and her work until later," he answered. "I must admit that I find her views objectionable, particularly her justification of the genocide of Native Americans on the grounds that they were 'primitive.' I also find her support of selfishness as misguided, since no society can function without a strong collective and a sense of compassion for one another."

The reader may wonder what he is referring to when O'Connor talks about Ayn Rand and Native Americans. On March 6, 1974, Rand spoke before the graduating class of the U. S. Military Academy at West Point. During a question and answer period, she was asked about negative aspects of American history. Regarding the indigenous population, Rand stated that they did not "have any right to live in a country merely because they were born here and acted and lived like savages." She elaborated, "The Indians did not have any property rights — they didn't have the concept of property" and that, therefore, "they didn't have any rights to the land." She also said, "What was it that they were fighting for, if they opposed white men on this continent? For their wish to continue a primitive existence, their right to keep part of the earth untouched, unused, and not even as property, but just keep everybody out so that you will live practically like an animal? Any white person who brings the elements of civilization had the right to take over this continent and it is great that some people did, and discovered here what they couldn't do anywhere else in the world and what the Indians, if there are any racially Indians today, do not believe to this day: respect for individual rights."

Whew! It is very difficult to get around the bigotry and ignorance of Rand's views on Native Americans. However, I will state that although Rand clearly had a prejudiced view of Native Americans and their culture, she was not what is usually called a racist as she condemned racism as "the lowest and most primitive form of collectivism."

2015: *Saints vs. Scoundrels*: "Ayn Rand vs. Flannery O'Connor"

The Eternal Word Television Network (EWTN) is a cable television network that presents programming from a Roman Catholic viewpoint. A series entitled *Saints vs. Scoundrels* worked out fictional confrontations between pairs of historical figures, one a professing and devout Catholic and another (the "scoundrel") with a very different worldview. Dr. Benjamin Wilker, a Catholic professor who teaches ethics and political science, hosted the show and varied actors played the historical figures. There were episodes pitting Jean-Jacques Rousseau against St. Augustine, King Henry VIII against St. Thomas More, and St. Francis of Assisi against Machiavelli.

In 2015, *Saints vs. Scoundrels* aired an episode in two parts that were both entitled "Ayn Rand vs. Flannery O'Connor." Why were these writers set against each other? Partly for what they had in common, partly for their strong differences. Both were women writers of the early to mid-20th century. As previously noted, Rand was a rock-hard skeptic and atheist. While Rand's characters tend to be either completely "good" (from an Objectivist perspective) or completely "bad," O'Connor's characters are much more apt to be morally mixed. O'Connor was a deeply devout Roman Catholic and her writing reflected Catholic beliefs.

In "Ayn Rand vs. Flannery O'Connor," Amber Lee Ettinger played Ayn Rand and Jessica Brydon played Flannery O'Connor.

As the episode starts, the audience sees chess pieces and books in what appears to be the office of a scholar. Rather disconcertingly, we see our host clean a handgun. Then Dr. Wilker tells the audience that we will meet two writers, one of them the devoutly Roman

Catholic author Flannery O'Connor and the other the atheist and dedicated anti-communist Ayn Rand.

The first to enter is Flannery O'Connor. Jessica Brydon has brown hair in a kind of stiff flip, harlequin-styled horn-rimmed spectacles, and wears a red sweater over a white dress. Reflecting the truth that the writer she plays spent much of her life disabled by lupus, she walks with the aid of metal crutches with wrist attachments. We soon learn (assuming we do not already know it) that this female writer has a very low opinion of the other female writer she will meet in this episode. Flannery asserts that Ayn Rand "makes Mickey Spillane look like Dostoevsky." The real Flannery O'Connor did indeed make this comparison. There is an element of irony in this put-down because Rand was an admirer of Spillaine and believed he was a good writer, especially in the area of plot structure. O'Connor goes on to tell us that Rand's characters are merely fictional mannequins upon which she "hangs bad ideas" and suggests anyone who comes across a copy of *Atlas Shrugged* should "throw it in a garbage pail." By contrast, Flannery O'Connor believes she herself is "good" at writing because she is "called by gift." She declares, "I write from Christian orthodoxy." O'Connor has found her suffering from lupus "more instructive than a long trip to Europe." There is further discussion of the Catholic author's life. Part 1 ends without Ayn Rand.

In Part 2, Ayn Rand soon enters. Her auburn hair is slicked down and she wears a gray-blue dress buttoned down the front. The host need do little prodding for Rand to expound on her philosophy that holds "reason as the only guide to action." The host wonders if she likes chess. She does. She once wrote to chess playing great Boris Spassky pointing out how the logical principles of chess is opposite the confusion of communism.

Ayn and the host verbally spar with Ayn boasting that she founded a philosophy in which she "revealed the truth" that the basis of morality is "not faith but reason." She said, "I created a new code of morality based on reason by which man's highest purpose is his own happiness."

In comes Flannery O'Connor. She introduces herself as "Mary Grace Flannery O'Connor." Unh-oh. Mary Grace was the name of a character in O'Connor's short story entitled "Revelation," an ugly, bookish, and disturbed young woman who leads a Christian woman to realize how weak her Christianity has been. She does it in a very violent and painful way so the introduction leads us to suspect Rand is in for similar treatment.

Discussion between the two authors quickly turns bitter as the Catholic accuses the atheist of turning "the sin of pride into the greatest virtue." Flannery O'Connor derides Rand's skills as an author, claiming Rand could have just written an essay consisting of John Galt's speech rather than write novels in which the characters are "billboards for your philosophy."

During the confrontation, the affair Ayn had with Nathaniel Brandon is used to assert that she deliberately caused unnecessary pain to her husband as well as to Barbara Branden. Things get worse from there until we see Flannery O'Connor with a gun in her hand — and pointing it at Ayn Rand!

All in all, it is a powerful and emotionally intense episode. Part of what makes it so powerful is that so much emotion comes out of philosophical and literary discussion.

The author of this book interviewed Amber Lee Ettinger about her work playing Ayn in this *Saints vs. Scoundrels* episode. Asked how she was selected to play Ayn in this show, Ettinger answered, "I had been studying with mentor/Acting Coach Marta DuBois for a couple of years in Los Angeles. She had helped with casting on a few of the previous episodes using some of the students in our class and she had asked me if I would be interested in playing Ayn Rand and I immediately said yes!"

Particular needs of the series made playing in it a special challenge. "The difference between the *Saints vs. Scoundrels* script and other TV film scripts that I have worked on in the past is that they're not easy conversations; they're literal debates happening between the saint and the scoundrel. The characters had lengthy monologues full of facts from their philosophies or their writings. So there was no way to ever really improve on the script — you had to get it word perfect. I rehearsed endless hours alone and with my teacher Marta and my co-star." Research for depicting the controversial figure was also demanding. "I spent countless hours on research and development and reading Ayn's books and watching every video I could find of her on YouTube," Ettinger remembered

What did Ettinger like most about playing Ayn Rand in this *Saints vs. Scoundrels* episode? "When we filmed this, it was the most rewarding role I had ever played," she replied. "It was an honor to portray her and tell her story. It was extremely hard to prepare for but afterwards, after that script in particular, I said if I can memorize this, work on an accent and have it word perfect on set, I can do anything!" Her depiction of Rand led to two more roles in the same show. "I've since worked on two other characters on *Saints vs. Scoundrels*, Edith Stein and, just this past summer, Simone de Beauvoir." Ettinger very much enjoyed playing Ayn in the series. "It was eye-opening for me," she asserts. "I think afterwards I really knew I loved what I do and wanted to keep at it."

What does Amber Lee Ettinger think of Ayn Rand? "Very controversial but I fell in love with her," she states. "I think that all that research and development made her a small part of me. I may not agree with all she has written but I have the utmost respect for her."

Years before the making of the episode, Jessica Brydon was taking a class with her acting teacher — also Marta Dubois! — who was reading a biography of Flannery O'Connor. Class was in session when she told Brydon, "If they ever make a movie about Flannery O'Connor, you should play her." Brydon was thrilled at this statement. "I was so young and latched onto any encouragement," she related to the author of this book. "I started writing a screenplay based on one of her biographies and read all her work."

Teacher Dubois was instrumental in Brydon's casting in this episode of *Saints vs. Scoundrels*. "I was cast to play Flannery O'Connor from a referral from acting teacher Marta Dubois," Brydon stated. "The people over at EWTN asked her if she knew anyone who might be a good fit to play Flannery and she mentioned me." Brydon auditioned and got the part.

What was most challenging about playing Flannery O'Connor in this episode? "Getting that soul right," Brydon declared. "She was so disappointed with Ayn Rand but still loved her so much." Another challenge was the very practical one of "learning to walk with her crutches." How did the actress meet this challenge? "I rented a pair for a month before filming, but to make it look authentic was challenging." Brydon elaborated that she felt it important to play the character authentically. "I was very focused on set because I wanted to get Flannery right," she related. The actress continued that she was permanently influenced by this part. "I try to keep some of the goodness I learned from her with me still," she said.

A "user reviewer" on IMDb reviewed both part 1 and part 2 of this episode. In the review of the first part, the person praised Ettinger's performance, writing, "Great job, Amber. She captured the toughness and resolve of Ayn Rand with precision. Some castings of Ms. Rand I have seen before portray her as too cold and almost mean." By contrast, this person said, "Amber drew up short of that and left some sense of humanity in the character which I believe was actually present in the person." In reviewing the second part, the person observed, "By dress, makeup, and hair Amber was transformed into a very Ayn Rand looking character. With very effective use of eyes, expressions, and voice Amber even manages to take the mind off her lovely face and focus attention on the words being spoken by the character."

Amber Lee Ettinger and Jessica Brydon used their considerable acting talents to make Ayn Rand and Flannery O'Connor come vividly to life in this *Saints vs. Scoundrels* episode. They both possessed deep understandings of their characters and the result is a show that is powerfully and memorably dramatic.

2017: *A Coisa Mais Simples do Mundo (The Simplest Thing in the World)*

A 20-minute film of Ayn Rand's short story about the psychological ramifications of writing was made in Brazil in 2017. As might be expected, it is in Portuguese but this author found an English-subtitled version on YouTube. Caio Amaral produced the film, directed it, wrote the script, did the cinematography, and the film editing. Alexandre Michanovich suppled the music. Its star, and only performer, is Fabio Augusto Barreto as writer Henry Dorn.

The movie starts with a close-up of our pensive hero's mustachioed face, hands on either side of his head. His thoughts are heard throughout the movie. Those thoughts commence: "This is going to be the easiest thing you've ever done. You just have to be stupid. Relax and be as stupid as you can." The hands come down from the sides of his head.

Rand's Henry Dorn thought of a book, *Triumph*, that he authored. This Henry Dorn thinks of a motion picture, *Triumph*, for which he wrote the screenplay. Like the original, this hero ruminates about whether or not his work was "terrible" or "brilliant" and concludes it is harder for him to accept its brilliance since it was a critical and commercial failure. He realizes he is more disturbed by a good review by one Marcelo Villaco, who praised *Triumph* as among the best films of the year because of its "touching love story." But Henry had not even intended to put a love story in the film! Henry restlessly paces around the cluttered and cramped room, taking time off to clip his fingernails and gaze outside at the evening skyline of a modern metropolis. He lays his head on the desk.

Returning to his laptop, he just does not type in even a single word but just goes back and forth in his mind between possible scenarios. He thinks of a scenario about a successful middle-aged man, whom Dorn compares to the title character of *Citizen Kane*, seducing a young woman. Then he changes the second character to a young man.

In a truly inspired twist, of course absent from its source material, the film has Dorn hit on the idea of modeling his work after *The Fountainhead* by Ayn Rand!

After more meditations, this agonizing episode of writer's block ends far more dramatically than the short story on which it was based: Henry Dorn jumps out of his window to a presumed certain death.

Interviewed by this author, Barreto recalled how he was cast as Henry Dorn. "A couple of friends referred me to the director who saw my portfolio and invited me," Barreto revealed.

What was most challenging about playing Henry Dorn? What was most enjoyable about it? "I think the most difficult and most pleasant thing was dealing with the dichotomy that is very present in the lives of most artists," Barreto answered. "Henry Dorn goes through a very common philosophical crisis among artists about the essence of their creation, their role in society, and about the modern need to be commercially successful in order to be considered a successful artist."

Barreto found playing Dorn a very positive experience. "I think the director and I were so connected and open to any surprises that we created an environment of a lot of fun and freedom which promoted really creative moments," the actor commented.

Filming the twenty minute long short did not take particularly long. "As we filmed some years ago, I don't remember precisely [how long was spent on it] but I think we recorded everything in about 30 hours of work counting the narration time," he said. "Obviously, the entire film production process is much longer from text adaptation [and] rehearsals to post production."

The actor clearly survived the death scene of his character and was not put in great danger by it. "I had to jump off a table in front of a green screen," Barreto cheerfully explains. "Afterwards it was a postproduction effects work."

Overall, *A Coisa Mais Simples do Mundo (The Simplest Thing in the World)* is astonishingly faithful to its source material. What's more, it clearly and convincingly captures the chaotic emotions swirling through a writer struggling with writer's block. In accomplishing what Ayn Rand accomplished with the short story, this short film constitutes a powerful tribute to Ayn Rand.

2018: *Anthem: The Graphic Novel*

An animated version of Rand's dystopian novel aired on television in 2018 under the title *Anthem: The Graphic Novel.* Jennifer Grossman, Atlas Society CEO, co-authored the screenplay along with Daniel Parsons, who was the artist of the cartoon series. Letitia Capili directed it. She and husband Rob Capili were responsible for visual effects. Keely Cat-Wells supplied all female voices and Mitchell Cockman supplied the male voices.

Ryan Rapsys and Scott McRae, who had often worked as a team on musical scores, created the musical score for *Anthem: The Graphic Novel.* "Rob and Letitia brought us on board," Rapsys told this writer. One reason they were brought on board was that both men admire Ayn Rand. "I have delved real deeply into her philosophy of Objectivism," Rapsys disclosed. "I wouldn't call myself an Objectivist but I definitely admire Ayn Rand."

What focus did Rapsys and McRae take in scoring this animated series? "It was a post-apocalyptic setting in which the world has gone back to being primitive so we tried to make music that was atmospheric but also otherworldly," Rapsys recalled. "We wanted it to sound like ancient music so Scott and I listened to ancient music and let that inspire us."

2021: *Red Pawn*

Paramount never made *Red Pawn* into a motion picture. However, an animated television series was made of it that aired in 2021. It was created, in large part, by the same people who made *Anthem: The Graphic Novel.* Letitia Capili directed *Red Pawn*, she and Rob Capili did its visual effects, and Rob Capili was the animator, film editor, and sound design and effects editor. Jennifer Grossman voiced Joan Harding/Frances. Dimitry Rozental voiced all the male characters.

Again Ryan Rapsys and Scott McRae made the musical score. "We brought Bryan Charles Wilson on as a cellist because he is a great cellist," Rapsys told this author.

What was the difference between scoring *Anthem: The Graphic Novel* and scoring *Red Pawn*? "We were intrigued by both projects," Rapsys asserts. "While *Anthem* had a kind of otherworldly score, we wanted a very romantic, classical, lush kind of music for *Red Pawn* and music that would suggest its Russian setting so that is how we tried to score it. We were influenced by the Russian composer Dimitri Shostakovich."

In an interview with the author of this book, actor Dimitry Rozental recalled how he was selected to voice the male characters in *Red Pawn*. "It was a public audition and there were many different actors," he remembered. "I went character by character and I did seven different parts, seven different voices right off the bat. I don't know how many actors they listened to in the auditions but they came back to me and I gave a few more characters." The first voice he did was that of the warden Kareyev who was nicknamed the Beast. "I read for him first," Dimitry related. "I understood his darkness, his brokenness, and the other characters all fell into it." Dimitry voiced over thirty-five different characters for the series.

He said that the sheer number of different voices in one show made it "a most interesting challenge of my Voiceover career."

Dimitry spent a total of six months working on *Red Pawn*. How did he change his voice enough to suggest over thirty distinct characters? "I recorded my voice and listened to it to make sure they were different," he explained. "I tried to do something new, something else, with each character. I would imagine this guy wears glasses, this guy is old, this guy is sick, and so on, depending on the way they were written in the story. Besides looking at physical and environmental reasons while creating my characters, I also connected with them emotionally, living through the situation moment to moment and letting it affect my performance as I empathized with each character and what was happening to him. Each character's story, how they represented themselves, gave me a chance to pick a particular voice."

Challenges made this work special. "It was definitely a rare situation so I had to push my imagination because it is so rare to create this many characters for one series," he observed. "I tried to make them distinct in my head and see them reflected in my voice. It was mind-blowing for me personally."

Dimitry Rozental's background may have helped suit him for this job as he has some things in common with Ayn Rand. For example, like Ayn Rand, he is ethnically Jewish. "I'm a Ukrainian Jew," he said, "I was born in 1977, in the Soviet times." A major interest also suited him for *Red Pawn*: "I'm a history buff and very interested in Russian history."

The project led Dimitry to research Ayn Rand. "I read a biography," he stated. "I approached the job with a very fresh way of understanding Objectivism." Does he admire Ayn Rand? "I'm definitely an admirer of the story of *Red Pawn* and how it made me feel. I like her ideas but I'm not deeply familiar with the philosophy of Objectivism. I understand that the goal of all of us is happiness and everyone is striving for a better life. I like the ideas of productivity and achievement. I can't say I'm leaning to Objectivism as I'm about as moderate as possible. Ayn Rand did a lot of work and I have to admire that. *Red Pawn* is an exciting story to read with its combination of a love triangle, action, massive amount of innuendoes, and really well-drawn characters."

Summing Up

As previously noted, Ayn Rand was a controversial figure in life and continues to be controversial decades after her death. She will continue to be idolized and despised. Her books will continue to briskly sell, drawing her both new fans and new critics. It is the hope of this author that readers will find *Ayn Rand at the Movies* interesting regardless of whether they love or hate Ayn Rand or, like the author, have a mixed view of her. After all, this book is not "about" Ayn Rand but about her relationship to the motion picture industry.

Ayn Rand loved movies. Movies were vital to her life. They were vital to her life in multiple ways. After all, she met the most important person in her life, Frank O'Connor, when the two of them worked on a movie.

Rand's contributions to films display aspects of her personality that work against the simplistic perception of her as a humorless ideologue and "mean girl." Ayn Rand was a complex person, perhaps far more complex than she knew she was. The motion pictures she scripted, the motion pictures she inspired, and the motion pictures about her all reflect the richness and depth of her personality and life experience.

It is the hope of this writer that *Ayn Rand at the Movies* will bring to light heretofore neglected facets of this fascinating philosopher and author.

References

Thanks to those who spoke with this author: John Handem Piette, Phillipe Coquet, Mary Gallagher, Resa McConaghy, Lindsey Hermer-Bell, David Martin, Ryan Rapsys, Dimitry Rozental, Galen Carter-Jeffrey, Fabio Augusto Barreto, Janne Peters, Michael Paxton, Jeffrey M. Hoffman, George O'Connor, Jessica Brydon, Amber Ettinger, Elia Cmiral,

"A Coisa Mais Simples do Mundo." (2017). https://www.imdb.com/title/tt6352292/

"A Last Survey." *The Ayn Rand Letter*, IV, 2, 3.

"Anthem." (2009). https://www.imdb.com/title/tt3705076/?ref_=fnal_tt_1

"Anthem." (2015).

"Anthem: The Graphic Novel." (2018). https://www.imdb.com/title/tt9476614/

"An Answer to Readers (About a Woman President)." *The Objectivist*. Dec. 1968, 1.

Arnold, Jeremy. "Love Letters." (1945) Turner Classic Movies. https://www.tcm.com/tcmdb/title/82008/love-letters#articles-reviews

"Ayn Rand." https://www.imdb.com/name/nm0709446/?ref_=fn_al_nm_1

"Ayn Rand." *History of Women Philosophers and Scientists*. https://historyofwomenphilosophers.org/project/directory-of-women-philosophers/rand-ayn-1905-1982/

"'Ayn Rand' Premiere Slated at Paramount." *Los Angelos Times*. Oct. 26, 1996.

Ayn Rand: A Sense of Life. https://www.amazon.com/Ayn-Rand-Sense-Directors-Vision/dp/B0002Q9VQ6

Ayn Rand: A Sense of Life. https://www.imdb.com/title/tt0118662/

Savlov, Marc. "Ayn Rand: A Sense of Life." *The Austin Chronicle.* Nov. 6, 1998.

Ayn Rand: A Sense of Life. http://aynrandasenseoflife.com

"Ayn: It Rhymes With Mine." Reeling Back. https://reelingback.com/articles/ayn_it_rhymes_with_mine

"Ayn Rand: A Sense of Life." (1996). https://www.imdb.com/title/tt0118662/?ref_=fn_al_tt_1

Crowther, Bosley. "Gary Cooper Plays an Idealistic Architect in Film Version of 'The Fountainhead.'" *The New York Times.* July 9, 1949.

"The Fountainhead." (1948). https://www.imdb.com/title/tt0041386/?ref_=fn_al_tt_1

Freedland, Jonathan. "The new age of Ayn Rand: how she won over Trump and Silicon Valley." *The Guardian.* April 10, 2017.

Kehr, David. "The Fountainhead." *Reader.* Oct. 26, 1985.

"Broadway Television Theatre The Night of January Sixteenth." (1952). https://www.imdb.com/title/tt0532452/

Carmen, John. "Mirren Captures Rand's Passions." *SFGate.* May 27, 1999.

Hinson, Hal. "We the Living." *The Washington Post.* Feb. 11, 1989.

"ITV Play of the Week: Night of January 16th." (1960).

"Ideal." (2004 Video). https://www.imdb.com/title/tt0773755/?ref_=nm_flmg_t_1_dr

"The King of Kings." (1927). https://www.imdb.com/title/tt0018054/?ref_=fn_al_tt_1

LaSalle, Mick. "Documentary Helps Make Sense of Rand's Life." *SFGate.* May 1, 1998.

Leonard, John. "The Passion of Ayn Rand." *New York.*

Levy, Emanuel. "Fountainhead, The (1949): King Vidor's Powerfully Erotic Melodrama, Starring Gary Cooper and Patricia Neal." Emanuel Levy Cinema 24/7. https://emanuellevy.com/review/fountainhead-the-1949/

"Love Letters." (1945). https://www.imdb.com/title/tt0037885/?ref_=fn_al_tt_3

"Lux Video Theatre Love Letters." (1955). https://www.imdb.com/title/tt0637763/

"Lux Video Theatre The Night of January Sixteenth." (1956). https://www.imdb.com/title/tt0637908/

Maslin, Janet. "'Ayn Rand: A Sense of Life': A View of the Philosopher." *The New York Times*. Feb. 13, 1998.

Mayhew, Robert. *Essays on Ayn Rand's The Fountainhead*. Lexington Books. Lanham, MD. 2007.

"The Night of January 16th." (1941). https://www.imdb.com/title/tt0033954/?ref_=nv_sr_srsg_0

"Night of January 16th." Turner Classic Movies. https://www.tcm.com/tcmdb/title/84899/night-of-january-16th#overview

"Of Living Death." *The Voice of Reason*. A Meridian Book.

"The Passion of Ayn Rand." (1999 TV Movie). https://www.imdb.com/title/tt0140447/?ref_=fn_al_tt_1

"The Passion of Ayn Rand. The Showtime Movie." BarbaraBranden.com. https://www.barbarabranden.com/movie.html

"*Playboy* Interview: Ayn Rand." *Playboy*. March 1964.

New York, New York. 1990.

Rand, Ayn. *The Early Ayn Rand: A Selection from Her Unpublished Fiction*. Signet Books. New York, New York. 2005.

Rand, Ayn. *We the Living*. Signet Books. New York, New York. 2011.

Rand, Ayn. *Three Plays: Night of January 16th, Ideal, Think Twice*. Signet Books. New York, New York. 2005.

"Saints vs. Scoundrels: Ayn Rand vs. Flannery O'Connor. Part 1." (2015). https://www.imdb.com/title/tt4656532/

"Saints vs. Scoundrels: Ayn Rand vs. Flannery O'Connor. Part 2." (2015). https://www.imdb.com/title/tt4371904/

"The Simpsons: A Streetcar Named Marge." (1992). https://www.imdb.com/title/tt0701048/

"The Simpsons: Four Great Women and a Manicure." https://www.imdb.com/title/tt1291165/

"Thought Control," *The Ayn Rand Letter*, III, 2, 2.

Vineyard, David. "The Night of January 16th." Mystery * File. https://mysteryfile.com/blog/?p=42365

W., A. "At Loew's State." *The New York Times*. Dec. 19, 1941.

"We the Living." (1942). https://www.imdb.com/title/tt0035130/?ref_=fn_al_tt_1

Winnert, Derek. "The Night of January 16th." https://www.derekwinnert.com/the-night-of-january-16th-1941-robert-preston-ellen-drew-nils-asther-classic-movie-review-10797/

Winnert, Derek. "We the Living." https://www.derekwinnert.com/we-the-living-1942-alida-valli-fosco-giachetti-rossano-brazzi-classic-movie-review-10260/

www.ingramcontent.com/pod-product-compliance
Ingram Content Group UK Ltd.
Pitfield, Milton Keynes, MK11 3LW, UK
UKHW021905190726
13853UKWH00002B/517